English Unlimited

ESOL, Access & Progression

B2 **Upper Intermediate**
Teacher's Pack

Alex Tilbury & Leslie Anne Hendra
with Sarah Ackroyd

CAMBRIDGE
UNIVERSITY PRESS

Acknowledgements

The authors would like to thank their editors, Alison Bewsher and Catriona Watson-Brown, for the perceptive feedback and detailed guidance they provided during the writing of this Teacher's Pack.

Leslie Anne Hendra would like to thank Michael Stuart Clark for all his help and patience through this project. She would also like to thank Valeria Finnigan, Dariel Lum and Omanie Elias for their encouragement and support over many, many years together.

Alex Tilbury would like to take this opportunity to say a big 'thank you' to those trainers who did so much to guide and inspire him early on in his teaching career, in particular Jon Butt, Mike Cattlin, Philip Dale, Nicholas Davids, Laurence Kinsella and Jonny Martin.

Sarah Ackroyd would like to thank all the editors who have provided invaluable support throughout.

The authors and publishers are grateful to:

Text design and page make-up: Stephanie White at Kamae Design

Video content: all the team at Phaebus Media Group

Illustrations by Kathy Baxendale, Mark Duffin, Julian Mosedale, Vicky Woodgate

The authors and publishers acknowledge the following sources of copyright material and are grateful for the permissions granted. While every effort has been made, it has not always been possible to identify the sources of all the material used, or to trace all copyright holders. If any omissions are brought to our notice, we will be happy to include the appropriate acknowledgements on reprinting.

For the tables on the DVD-ROM and the text on pages 4 and 22 of the Teacher's book © *Common European Framework of Reference for Languages: Learning, teaching, assessment* (2001) Council of Europe Modern Languages Division, Strasbourg, Cambridge University Press

Contents

Introduction

Teaching notes

The thinking behind *English Unlimited*

The aim of *English Unlimited* is to enable adult learners to communicate effectively in English in real-life situations. To achieve this, *English Unlimited* is:

1 a **practical** course
2 an **authentic** course
3 an **international** course
4 a **flexible** course

1 A practical course

Each unit of *English Unlimited* is designed to help learners achieve specific **communicative goals**. These goals are listed at relevant points throughout the Coursebook. For example, you and your learners will see these goals at the top of the first lesson in Unit 3:

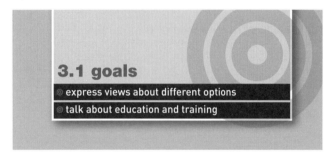

3.1 goals
◉ express views about different options
◉ talk about education and training

All the goals are of a practical 'can do' nature, chosen to enable Upper Intermediate learners to deal with a wide range of situations and topics in English. Of course, a substantial amount of each unit is dedicated to learning vocabulary and grammar – but the goals come first. We've identified goals which we think will be useful for Upper Intermediate learners to work on, and then selected vocabulary and grammar to help them do this.

Where exactly do the goals come from?

The goals for the course have been taken from the **Common European Framework of Reference for Languages (CEF)**, and adapted and supplemented according to our research into the needs of Upper Intermediate learners.

The goals in the Coursebook are based on the CEF goals but they have been reworded to make them less 'technical' and more motivating and accessible for learners and teachers.

What is the CEF?

The CEF uses 'Can Do' statements to describe the abilities of learners of English (or any other language) at different levels. The focus is on **how to do things in the language**, rather than on abstract knowledge of the language itself. For example, here are some CEF goals which describe learners' speaking abilities at the end of Upper Intermediate:

- Can understand detailed instructions reliably
- Can help along the progress of the work by inviting others to join in, say what they think, etc.
- Can outline an issue or a problem clearly, speculating about causes or consequences, and weighing advantages and disadvantages of different approaches

The CEF originated in Europe but is used increasingly widely around the world as a guide for curriculum design and assessment. It can be used with learners of any nationality or first language.

What's the level of the course?

The CEF is divided into six main **levels**, sometimes with 'plus' levels in between. This table shows the CEF levels and how they relate to the Cambridge ESOL exams:

CEF levels		Cambridge exams
C2	'Mastery'	CPE
C1	'Operational proficiency'	CAE
B2+		
B2	'Vantage'	FCE
B1+		
B1	'Threshold'	PET
A2+		
A2	'Waystage'	KET
A1	'Breakthrough'	

English Unlimited Upper Intermediate is based on 'Can Do' statements at the B2 level of the Common European Framework. It takes learners to the C1 or 'Operational proficiency' level of competence.

2 An authentic course

Because it is based on practical goals, *English Unlimited* teaches authentic language – that is, the kind of language which is really used by native speakers and proficient non-native speakers of English in everyday situations. An important tool for identifying useful language to include in the course has been the **Cambridge International Corpus (CIC)**.

What is the CIC?

The CIC is an electronic collection of more than a billion words of real text, both spoken and written, which can be searched by computer to discover the most common words, expressions and structures of the language, and the kinds of situation in which they are used.

How has it been used in the course?

The CIC has been used throughout *English Unlimited* to ensure that, as far as possible given the level of the course, learners are taught **the most frequent and useful words and expressions** for meeting their communicative goals.

The CIC has also been used in the preparation of **grammar** sections, both to select structures to be taught and to identify realistic contexts for presentation. For example, the past perfect simple (Unit 2) is presented in expressions with 'saying' and 'thinking' verbs (*I thought you'd cancelled the meeting*), while the structure *will be + -ing* (Unit 13) is placed in the context of informative talks and presentations (*I'll be talking about three topics*).

A further use of the CIC is in the **Keyword pages** which appear in odd-numbered units. Each Keyword page focuses on one or more of the most frequently used words in English and teaches its most common meanings, as well as useful expressions based around it.

How else is English Unlimited *an authentic course?*

In addition to being informed by the CIC, *English Unlimited* contains a large amount of **unscripted audio and video material**, recorded using non-actors, both native and non-native speakers. Many other listening texts have been scripted from recordings of real conversations.

What are the benefits for learners of using 'authentic' listening material?

Listening to spontaneous, unscripted speech is the best way to prepare learners for the experience of understanding and communicating in English in the real world. We also find that authentic recordings are more motivating and engaging for learners in general.

3 An international course

In what ways is English Unlimited *'international'?*

Firstly, *English Unlimited* is an **inclusive** course, catering for learners of different backgrounds from all around the world. We have taken care to select topics, texts and tasks which will appeal to a broad range of learners. We've tried to avoid topics which learners may find uncomfortable, or simply uninteresting, and we don't assume a knowledge of a celebrity culture, but focus instead on more universal themes, accessible to all.

English is most often used nowadays between non-native speakers from different places. How does the course take this into account?

A second strand to the 'internationalism' of the course is that it includes features which will help learners become more effective communicators in international contexts.

In every even-numbered unit there is an **Across cultures** page which focuses on a particular topic of cultural interest. The aim of these pages is to increase learners' awareness of how the values and assumptions of people they communicate with in English might differ from – or be similar to – their own. Learners who have this awareness are likely to be more sensitive and effective communicators in international environments.

Listening sections use recordings of **speakers with a range of accents** in order to familiarise learners with the experience of hearing both native and non-native speakers from a wide variety of places. Regardless of accents, care has been taken to ensure that recordings are of appropriate speed and clarity for learners at this level, and that they are error-free. All non-native speakers are competent users of English and should provide learners with strong and motivating role models to help them progress and achieve greater confidence in English.

For the purposes of language production, taught grammar, vocabulary and pronunciation follow a British English model, but by exposing learners to a wide range of accents and models, we are helping to enhance their ability to use English in real international contexts.

4 A flexible course

The next five pages show how a typical unit of *English Unlimited* is organised.

As you'll see, the first five pages are connected to each other and make up the 'core' of the unit. After that, there is the **Explore** section, two pages of activities which have a topical or linguistic link to the unit, but which can be used separately. On the last page of each unit is the **Look again** page, comprising review and extension activities, which can be done by learners either in the classroom or for homework.

This means that *English Unlimited* can be adapted not only for lessons of different lengths, but also for shorter and longer courses. For example, just using the 'core' of each unit would be suitable for a course of about 50 hours, while using all the material, including the **Explore** and **Look again** pages, would give a course length of 80 or 90 hours.

The flexibility of *English Unlimited* is further enhanced by an extensive range of supplementary materials. These include **grammar reference and extra practice** at the back of the Coursebook, the **Teacher's DVD-ROM** containing three extra activities for each unit of the Coursebook, **Achievement and Progress tests**, and the **Self-study Pack**, which offers more than 50 hours of additional language and skills practice material in the Workbook and on the Self-study DVD-ROM.

In the rest of this introduction you'll find:
- a plan showing how a unit is organised *pages 6 to 10*
- more detailed notes on the different sections of the units *pages 11 to 15*
- information about the other components of the course *pages 16 to 21*
- more detailed information about the CEF *page 22*

We hope that you and your learners will enjoy using *English Unlimited.*

Alex Tilbury
Leslie Anne Hendra
David Rea
Theresa Clementson

How a unit is organised

The course consists of 14 units, each of which has eight pages.

The first two pages are a single lesson with goals based on the CEF. You can, of course, spread the material over more than one lesson if you want.
⊘ *about 90 minutes*

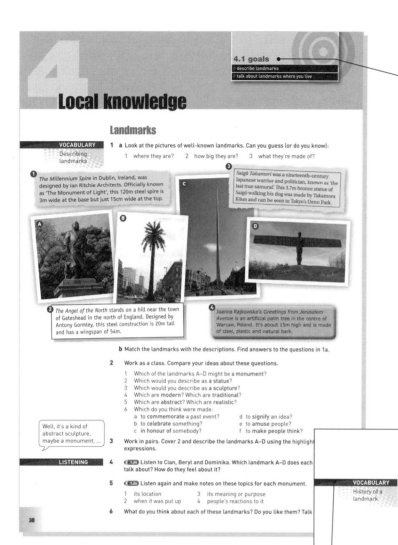

4

4.1 goals
• describe landmarks
• talk about landmarks where you live

Local knowledge

Landmarks

VOCABULARY
Describing landmarks

1 **a** Look at the pictures of well-known landmarks. Can you guess (or do you know):

1 where they are?   2 how big they are?   3 what they're made of?

① *The Millennium Spire* in Dublin, Ireland, was designed by Ian Ritchie Architects. Officially known as 'The Monument of Light', this 120m steel spire is 3m wide at the base but just 15cm wide at the top.

③ *Saigō Takamori* was a nineteenth-century Japanese warrior and politician, known as 'the last true samurai'. This 3.7m bronze statue of Saigō walking his dog was made by Takamora Kōun and can be seen in Tokyo's Ueno Park.

② *The Angel of the North* stands on a hill near the town of Gateshead in the north of England. Designed by Antony Gormley, this steel construction is 20m tall and has a wingspan of 54m.

④ Joanna Rajkowska's *Greetings from Jerusalem Avenue* is an artificial palm tree in the centre of Warsaw, Poland. It's about 15m high and is made of steel, plastic and natural bark.

b Match the landmarks with the descriptions. Find answers to the questions in 1a.

2 Work as a class. Compare your ideas about these questions.

1 Which of the landmarks A–D might be a **monument**?
2 Which would you describe as a **statue**?
3 Which would you describe as a **sculpture**?
4 Which are **modern**? Which are **traditional**?
5 Which are **abstract**? Which are **realistic**?
6 Which do you think were made:
   a to **commemorate** a past event?   d to **signify** an idea?
   b to **celebrate** something?   e to **amuse** people?
   c in **honour** of somebody?   f to **make people think**?

Well, it's a kind of abstract sculpture, maybe a monument, ...

3 Work in pairs. Cover 2 and describe the landmarks A–D using the highlighted expressions.

LISTENING

4 🔊 1.24 Listen to Cian, Beryl and Dominika. Which landmark A–D does each talk about? How do they feel about it?

5 🔊 1.24 Listen again and make notes on these topics for each monument.

1 its location   3 its meaning or purpose
2 when it was put up   4 people's reactions to it

6 What do you think about each of these landmarks? Do you like them? Talk

30

Lessons include **vocabulary** and/or **grammar**, as well as practice in **reading**, **listening** and **speaking**. Lessons always finish with a communicative speaking task.
See pp11–13 for details of language and skills sections.

Every unit has a focus on **pronunciation**.
See p12 for details.

4.1

A big impression

VOCABULARY
History of a landmark

1 Do the highlighted expressions in a and b have similar or different meanings? If they differ, explain how.

a	b
1 It was **erected** to celebrate the Millennium.	It was **put up** during the 1990s.
2 It was **unveiled** at the very end of 1999.	It was **opened to the public** in 2006.
3 It was **heavily criticised** at first.	It was **badly received**.
4 It **caused a lot of controversy**.	It **made a big impression** on people.
5 People **didn't know what to make of it**.	People were **baffled by it**.
6 People **grew to love it**.	People **warmed to it** after a while.
7 It **became a landmark**.	It **became a tourist attraction**.
8 People **see it as part of the landscape**.	People **regard it as an eyesore**.

2 **a** Choose expressions from 1 to complete the description of the Eiffel Tower. In some cases, more than one answer is possible.

AT 324 METRES HIGH, THE EIFFEL TOWER is the tallest structure in Paris. It ¹____ between 1887 and 1889 as the entrance arch for the 1889 Exposition Universelle ('World Fair'). Its designer, Gustave Eiffel, had originally planned to build the tower in Barcelona, but it was decided that his idea would not suit the city. Eiffel therefore took his design to Paris instead, and the Tower ²____ on 6 May 1889.

The Tower ³____ when it was first built. The newspapers of the day were filled with angry letters, with many people calling the Tower ⁴____. Other people ⁵____ it, unsure whether the Tower was intended to be a work of art or a demonstration of engineering.

The city planned to allow the Tower to stand for twenty years and then tear it down, but with time people ⁶____ it and it became both ⁷____ and ⁸____. Today, the Tower is widely regarded as a striking piece of structural art. Since its construction, it's been visited by more than 200 million people.

b Compare your answers in groups.

PRONUNCIATION
Weak forms

3 **a** 🔊 1.25 Some very common words have weak forms: when they're not stressed, you can say them with a schwa sound /ə/. Listen and notice the weak forms in this sentence.
It was erected to celebrate the Millennium.
Practise saying the sentence.

b Words we usually say as weak forms include:

• articles *a, an, the*   • forms of *be*   • prepositions *as, at, for, from, of, to*

Look at the other sentences in 1. Write /ə/ above the words you'd probably say as a weak form.

c 🔊 1.26 Listen and look at the script on p146 to check. Practise saying the sentences.

SPEAKING

4 **a** Work alone. Choose two or three landmarks in your region or country. For each one, think about these questions.

1 What does it look like? How would you describe its style?
2 Why was it built? What do you think it represents?
3 When was it built? Is it popular with local people and tourists?
4 Has its reputation changed over time?
5 What do you think about it? Why?

b Talk in groups. Can you add any more information to each other's descriptions? Which places would you most like to see?

31

Two voices

Umm Kulthum (1904–1975) was a singer famous in Egypt and throughout the Arabic-speaking world.

4.2 goals
- talk about well-known people where you live
- describe someone's life and work

1 **a** Look at the photos and read the captions. Which six of these things do you think could be mentioned in an article about: Umm Kulthum? Bohumil Hrabal?

Prague Cairo radio concerts an accident or suicide real events a huge funeral lyrics an Oscar records a single sentence up to six hours banned books

b Work in two groups.

Group A – read the article about Umm Kulthum below.
Group B – read the article about Bohumil Hrabal on p119.

Find out which six things are mentioned in your article.

Bohumil Hrabal (1914–1997) was one of the Czech Republic's best-known and best-loved writers.

Article | Discussion   Log in/create account

Umm Kulthum

Umm Kulthum was probably the most famous singer of the Arab world in the 20th century. Even today, more than three decades after her death, she is known as 'the Voice of Egypt' and 'the Star of the East', and her music can often be heard on radio and television.

She was born in a village in northern Egypt in around 1904 and showed an extraordinary singing talent from an early age. When she was 12 years old, she started performing in a small group directed by her father. Four years later, she was noticed by Zakariyya Ahmad, a famous musician, who invited her to Cairo. There, she was introduced to the poet Ahmad Rami, who went on to write 137 songs for her. She had her first real success when she began performing at the Arabic Theatre Palace.

By 1932, Umm Kulthum had become so popular that she began a long tour of the Middle East, performing in cities such as Damascus, Baghdad, Beirut and Tripoli. Her radio concerts, held on the first Thursday of every month, were famous for emptying the streets of some of the world's busiest cities as people rushed home to listen.

Umm Kulthum's songs are about the universal themes of love and loss. A typical concert would consist of two or three songs performed over a period of up to six hours. The duration of her songs varied from concert to concert and was based on the interaction between singer and audience. One of her techniques was to repeat a single line of a song's lyrics again and again, slightly changing the emphasis each time to bring her listeners into a euphoric state. It is said that she never sang a line the same way twice.

Umm Kulthum gave her last concert in 1973. She died in Cairo on February 3, 1975. Her funeral was attended by one of the largest gatherings in history – over four million people. In Egypt and the Arab world, she is remembered as one of the greatest singers and musicians who ever lived. Since her death, it is estimated that about a million copies of her records have been sold every year.

---

2 **a** Read again. Note down one or two details about each of the six things in your article.

b In A/B pairs, tell each other about Umm Kulthum and Bohumil Hrabal. What do you find most interesting about each person?

3 Match 1–8 with a–h to make sentences from the articles.

1 She was probably the most famous	a repeat a single line of a song's lyrics.
2 She had her first real success when	b Best Foreign Film in 1967.
3 One of her techniques was to	c a collection of short stories.
4 He started out as	d singer of the Arab World.
5 He had his first breakthrough with	e 1991.
6 One of his most famous works is	f a story written in a single sen...
7 The movie won an Oscar for	g she began performing at the... Theatre Palace.
8 The first of his collected writings came out in	h a poet.

4 Think of two or three famous writers or performers in your part of the wor... Choose expressions from 3 and talk in groups about:

- what they're famous for.
- how and why they became famous.

Well, Jang Nara is famous in South Korea. She had her first breakthrough with the hit song ...

The next two pages are another lesson with goals based on the CEF.
⏱ *about 90 minutes*

She's known as ...

1 Read the information about using the passive, and sentences 1–6. Find an example of:

a present simple passive
b past simple passive
c present perfect passive
d passive after a modal verb

In English, you usually put the person or thing you want to talk about (the **topic**) at the beginning of a sentence. New information (the **comment**) comes after it:

topic	comment
Umm Kulthum	was probably the most famous singer of the Arab world in the 20th century.

Notice how the writer chooses **active** or **passive** to keep Umm Kulthum, and things closely related to her, as the topic:

1	She	is known as 'the Voice of Egypt' and 'the Star of the East'.	PASSIVE
2	Her music	can often be heard on radio and television.	PASSIVE
3	She	showed an extraordinary singing talent.	ACTIVE
4	She	started performing in a small group directed by her father.	ACTIVE
5	She	was noticed by Zakariyya Ahmad, a famous musician.	PASSIVE
6	A million copies of her records	have been sold every year.	PASSIVE

2 Find and complete five common passive expressions from the last two paragraphs of the Umm Kulthum article.

1 The duration of her songs was b_____ on
2 It is s_____ that
3 Her funeral was a_____ by
4 She is r_____ as
5 It is e_____ that

3 **a** Read the profile of Jang Nara from a website for people interested in South Korean culture. At the moment, all the sentences are active. Decide which should be active and which passive, and rewrite the profile.

Profile **Jang Nara, entertainer (1981 – present)**

✻ Jang Nara was born in Seoul in March 1981. People consider her one of the best entertainers in South Korea.

✻ She started out as an actress in her primary school days, when theatre producers invited her to appear in the play *Les Misérables*. Later, in high school, she modelled in a number of television ads.

✻ Jang had her first real success as a singer in 2001, when a record company released her debut album. They sold 300,000 copies of the album, and the Korean music world awarded her Best New Singer of that year.

✻ At the same time, her acting career continued to develop. Korean TV companies hired her to star in popular sitcoms and dramas, and a Chinese television station also invited her to star in the successful drama *My Bratty Princess*. She is very popular in China, where they know her as 'Zhang Na La'.

✻ In addition, people have recognised her for her charity work in different countries. One Chinese charity appointed her a goodwill ambassador, the first foreigner to receive this honour.

---

b 🔊1.27 Listen to check. Did you have the same ideas?

4 **a** Choose a person you think should be included on a website for people who are interested in your country, its history and culture, for example:

an artist a successful business person a scientist a sportsperson a leader

Write a profile of the person for the website. Use passive expressions from 1 and 2.

b Read each other's profiles and ask questions to find out more.

There is a **Grammar reference** and **extra grammar practice** for every unit at the back of the Coursebook.

> ⏱ *The last four pages of a unit will take about 45 minutes each.*

The fifth page is the heart of the unit, the **Target activity**. Learners prepare for and carry out an **extended task** which is designed to combine and activate language taught in earlier lessons in the unit. *See p13 for details.*

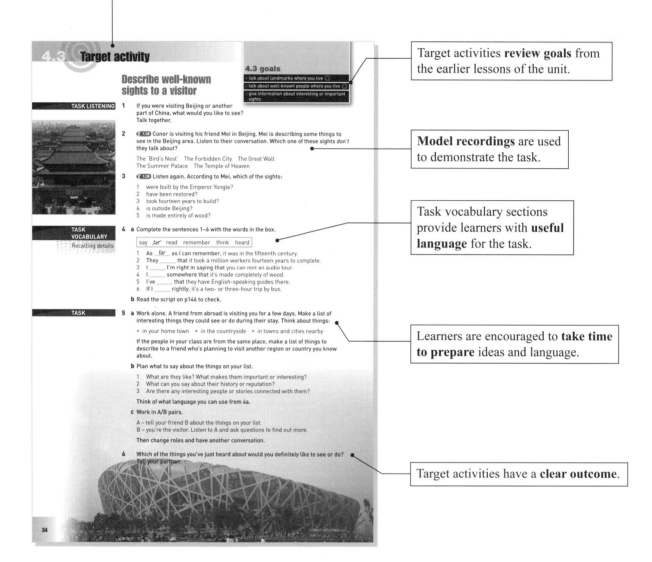

Target activities **review goals** from the earlier lessons of the unit.

Model recordings are used to demonstrate the task.

Task vocabulary sections provide learners with **useful language** for the task.

Learners are encouraged to **take time to prepare** ideas and language.

Target activities have a **clear outcome**.

The **Explore** section is made up of activities which extend and broaden the topics, language and skills taught in the core part of each unit. On the first page is **Across cultures** or **Keyword** in alternate units. On the second page is either **Explore writing** or **Explore speaking**.

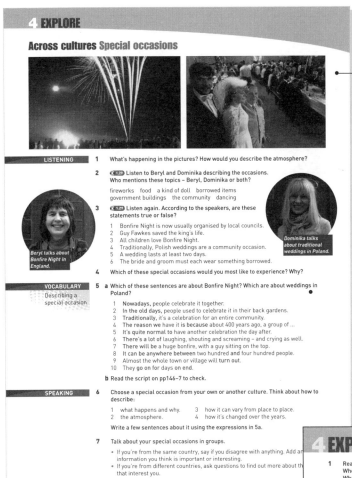

Even-numbered units have **Across cultures** pages which give learners the chance to think about and discuss how cultures differ – or are similar – around the world. *See p13 for details.*

Even-numbered units have **Explore writing** pages which enable learners to write a range of different text types. *See p14 for details.*

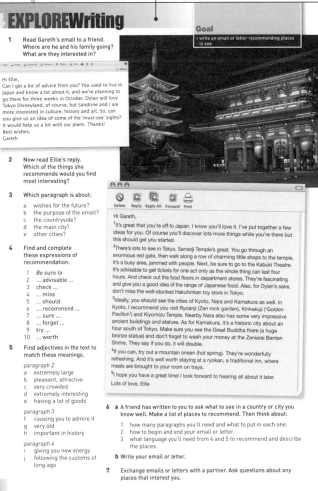

Odd-numbered units have **Keyword** pages. Each one focuses on a common English word, teaching and practising the main meanings and useful expressions. *See p14 for details.*

Odd-numbered units have **Explore speaking** pages dedicated to developing learners' speaking skills and strategies. *See p14 for details.*

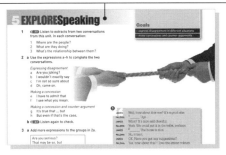

The last page of each unit, **Look again**, is a series of short classroom activities for reviewing and extending the language from the unit. *See p15 for details.*

Review activities include **vocabulary** and **grammar** from the unit.

Spelling and sounds activities help learners make connections between English spellings and how to pronounce them.

Notice activities draw out further useful language from the unit's reading or listening texts.

At the end of each unit is a **Self-assessment** for learners to complete.

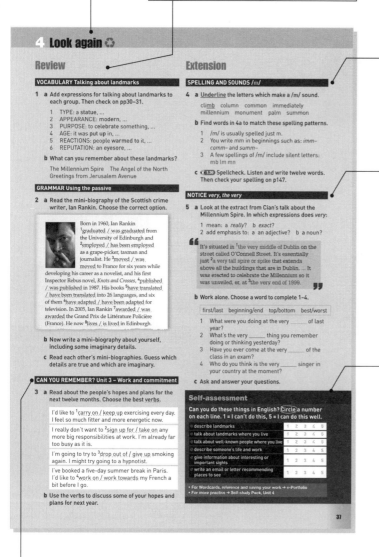

Can you remember? activities review a language point from the previous unit.

A more detailed look at the features of *English Unlimited*

Vocabulary

English Unlimited provides learners with **a wide variety of vocabulary**, chosen to meet each unit's communicative goals. In most units, there are three or four vocabulary sections in the first two lessons and Target activity, and vocabulary is also presented and practised on **Keyword**, **Across cultures**, **Explore writing** and **Explore speaking** pages.

Vocabulary includes:
- **words** like *delighted, mortified, intrigued*
- **collocations** like *set goals, get feedback*
- **stems** like *I'm in two minds about ...*
- **fixed expressions** like *It's tried and tested.*

The focus on longer items as well as single words will enable learners to express themselves more fluently, naturally and effectively.

The course provides a balance of:
- more frequent vocabulary, selected and checked using the Cambridge International Corpus (CIC);
- topical and functional items which learners need in order to achieve particular goals. For example, words like *statue* and *monument* are not especially frequent statistically, but are obviously necessary for the fulfilment of goals such as 'describe landmarks' and 'talk about landmarks where you live'.

Taught vocabulary is generally drawn from texts which learners have already read or listened to as part of a skills section of a lesson. In other words, vocabulary is **placed in clear contexts** which help learners work out what it means, and how it's used.

Grammar

Each unit of the course teaches the grammar essential to achieving the **communicative goals**.

The points of the grammar syllabus have been selected and placed in particular units to help learners meet these goals. For example, the passive is focused on in Unit 4 because it's particularly useful as a way of controlling the topic of short, biographical texts about people's lives and work. Similarly, past and present participle clauses are taught in Units 5 and 7 as they are very useful for describing physical objects and scenes.

Before focusing on grammar explicitly, learners are first exposed to grammar **in context** through reading and listening texts. Then meaning and form are highlighted using **a 'guided discovery' approach**, which actively involves learners in finding out about the grammar for themselves while also providing plentiful support and opportunities for you to monitor and assist:

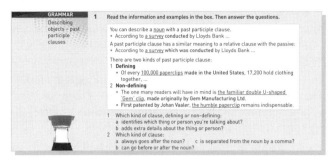

Thorough **controlled practice** is provided to check learners' understanding of the language and provide initial practice, while maintaining and developing the topic of the lesson:

Lessons end with a speaking task (or, occasionally, a writing task) which gives learners the chance to use the language of the lesson, including the grammar, in **freer practice**.

Grammar reference

In each grammar section, you'll see a label like this ...

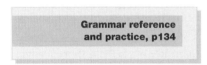

Grammar reference and practice, p134

... which directs learners to a **Grammar reference section** at the end of the book, accompanied by **extra practice exercises**.

Each Grammar reference section sets out the **meaning, form and pronunciation** of the point in question, using simple language and a range of examples:

The extra practice exercises can be either done in class as the need arises, or set as homework.

Pronunciation

There is one pronunciation section in each unit.

These sections have both **receptive and productive aims**:
- to help learners understand natural spoken English;
- to build confidence by isolating and practising specific, manageable features of spoken English;
- to help learners speak more intelligibly.

Note that although native-speaker voices are used to model features of pronunciation, the primary goal of these sections is **intelligibility** and not (necessarily) achieving a native-like accent.

Pronunciation sections address areas which will be useful for all Upper Intermediate learners to work on, regardless of their first language: **'unmarked' and contrastive stress, weak forms, elision, intrusion**, dividing speech into **groups of words**, and the use of **prominence**.

Each pronunciation section is based on **a short extract** drawn from a listening sequence. Learners are encouraged to **notice** a language feature and then **practise** it:

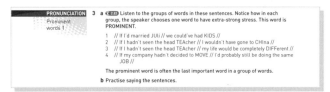

Key pronunciation areas may be touched upon **two or three times** during the course rather than being 'one-offs', thereby building learners' familiarity and confidence. Interest is maintained by slightly increasing the level of challenge on each occasion. For example, the activity above from Unit 8 asks learners simply to notice and repeat groups of words and prominence, while the activity below, from Unit 11, asks learners to make their own choices about dividing expressions into word groups and assigning prominence:

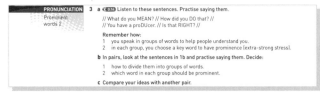

Learners can also practise the **individual sounds** they have problems with, using the phonemic chart on the Self-study DVD-ROM. In addition, on the e-Portfolio **word list**, learners can check their pronunciation of words and expressions against British and American English recordings.

Listening

There is usually at least one major listening section in the first two lessons of each unit, and other listening activities occur frequently on pages such as **Target activity**, **Across cultures** and **Explore speaking**.

A wide range of recordings, both **authentic** and **scripted**, is used, including monologues, topical conversations between friends and colleagues, conversations in service situations, phone calls and interviews.

Authentic recordings are unscripted and feature both native and non-native speakers from a variety of backgrounds. These provide exposure to a range of accents and to features of real spoken English, such as vague language and hesitation devices.

Scripted recordings are based on real-world recordings and corpus data to guarantee the inclusion of natural expressions and features of English. They are often used to contextualise functional language, such as expressions for discussing solutions or signposting a talk.

Texts are exploited using **a range of tasks** designed to develop specific listening skills, build confidence and prepare learners for less-graded authentic texts. For example, this sequence includes:
- prediction (1a);
- listening for gist (1b, 2);
- listening for specific information (3);
- an opportunity for learners to respond to the recording in a natural way (4).

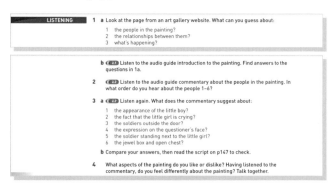

Reading

Units usually have at least one major reading section in the first two lessons. Smaller reading texts are used in some **Target activities** and can be found in **Across cultures** and **Explore writing** pages.

A wide range of text types is used, both **printed and electronic**: newspaper, magazine and online articles, web postings, brochures, interviews and personal correspondence.

Reading texts:
- are drawn from sources around the world in order to appeal to as many learners as possible;
- are authentic, or based on authentic texts, ensuring that learners are exposed to natural language and preparing them for the experience of reading outside the classroom;
- recycle known language in order to build learners' confidence in reading;
- are slightly above learners' productive language level, so that learners have opportunities to notice new language;
- provide a context for vocabulary and grammar which is to be taught.

Texts are exploited using **a range of tasks** appropriate for the level and text type. For example, this sequence includes:

- personal orientation to the topic of the text (1);
- reading for gist (2);

- reading in detail (3);
- an opportunity for a natural, personal response to the text (4).

For further reading practice, the Self-study Pack contains seven **Explore reading** pages, each of which focuses on a different real-life reading scenario.

Target activity

The target activity is **an extended speaking task**, which **recycles some or all of the goals, vocabulary and grammar of the previous two lessons**. It is the conclusion of the first five, topically linked pages of the unit.

As part of the task preparation, the Target activity also provides further listening or reading skills development, and further language input. Target activity pages have **three sections**.

Task listening and **Task reading** sections have three objectives: they provide a model for the task which students do later on, they provide a context for the vocabulary which is presented afterwards, and they provide further receptive skills development:

The **Task vocabulary** is drawn from the listening or reading above, and focuses on useful language for the task to follow:

In the **Task** section, learners are given the chance to think about the ideas and the language they want to use before they begin, meaning that they will be able to focus on accuracy as well as fluency when they do the task itself:

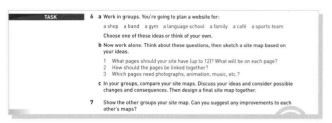

You can support your learners during task preparation by encouraging them to look back at the relevant vocabulary and grammar sections from the preceding lessons.

Across cultures

More and more people around the world are learning English in order to live, work, study and travel in other countries. The increasingly global nature of business, travel, education and personal relations in today's world means that **intercultural awareness** is an area of growing interest and need for learners everywhere. The Common European Framework of Reference for Languages (CEF) identifies intercultural awareness as a key sociolinguistic competence (chapter 5.1.1–3). Learners who are interculturally competent are more sensitive and effective communicators in international situations.

To this end, the **Across cultures** pages are intended to help learners to:

- communicate better with people from a range of cultural backgrounds;
- be more aware of the kinds of differences and similarities that can exist both between and within cultures;
- reflect on aspects of their own and other cultures in an objective, non-judgemental way;
- contribute to an exchange of ideas about cultures by drawing on their own observations and experiences.

The course has seven **Across cultures** pages in **even-numbered units** (alternating with Keyword). Each looks at a particular topic from an intercultural perspective:

Unit	
2	Aspects of culture
4	Special occasions
6	Ways of communicating
8	Languages
10	Rights and obligations
12	Health and healthcare
14	Recruitment

Across cultures pages are structured like an ordinary lesson. They typically include a brief lead-in, a listening or reading text for further skills development, and some language input to support learners in a final speaking stage where they talk about their own and other cultures.

Listening stages usually use **authentic recordings** of people talking about their own countries and cultures. These are intended to engage learners' interest and promote discussion, rather than representing the only 'truth' about a given culture. Indeed, learners with experience of the same culture are encouraged to agree, disagree and add further information.

Keyword

The **most frequent words** in English tend to have a number of different meanings and to occur in a range of patterns and expressions. Each odd-numbered unit of the course has a self-contained Keyword page which focuses on one of these words, clarifies its **key meanings** and **useful expressions** as identified by corpus research, and practises them.

The meanings and expressions of the keyword are often illustrated using examples from the current unit and previous units:

This is followed by controlled and freer practice:

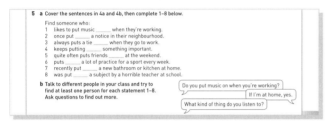

Explore writing

Explore writing pages occur in **even-numbered units** (alternating with Explore speaking).

This page is dedicated to improving learners' writing skills through a sequence of activities which build towards a practical, purposeful writing task. As with Explore speaking, the page will have a topical link with the rest of the unit.

Specifically, Explore writing pages will help learners to:

- **write a range of text types** appropriate to the level, e.g. an email recommending places to see, a dramatic story, a web posting putting forward an argument, a proposal;
- **understand genre-specific conventions**, e.g. the language and content of a complaint, the language and organisation of a proposal, ways of making a story dramatic;
- **develop confidence** in writing by planning and discussing ideas with peers, talking about and improving texts together, and building from shorter to longer texts.

Each page contains one or more models of the text type learners will produce at the end of the lesson. The sequence of exercises will usually require learners to:

- **read the model texts** for meaning;
- **notice** specific language features in the texts;
- **practise** using the new language in writing;
- **plan** a piece of writing, e.g. learners may be asked to generate ideas in pairs or groups, then organise their ideas into paragraphs;
- **write** their own texts;
- **read** each other's texts and **respond** where possible (either orally or in writing);
- work to **improve** their own or each other's texts.

You can, of course, set some of the later stages of the writing process as homework if you prefer.

In many cases, the goals for these pages refer to both traditional and electronic media (e.g. 'write a formal **letter** or **email** of refusal'), meaning you can choose to ask your learners to write either on paper or on computer if the facilities are available.

Explore speaking

Explore speaking pages occur in **odd-numbered units** (alternating with Explore writing).

Explore speaking is a complete, free-standing page which aims to equip learners with **skills and strategies for improving their spoken interaction** in a wide range of situations. It addresses real-life, immediate needs of Upper Intermediate learners, such as:

- using vague expressions to describe categories of things;
- showing different attitudes and feelings;
- making concessions and counter-arguments;
- speaking tactfully in different situations;
- giving emphasis to different kinds of information;
- checking that people understand.

Each Explore speaking page includes:

- **a listening text** containing the target language. The listening, which generally links to the topic of the unit as a whole, provides a clear context for the target language;
- **the listening script** on the same page. This enables learners to see and study the target language right away without having to flick to the back of the book;

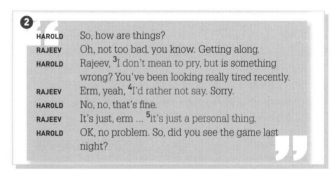

- activities in which learners **notice the target language** in different ways, such as categorising expressions according to their function;
- **controlled practice exercises** which build familiarity and confidence with the target language;
- **a freer practice task**, such as a role play, which gives learners the chance to use the target language in a real-life situation.

Look again

The Look again page is divided into two columns, **Review** and **Extension**. Although some sections can be set as homework, the page is intended as a series of communicative activities for learners to do in class. The Look again page also includes a final **Self-assessment** for the unit.

Review

The **three Review activities** will help learners to recycle language from both the current and previous unit:

1 Vocabulary – provides further communicative practice of a key area of functional or topical language from the unit.

2 Grammar – provides further communicative practice of the key grammar point in the unit.

3 Can you remember? – recycles a key language focus from the preceding unit to help learners reactivate and better retain the language.

Extension

The **two Extension activities** focus on useful aspects of language, extending learners' knowledge beyond what is taught in the main body of the unit.

4 Spelling and sounds – this section is intended to meet the need of learners and teachers for a systematic approach to English spelling.

It takes a 'sounds to spelling' approach in the belief that the most useful guide for Upper Intermediate learners is to help them spell words when they hear them. It looks at different spellings of consonants such as /dʒ/, /m/ and /g/ (including silent letters and consonant doubling), vowels such as /e/, /ʌ/ and /ʊ/, and vowel digraphs such as /eɪ/, /eə/ and /əʊ/.

Spelling and sounds will help students to:

- become aware of sound / spelling correlations, helping to improve both spelling and pronunciation;
- learn general rules for spelling in manageable amounts;
- develop accuracy in spelling and therefore confidence in writing;
- revise words encountered in the current and previous units.

5 Notice – this section further exploits reading and listening texts from the unit by briefly looking at and practising a useful and regularly occurring language feature, e.g. nouns linked with *and* and *or* (binomials), the uses of *very* and *the very*, verbs with *off*, a set of expressions about planning and spontaneity.

Self-assessment

Each unit concludes with a Self-assessment box for learners to complete either in class or at home. Many learners find it useful and motivating to reflect on their progress at regular intervals during a course of study.

For teachers, the Self-assessment will be a valuable means of gauging learners' perceptions of how much progress they've made, and of areas they need to work on further. Self-assessments can also be useful preparation for one-to-one tutorials in which the learner's and teacher's perceptions of progress are compared and discussed.

The Self-study Pack

About the Self-study Pack

English Unlimited Upper Intermediate Self-study Pack offers a wealth of activities for learners to **reinforce what they have learned in class**. It has been designed to offer **flexibility and depth** to your English teaching, whatever the specific needs of your learners. The Workbook and Self-study DVD-ROM provide a wide range of language and skills practice activities to accompany each unit of the Coursebook, so you can:

- set homework tasks based on the Coursebook lessons;
- supplement your lessons with further language and skills practice;
- use authentic video activities in class, or get learners to watch in their own time.

Your learners can:

- consolidate their knowledge of language and skills taught in class;
- practise and check their pronunciation;
- learn and practise essential speaking skills;
- create tests on specific language areas quickly and easily, which allows learners to focus on either grammar-based or vocabulary-based questions or both from any unit or combination of units;
- check their progress and get feedback on their level of English and any specific areas of difficulty;
- record and listen to themselves speaking in everyday conversations, using the audio materials.

In the Workbook

English Unlimited Upper Intermediate Workbook contains:

- activities which practise and extend the vocabulary and grammar taught in the Coursebook units;
- further reading and writing skills practice;
- numerous opportunities in each unit for learners to personalise what they are learning to their own interests and situations.

The first three pages of each unit consist of **vocabulary and grammar practice activities** to consolidate and reinforce what has been taught in the Coursebook, which can be either used in class or set for homework. **Over to you** activities suggest ways for learners to practise and personalise the language and skills they have learned in a more open way.

Explore reading, in even-numbered units, offers practice in reading, understanding and responding to a range of everyday texts, such as news and popular science articles, information websites and emails. As Upper Intermediate learners are expected to be able to deal with quite long and in-depth reading tasks, each Explore reading section is two pages long. This allows for an extended reading task, followed by detailed comprehension, language and exploitation work.

Explore writing, in odd-numbered units, gives learners key pointers on structure and language, to enable them to produce a wide range of written texts, such as a web posting, a letter to a newspaper or a statistical report. Taken alongside the Explore writing pages in even-numbered units of the Coursebook, this means that there is a dedicated writing lesson for every unit of the course.

The last page (or sometimes two pages) of each unit has a set of activities that link up directly with the authentic video on the Self-study DVD-ROM. Learners have the chance to watch and listen to real people from around the world, talking about topics connected to the unit.

On the Self-study DVD-ROM

The *English Unlimited Upper Intermediate Self-study DVD-ROM* offers your learners over 300 interactive activities which they can use to practise and consolidate what they have learned in class, while providing a number of easy ways to check their progress at every step of the course.

Just click on the icon for each unit and the learners will find a wide range of engaging and easy-to-use activities, from picture matching and drag-and-drop categorisation to cloze exercises. Learners are also able to record themselves, practising pronunciation or taking part in conversations, and compare their recordings with the original audio. If learners have used their e-Portfolio from the Coursebook, they are able to save their conversation recordings direct to their e-Portfolio.

Each unit's activities practise and extend the vocabulary, grammar, pronunciation and Keyword areas focused on in the Coursebook. Learners can also generate tests quickly and easily, using the Quick check test question bank. They can choose which units they want to test and how many questions they want the test to consist of, and Quick check will randomly select from the 700 questions in the bank.

Learners can also keep track of their progress as they work through the course with the Progress page, which shows which exercises they have attempted and their scores. Learners can therefore quickly see the language areas where they need to do more work and can retry the relevant exercises.

In addition to language practice, each unit of the Self-study DVD-ROM also contains Explore speaking and Listening activities. Explore speaking trains learners to notice key speaking skills, such as using stress to show disbelief or expressions such as *whatever*, *anyway* and *right* as discourse markers, and then incorporate these techniques into their own spoken English. Listening activities expose learners to useful everyday listening texts, such as a lecture, a radio phone-in show and a job interview.

In most language courses, it is rare for learners to get the chance to listen to themselves in conversation, but if there is a microphone available, this can be done easily using the recorded dialogues on the DVD-ROM. Learners listen to the dialogues, take a closer look at the language used, and then have the opportunity to record themselves and play back to hear how they sound in the conversations. If they have installed the e-Portfolio from their Coursebook, they can save this conversation directly to the My work section. Learners can also record and listen to themselves during any exercise, for example, to practise pronunciation.

In every unit of the Self-study DVD-ROM, you will also find video, which can be used with the whole class or by the learners themselves outside class, using the last page (or two) of each unit of the Workbook, or just watching them to get extra exposure to real language. At Upper Intermediate level, there are two types of authentic video:

- 11 sets of **Interviews** including topics such as: *A holiday to forget*, *Virtual world* and *How not to get the job*.

- three short **Documentaries**, each starring one or two experts in their field discussing engaging topics. The three documentary subjects are:

  - *The sculptors*
  - *The human rights lawyer*
  - *The Antarctic researcher*

These videos on the Self-study DVD-ROM are available in full-screen version with optional subtitles, or inset alongside an onscreen transcription. In the full-screen version, subtitles can be easily toggled on and off, so learners can find extra support for any part of the video if they need it.

The e-Portfolio

The *English Unlimited Upper Intermediate e-Portfolio* is an interactive DVD-ROM which learners can use as a progress check, a reference tool and a store of written and spoken texts. It contains useful features to help reinforce learning and record and encourage progress. Learners click on one of the four icons on the start-up menu to start using these features.

Self-assessment

The **Self-assessment** feature allows learners to reflect on their own progress through the course. They do this by choosing a number between one and five to assess how well they feel they can complete each communicative goal from the Coursebook units. This encourages learners to take responsibility for their own progress and also motivates them by giving a visual record of the goals which they feel they are able to achieve. These rankings are recorded and can be revised when learners feel they have made improvements.

Word list

The **Word list** feature gives learners a comprehensive reference tool for checking the spelling, meaning and pronunciation of the words and expressions presented in the Coursebook. Learners can search by Coursebook unit or by topic group. Clear definitions show how each word or expression is used in the Coursebook, and both British and North American pronunciation guides allow learners to listen and compare with their own pronunciation.

The Word list also allows learners to enter and save new information about each word or expression. They can make notes on a word or expression, or add an example sentence which they have heard or read. New words that learners discover for themselves can also easily be added to the list, giving learners the chance to extend and personalise the Word list.

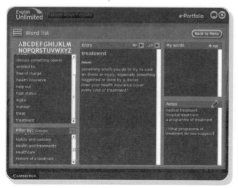

My work

The **My work** feature gives learners a convenient repository in which they can build a portfolio of their work as they progress through the course. Divided into **Reading and writing** and **Speaking and listening** folders, My work allows learners to import recorded examples of speaking and written work directly from the Self-study Pack or to import documents and files directly from their computer.

Developing a bank of their own written and spoken work provides another opportunity for review over a longer term and can be exceptionally motivating for learners. My work also offers a simple solution for English courses in which the production of coursework counts towards a learner's end-of-course grade.

Word cards

The **Word cards** feature encourages the review of words and expressions from the Coursebook. A series of words and expressions can be generated randomly by unit or topic, with the number of 'cards' set by the learner. Cards are then dragged and dropped into categories based on how well the learner can recall the word. A learner can check the meaning of the word by turning over the card. There is also the option for learners to include new words which they have added in the Word list. This is a fun and easy-to-use way of reinforcing vocabulary acquisition.

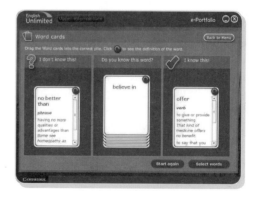

The Teacher's Pack

We understand that no two teachers or classes are alike, and that the role of a Teacher's Pack accompanying a language course is to cater for as diverse a range of pedagogical needs as possible. The materials in this Teacher's Pack serve to enhance the flexibility of *English Unlimited* to meet the needs of teachers who:

- are teaching courses of different lengths;
- want to supplement the Coursebook materials;
- have different class sizes and types;
- are teaching in different parts of the world;
- are addressing different assessment needs;
- want to use video materials in the classroom.

English Unlimited Upper Intermediate Teacher's Pack offers a **step-by-step guide to teaching** from the Coursebook, **more than 50 photocopiable activity worksheets** to extend and enrich your lessons and a **complete testing suite**. The Teacher's Pack consists of the **Teacher's Book** and the **Teacher's DVD-ROM**.

In the Teacher's Book

Teacher's notes

In the Teacher's Book, there are more than 100 pages of teacher's notes (pp23–126) to accompany the Coursebook material. These notes are a comprehensive and easy-to-follow guide to using the *English Unlimited Upper Intermediate Coursebook*, and have been written with a broad range of class types and teaching styles in mind.

Each unit's notes take you smoothly through the different stages of the Coursebook lessons. Answers are clearly highlighted, and the Individual, Pair and Group work symbols show at a glance what interaction is suggested for each stage.

On most pages, there are instructions for alternative activities, clearly boxed, to offer greater variety and interest. There are also suggestions throughout for adapting activities to stronger and weaker classes, multilingual and monolingual classes, and to different class sizes and environments.

On the Teacher's DVD-ROM

A teacher-friendly resource

English Unlimited Upper Intermediate Teacher's DVD-ROM offers a large suite of language and skills practice, assessment and video materials in an easy-to-use package. It also contains unit-by-unit PDF files of the Teacher's Book.

It is designed to offer flexibility to teachers who may want to use materials in digital and paper format. So you can:

- display activity worksheets and tests on a screen or whiteboard as well as distributing paper copies to learners. This is useful if you want to: demonstrate an activity; go through answers with the whole class; zoom in on an area of a worksheet; display Progress or Achievement tests as learners attempt them, or when you go through the answers;
- display answers to Progress tests, so that learners can mark their own papers;
- print out just the unit of the Teacher's Book that you are using, rather than carrying the book around;
- display answer keys to Coursebook exercises from the Teacher's Book;
- watch videos with your learners.

Photocopiable activities

There are 42 photocopiable activity worksheets on the Teacher's DVD-ROM (three for each unit), ready to print out and use straight away. These offer extra vocabulary, grammar and pronunciation practice, extra reading and writing work, role plays and games which further activate the language that learners have been introduced to in the Coursebook, and build their fluency, confidence and communication skills.

Each activity is accompanied by a page of clear, step-by-step instructions, with answer keys and extra teaching ideas. At the end of each unit of the Teacher's notes, there is a page to help you find the activities you need, and there are also boxes in the unit notes which suggest when particular activities might be used.

Progress and Achievement tests

The *English Unlimited* testing suite consists of 14 unit-by-unit Progress tests and three skills-based Achievement tests to motivate your learners and give you and them a clear idea of the progress that they are making. These and other methods of assessment are discussed in detail on pp20–21.

Videos

The video from each unit of the Self-study Pack is also included on the Teacher's DVD-ROM, as this is easily adaptable for use in class, either using the video exercises from the Workbook, or just for extra listening practice and class discussion. The 11 Interviews and three Documentaries are each linked topically to the unit, and so they offer extension and consolidation of the work done in the Coursebook, as well as giving learners the chance to listen to authentic, spontaneous speech from a range of native and non-native English speakers. The subtitles toggle on and off, so you can easily show any sections of text which learners find difficult to understand.

The book on the disk

English Unlimited Upper Intermediate Teacher's DVD-ROM also contains the whole Teacher's Book in PDF format, so that you can print out the unit or section that you want, instead of carrying the book around with you.

There are also CEF tables, which show how *English Unlimited Upper Intermediate* completes CEF level B2 by mapping the relevant 'can do' statements from the CEF to specific pages and tasks in the Coursebook.

Assessing your learners with *English Unlimited*

There are many ways of assessing learner progress through a language course. For this reason *English Unlimited* offers a range of testing and assessment options, including progress tests, skill-based achievement tests, assessment using the e-Portfolio, self-assessment and continuous assessment.

Tests on the Teacher's DVD-ROM

There are two types of test available as PDFs on the Teacher's DVD-ROM: Progress and Achievement tests.

Progress tests

There is one Progress test for each of the 14 units of the course. These assess the learners' acquisition of language items taught in the main Coursebook material. Each test carries 40 marks and includes questions assessing grammar and vocabulary items taught in the unit. These are not intended to be 'high stakes' tests but rather quick checks that will help the teacher and learner judge which language points have been successfully acquired and understood, and which areas individual learners or the whole class may need to study again.

We suggest that each test should take no more than 30 minutes in the classroom. Tests can be copied and distributed to each learner and taken in class time. The tests are designed for quick marking with the provided Answer Key. Teachers may choose to mark tests, or, alternatively, learners can mark each other's work. A mark can be given out of 40. If particular problem areas are identified, learners can be directed to do extra work from the Self-study Pack.

Achievement tests

There are three Achievement tests, designed to form the basis of formal learner assessment.

- **Achievement test 1** can be taken after Unit 4.
- **Achievement test 2** can be taken after Unit 9.
- **Achievement test 3** can be taken after Unit 14.

These tests are based on the four skills: Reading, Listening, Writing and Speaking.

Reading tests

Each test is based on a short text and we advise allowing no more than 15 minutes for each test. As with the Coursebook and Listening tests, there may be a few unfamiliar items in the text, but the tasks are graded so unknown items should not hinder the learners' ability to answer the questions. The teacher may mark the tests or it may be acceptable for learners to mark each other's work.

Listening tests

The audio tracks for these are found at the end of the three Class Audio CDs. Achievement test 1 is track 31 on CD1; Achievement test 2 is track 29 on CD2; Achievement test 3 is track 37 on CD3.

We suggest carrying out tests under controlled conditions, with the recording played twice. Each test should take no longer than ten minutes. As with the Coursebook audio, there may be a few unfamiliar language items in the listening text, but tasks are graded to the level of the learner, so unknown items should not hinder the learners' ability to answer the eight questions. The tests are simple and quick to mark. They can be marked by the teacher or it may be acceptable for learners to mark each other's work.

Writing tests

Learners are set a writing task based on themes from the Coursebook and the teacher assesses work using the Writing assessment scales provided. Tasks are designed to simulate purposeful, real-life, communicative pieces of writing. The teacher should endeavour to identify the band the work falls in for each category. This marking scheme can give learners a profile of the strong and weak points of their written work, creating a virtuous circle of improvement through the course.

If the tests are to be used under timed conditions in class, 40 minutes should be allowed for the learners to produce their texts – planning and redrafting may be encouraged by the teacher at the outset.

Another way is to set the tasks as assessed writing assignments to be done as homework. In these cases, the teacher should interpret the band scales according to the time available and the availability of dictionaries and other reference materials.

The option chosen will depend on your learning environment. A timed test may help you assess learners under equal conditions, but can be a rather artificial, pressured environment. Written homework assignments are less controlled, but could be a better way of encouraging learners to work at their writing and feel satisfied with a polished piece of written work. The Explore writing tasks in the Coursebook and Self-study Pack may also be used as assessed assignments and marked using the assessment scales.

Speaking tests

These are designed to be carried out by an assessor, who may be the learners' regular teacher or another teacher in the institution. Learners do the tests in pairs. The ideal environment is for the test to take place in a separate room from the rest of the class, who can be engaged in self-study work while the testing is taking place. It is best if seating is set up as a 'round table' if possible, rather than the assessor facing both learners across a desk, so as not to suggest an interrogation! Each test takes 14 minutes.

The assessor should be familiar with the Speaking assessment scales for the Speaking tests before the test and have a copy of the Mark Sheet for each learner with their names already filled in. Screen the Mark Sheets from the learners.

The assessor will need the Teacher's Notes, which provide a script of prompts for the test. Each test is in two parts. In the first part (three minutes), the assessor asks the learners in turn a selection of questions from the Notes, based on themes from the Coursebook. The assessor may depart from the script to elicit further responses, maintaining a friendly, encouraging manner. The assessor may begin to note down some marks based on the scales for each learner.

In Part 2 (six minutes), learners are provided with prompts for a communicative task, which they carry out between themselves. Learners may need some encouragement, or to have the instructions explained more than once.

During this section, the assessor should withdraw eye contact, making it clear that the learners should talk to each other, listen closely and revise the marks from Part 1, gradually completing the grid.

In part 3 (five minutes) the assessor asks learners questions related to the task in part 2. The assessor may now make any final necessary adjustments to the learners' marks.

The assessor should not correct learners at any point during the test.

Filling in the Mark Sheets

Once all four papers of the Achievement tests have been carried out, the teacher can provide marks for each learner. This includes analytical marks for the Speaking and Writing tests, and an average mark out of five for each one; and marks out of eight for the Reading and Listening tests. This gives the learners a snapshot of their performance in the four skills. The learners should be encouraged to reflect on what they found easy or difficult, and given strategies to improve performance in different skills. The marks can be used as the basis for course reports or formal assessment.

Self-assessment

Assessment is not just about tests. Self-assessment encourages more reflective and focused learning. *English Unlimited* offers a number of tools for learner self-assessment:

- Each unit of the Coursebook ends with a self-assessment grid in which learners are encouraged to measure their own progress against the unit goals, which in turn are based on the can-do statements of the Common European Framework of Reference for Languages.
- Progress with the activities on the Self-study DVD-ROM can be analysed in detail on the Progress screen.
- The Self-study DVD-ROM also contains Quick Check tests, using a bank of 700 multiple-choice questions. Learners select which units they want to be tested on and how long they want the test to be – new tests will be randomly generated each time.

Using the e-Portfolio

Portfolio-based assessment is a useful tool for both self-assessment and formal assessment, particularly for teachers seeking an alternative to traditional timed writing tests. The e-Portfolio allows learners to:

- assess their progress against can-do statements and revise their assessments later in the course depending on progress made;
- build up a personal e-Portfolio of written work associated with the course. The learner may then select their best work, as an alternative to tests, or at the end of the course to be provided as a Portfolio. This may include word-processed documents, project work and even audio files. Some of the Explore writing tasks may lend themselves well to portfolio work, and in some classrooms, learners may be asked to record personal audio files based around speaking tasks in the Coursebook. The satisfaction of producing a polished *spoken* text is a rare one in a language course, but if the learner or the centre has access to a microphone, it is relatively easy to do.

Written texts and audio in a learner's e-Portfolio may be assessed using the same analytical scales as the Writing and Speaking Achievement tests. You can find more information about the e-Portfolio on p18.

Continuous assessment

Finally, some teachers and institutions may prefer to dispense with tests and adopt a form of continuous assessment. This can be demanding on the teacher's time but perhaps no more so than the marking load created by frequent formal tests. The important thing is to explain the system to learners early in the course, and regularly show them their Mark Sheets to indicate how they are getting on. How actual assessment is carried out may differ between institutions, but here are some guidelines and ideas:

- It is possible to assess learners using the Speaking assessment scales regularly through the course. The Target activities, where learners are involved in more extended discourse, offer an opportunity for this.
- Tell learners when their speaking is being assessed and the teacher can monitor particular groups.
- Learners should be assessed several times during the course or they may rightly feel they were let down by a single bad performance, even if the assessment is not 'high stakes'.
- An atmosphere of gentle encouragement and striving for improvement should always accompany this kind of assessment. Some learners can get competitive about this, which can have a negative effect on class atmosphere and demotivate less-confident learners.
- The Explore writing tasks can be used for continuous written assessment, using the Writing assessment scales.

A final word

Testing and assessment can be a vital tool for teachers and learners in assessing strengths and weaknesses, building awareness and encouraging improvement. But it can be frustrating for a learner to feel that they are being assessed too often, at the expense of actually learning, and whilst there are certainly learners who like being tested, there are many others who certainly don't!

English Unlimited aims to help learners communicate in real-life situations, and the testing and assessment tools provided should be used with that purpose in mind. Testing and assessment should never take precedence over learning, but serve as useful checks on the way to increasing confidence, competence and fluency.

The Common European Framework of Reference for Languages (CEF)

A goals-based course

English Unlimited is a practical, goals-based course for adult learners of English. The course goals are taken and adapted from the language-learning goals stated in the Common European Framework of Reference for Languages (CEF).

The goals of the CEF are divided into a number of **scales** which describe abilities in different kinds of communication. We've chosen the scales which we felt to be the most useful for adult general English learners at Upper Intermediate level. These are:

Speaking
Describing experience
Putting a case
Addressing audiences
Conversation
Informal discussion
Formal discussion and meetings
Goal-oriented co-operation
Transactions to obtain goods and services
Information exchange
Interviewing and being interviewed
Planning
Compensating
Monitoring and repair
Turntaking
Co-operating
Asking for clarification

Writing
Creative writing
Reports and essays
Correspondence
Processing text

Listening
Overall listening comprehension
Understanding conversation
Listening to announcements and instructions
Listening to audio media and recordings

Reading
Overall reading comprehension
Reading correspondence
Reading for orientation
Reading for information and argument

Where the goals are met

As you'll see in the example unit on pp6–10, goals are given for the two lessons at the start of each unit, for the Target activity, and on the Explore speaking and Explore writing pages. They are also listed in the Self-assessment, which learners do at the end of the Look again page.

Listening and reading goals are not usually given on the page, as they are addressed repeatedly throughout the course. The CEF tables on the Teacher's Pack DVD-ROM show which parts of the course deal with the listening and reading goals.

Find out more about the CEF

You can read about the CEF in detail in *Common European Framework of Reference for Languages: Learning, teaching, assessment* (2001), Council of Europe Modern Languages Division, Strasbourg, Cambridge University Press, ISBN 9780521005319.

1 Talented

1.1

Goals: talk about people's success
discuss and evaluate ideas

Core language:

VOCABULARY   Routes to success
VOCABULARY   Reacting to ideas

Practice makes perfect?

READING

1   👥👥 *Personal introductions.* Learners introduce themselves to each other and find out about 1–3.

> **Alternative**
>
> *Mingle activity.* Learners move freely around the room, asking each other the questions. They try to talk to at least five or six other learners in the class. Then they sit down and, in pairs/groups, tell each other what they can remember about the other people in the class.

To round off this stage and introduce the topic of the reading, elicit from the class at least one thing that each learner is good at.

2   *Reading for main ideas.* Read through the four sentences with the class to familiarise learners with them. Then learners read the article and choose the correct options in the sentences.

> 1 beginning   2 practice   3 enthusiasm   4 mature

3   *Reading for details.* Learners read again to find out about the four topics.

> 1 Setting particular goals, getting feedback straight away, concentrating equally on technique and results
> 2 Students should focus on the things that interest them earlier on, in order to get more practice and feedback.
> 3 Because, in a team with players from a particular calendar year, the January-born players will be older and therefore stronger.
> 4 They receive more training, practice and feedback, and therefore also have more self-esteem.

> **Alternative for weaker classes**
>
> While going through the answers to this task, ask learners which parts of the article the answers are based on.
>
> 1 the last sentence of the second paragraph
> 2 the last sentence of the third paragraph
> 3 the first half of the final paragraph
> 4 the last sentence of the final paragraph

VOCABULARY Routes to success

4   👥/👥👥 *Presentation.* Learners match the verbs with the correct endings to make expressions from the article. Make sure learners realise that the verbs/endings are set in pairs, so that they only have to choose between two possibilities each time.

> 1 set specific goals   2 get feedback
> 3 concentrate on results   4 possess talent
> 5 put in a lot of practice   6 build up experience
> 7 have the will to succeed   8 follow your interests
> 9 receive training   10 have high self-esteem

Ask questions to check that learners understand some of the more challenging expressions:

- *Which word means 'information about how well (or badly) you did something'?* (feedback)
- *In what ways do people at school or university get feedback?* (grades, exam results, written reports, tutorials, etc.)
- *Which expression means 'concentrate on things you like or are interested in'?* (follow your interests)
- *Which expression means 'have a good opinion about yourself or your abilities'?* (have high self-esteem)
- *How do 5 ('put in a lot of practice') and 9 ('receive training') differ in meaning?* (5 is something you do yourself, independently; 9 suggests that you have help from a trainer, coach, instructor, etc.)

5   👥 *Memorisation.* Learner A chooses expressions from 1–10 at random and says the second part of each expression. Learner B (book closed) listens and replies with the whole expression. Then they swap roles.

SPEAKING

6   👤 *Preparation for discussion.* Learners read and think about how to answer the questions. Encourage them to think about how they can use the expressions from 4.

👥/👥👥 *Discussion.* Learners discuss and compare their answers to the questions.

Round-up. Ask a few learners to tell the class about someone they know who's been very successful (question 2).

I'm not really convinced

LISTENING

1   *Listening for main ideas.* Direct learners' attention to the picture and explain that they're going to listen to Jennifer and Derek talking about the article. Read through the three questions, then play recording **1.1**. Learners listen and answer the questions.

> 1 Derek's started playing golf. He doesn't enjoy it.
> 2 Jennifer's read the article. Derek hasn't.
> 3 Jennifer seems to be convinced. Derek isn't sure.

2 a   *Listening for details.* Play recording **1.1** again. Learners listen again and identify Derek's attitude to three particular ideas from the article.

> 1 It's not a new idea. Also, practice isn't everything: talent is important, too.
> 2 He doesn't understand it and isn't sure it's true.
> 3 It makes sense. He hadn't thought about it in this way before.

b 👥/👥👥 Learners compare, then read script **1.1** on p141 to check and complete their answers.

VOCABULARY Reacting to ideas

3 a 👥/👥👥 *Presentation.* Learners match the sentences 1–5 from the conversation with the meanings a–e.

> 1 d   2 c   3 a   4 b   5 e

b 👥/👥👥 Learners match five more sentences 6–10 from the conversation with the meanings a–e.

> 6 b   7 c   8 a   9 d   10 e

4 👤 *Practice.* Learners spend a few minutes planning a personal response to the ideas in the article, choosing expressions from **3**.

👥/👥👥 Learners describe and explain their responses.

SPEAKING

5 👥/👥👥 *Discussion.* Learners look at the summaries one by one on p118 and say what they think about the ideas expressed in them.

Alternative

'Carousel' discussion. Divide the class into five groups and give a copy of *one* of the summaries to each group. Groups discuss the summary for a few minutes. Then move the summaries round so each group has a new summary to discuss. Repeat until all the groups have had a chance to discuss all five summaries.

Round-up. Elicit different groups' opinions about each of the summaries. Find out if there's a consensus opinion across the class or if people have sharply differing opinions.

 You could use photocopiable activity 1A on the Teacher's DVD-ROM at this point.

1.2

Goals: talk about things you're good at
describe and evaluate skills

Core language:

GRAMMAR	Present perfect simple and progressive
VOCABULARY	Skills
PRONUNCIATION	Stress

I've always been good at …

LISTENING

1 *Pre-listening discussion.* To introduce the listening, briefly look at the pictures A–C in turn. Find out how much experience learners have of each activity, how easy they (would) find it, and why. For example, for Picture A, ask: *Has anyone ever been sailing? Are you good at it? Would you like to try it? What skills would you need to be a good sailor?*

Listening for main ideas. Play recording **1.2**. Learners listen and do the matching, then answer the question for all three speakers as a class.

> 1 Darya C   Cian A   Hyun-Ae B
> 2 Darya: *both*
>   Cian: *life outside work*
>   Hyun-Ae: *both*

2 👥/👥👥 *Listening for details.* Learners read through 1–6 and tell each other what they can remember about each point. Then play recording **1.2** again. Learners listen to check and complete their answers.

> 1 *When she was a child*
> 2 *When shopping and in her work as a civil engineer*
> 3 *His university and his country*
> 4 *A couple of hours*
> 5 *Moving from place to place made her skilled at meeting new people.*
> 6 *Running a social club for the elderly*

3 👥/👥👥 *Responding to the text.* Learners discuss the question.

Round-up. Ask a few pairs/groups to share their opinions with the whole class.

GRAMMAR Present perfect simple and progressive

4 👥/👥👥 *Presentation.* Learners read sentences 1–5 and then match them with descriptions a–e in the box below. Draw learners' attention to the rule that verbs describing states are generally not used in progressive forms.

> a 2   b 3   c 1   d 5   e 4

5 a 👤 *Practice.* Learners complete the profile using the verbs in brackets in the present perfect simple or progressive.

👥/👥👥 Learners compare their answers. Then go through the answers as a class, asking learners to explain them, referring to the four categories in the grammar box.

> 1 *'ve always been (c: 'be' is a stative verb, so we use the simple rather than the progressive.)*
> 2 *'ve been doing (e: We could use the simple, but the progressive sounds more natural.)*
> 3 *'ve completed (a)*
> 4 *'ve won (a)*
> 5 *'ve been advertising (e: We could use the simple, but the progressive sounds more natural.)*
> 6 *'ve given up (b)*
> 7 *'ve become (b)*
> 8 *'ve been experimenting (d)*

Note: Grammar practice

You could do the grammar practice on p131 at this point.

---

b 👤 Learners write a paragraph like Esmeralda's about things they're good at. As they write, monitor closely to help learners and check their use of the present perfect simple and progressive.

SPEAKING

6 a 🗣/🗣🗣 *Discussion.* Learners put away their writing from **5b** and tell each other about things they're good at and what they've done. Encourage learners to ask each other questions to find out as many details as they can. Demonstrate by having a more confident learner tell the class about the things they are good at. Ask questions and prompt other learners to ask questions.

b 🗣/🗣🗣 *Report.* Put learners into new pairs/groups. Learners report what they found out about the people in their previous pair/group in **a**.

 You could use photocopiable activity **1B** on the Teacher's DVD-ROM at this point.

Transferable skills

VOCABULARY Skills

1 a *Presentation.* With the whole class, match the groups of expressions 1–3 with the labels a–c.

> *a 3 b 1 c 2*

b 🗣/🗣🗣 Learners add more expressions to each group.

> 1 have good eyesight, have a good sense of balance, have quick reflexes
> 2 have plenty of imagination, have a lot of self-discipline, be well organised
> 3 be able to delegate, be able to manage groups, be sensitive to people's feelings

2 👤 *Practice.* Learners look at all the expressions and think about which skills Darya, Cian and Hyun-Ae from the Listening have.

🗣/🗣🗣 Learners compare their ideas.

PRONUNCIATION Stress

3 a *Books closed.* Write on the board: *be good with numbers.* Ask: *Which words would you usually stress?* (*good, numbers*) Underline the stresses on the board: *be good with numbers.* Ask: *Why do we stress these words?* (Because they carry the main meaning of the expression.)

🗣/🗣🗣 *Books open.* Learners look at the other expressions in **1** and mark the stresses. They focus on the highlighted expressions only.

b Play recording **1.3.** Learners listen while looking at the script on p141 to check their answers.

> 1 be strong, have plenty of endurance, be physically fit, have good eyesight, have a good sense of balance, have quick reflexes
> 2 be good with numbers, be able to think logically, be focused, have a lot of self-discipline, have plenty of imagination, be well organised
> 3 be a good listener, be an effective communicator, have the ability to compromise, be able to delegate, be able to manage groups, be sensitive to people's feelings

c Discuss the questions as a class. On the board, make a list of kinds of word which are usually 1) stressed, and 2) not stressed. Ask learners to give a few examples of each kind of word.

> 1 stressed: nouns, verbs, adjectives, adverbs, question words, 'not' (= 'content words')
> 2 not stressed: pronouns, articles, prepositions, conjunctions, modal verbs (= 'grammar words')

SPEAKING

4 Write on the board *transferable skills.* Learners read the extract from a website to find the answers to the two questions.

> 1 Skills from one part of your life which you can use in another part of your life. When people use this term, they're usually thinking about skills which can be transferred to work from outside (e.g. a hobby) or from one kind of work to another (e.g. when you change occupations).
> 2 Probably yes. The extract implies that everyone must have transferable skills to some degree.

5 a *Preparation for discussion.* For each job, learners think about what transferable skills they have. They decide which job they'd be most suited to.

Alternative

If necessary, change the selection of jobs to suit the ages, interests and backgrounds of your learners. Write them on the board.

---

b 👥👥 *Discussion.* Learners explain their ideas and decide who would be most suited to each job. Remind them to use expressions from **1a** and **b**.

Round-up. Ask the class who they chose for each of the six jobs, and why.

💿 You could use photocopiable activity 1C on the Teacher's DVD-ROM at this point.

1.3 Target activity

Goals: talk about people's success ♻
describe and evaluate skills ♻
give advice about an interest or occupation

Core language:

TASK VOCABULARY	Giving advice
1.1 VOCABULARY	Routes to success
1.2 VOCABULARY	Skills

Give advice about an interest or occupation

TASK LISTENING

1 👥 / 👥👥 *Pre-listening discussion.* To focus on the context of the listening, learners read the information about VideoJug and discuss the two questions.

2 a 👥 / 👥👥 *Prediction.* Tell learners they're going to listen to a VideoJug interview with a video game designer. Learners read through the five questions and discuss possible answers.

b *Listening for detail.* Play recording **1.4**. Learners listen to find answers to the questions, taking notes if they wish.

👥 / 👥👥 Learners compare their answers, then check and complete their answers by listening again and/or reading script **1.4** on pp141–2.

> 1 Harry doesn't feel specific gaming qualifications are necessary. He recommends a broad qualification combining sciences and humanities.
> 2 You can apply for a job as normal (though it's hard to succeed at this without experience), do work experience (presumably unpaid) or get known to the company by doing games testing.
> 3 No, though it is helpful.
> 4 No, though it is helpful.
> 5 Keep it to yourself. Try to get the game made once you've got a position in a games company, or try to make the game yourself.

TASK VOCABULARY Giving advice

3 👥 / 👥👥 *Presentation.* Learners read eight pieces of advice from Harry and match each with a question 1–5 from **2a**.

1 question 4	2 question 1	3 question 4	4 question 3
5 question 2	6 question 2	7 question 5	8 question 5

4 👤 *Practice.* Learners write four or five sentences about an interest or occupation using expressions from **3**.

Optional extra

Discussion. Put learners in pairs to listen to each other's sentences from **4** and ask follow-up questions about any points which interest them. If you do this, be sure to put learners into new pairs for the Task below.

TASK

5 a 👥👥 *Preparation for interview.* Learners tell their partner what the topic of the interview will be.

b 👤 Learners think of interview questions for their partner on their partner's chosen topic, and write the questions down. Draw learners' attention to the list of possible prompts given.

c 👤 Learners swap interview questions so they can now see the questions they're going to be asked in the interview. They plan how to answer the questions. Encourage learners to think about how they can use the expressions from **3**. You can also remind them to use expressions from VOCABULARY Routes to success and VOCABULARY Skills.

6 a 👥👥 *Interview.* Learners do two interviews, taking turns to be the interviewer and interviewee. Encourage interviewers to go beyond the questions they thought of in **5b**, listening carefully to the answers they get, asking follow-up questions and exploring areas of interest.

b 👥👥 *Task repetition.* In the same pairs, do the interviews again, this time recording them on audio or video.

👥👥 Listen to or watch the interviews as a class. In groups, learners identify the topic of each interview and think of one further question they'd like to ask the interviewee.

Alternative

Reporting an interview. If **6b** is not feasible, learners get into new pairs and tell each other what topics they asked about in their interviews and what they found out.

---

1 Explore

Meanings of *think*

1 a 👥 / 👥👥 *Prediction*. Learners look at the four cartoons and think about what could go in the empty speech bubbles. Ask different pairs/groups to tell the class about their ideas.

b 👥 / 👥👥 *Presentation*. Learners find one sentence to go in each cartoon.

> 1 B (We're thinking of having a party on Friday. Are you free then?)
> 2 A (You think too much. Just choose one and let's go!)
> 3 C (We really need to think of some ways to save money.)
> 4 D (So, what do you think of the octopus?)

c 👥 / 👥👥 Learners match each meaning of *think* 1–4 with a pair of sentences A–D from **b**.

> 1 D   2 C   3 B   4 A

d 👥 / 👥👥 Learners look again at the sentences in **b** and work out which patterns go with each meaning.

> a 2   b 4   c 1, 3

At this point, it might be useful to summarise on the board:

1 have an opinion or believe something: think of, think about
2 create an idea or a solution to a problem: think of
3 consider doing something: think of, think about
4 use your mind to consider a topic: think about

Language notes

- *Think* can also of course be followed by a clause: *I think that's true* (meaning 1), *I'm thinking maybe we should go* (meaning 3).
- In meaning 1, *think* describes a state and is therefore not usually used in the progressive form. In meanings 2–4, *think* describes an activity and is commonly used in both simple and progressive forms.
---

2 a 👤 *Practice*. Learners read the questions and decide which meaning of *think* is being used in each case. They decide which prepositions (*of*, *about* or both) can be used.

> 1 about   2 of/about   3 of/about   4 of

Then learners write two or three questions with *think* for their classmates, taking care to use the prepositions *of* and *about* as appropriate.

b 👥 / 👥👥 Learners ask and answer all the questions.

Common expressions with *think*

3 a 👥 / 👥👥 *Presentation*. Tell learners that they'll now look at a number of common expressions with *think*. Learners focus on the highlighted expressions in 1–10 and try to work out their meanings.

After a few minutes, elicit and check learners' ideas, or give out dictionaries so they can check for themselves.

> 1 think straight – think in a clear and logical way
> 2 think aloud – think and say what you're thinking at the same time
> 3 think highly of … – have a good opinion of …, respect …
> 4 not think much of … – have a low opinion of … (the opposite of 3)
> 5 think back to … – remember, think about the past
> 6 think ahead to … – plan, think about the future
> 7 think twice about – think very carefully because you have doubts
> 8 think long and hard about … – think carefully, for a long time
> 9 think on one's feet – make a decision quickly, often while in the middle of an activity
> 10 think for oneself – make your own decisions, form your own opinions

b 👥 *Memorisation*. Learner A chooses expressions with *think* from **a** in random order and gives definitions. Learner B (book closed) listens to A's definitions and replies with the expressions. Then they swap roles.

4 👥👥 *Practice*. Learners talk about 1–10 one by one, explaining to what extent the sentence is true for them, and why.

1 *Pre-listening discussion*. To introduce the context for the listening, draw learners' attention to the picture. Then discuss the question with the learners and make a list of their ideas on the board.

2 *Listening for main ideas*. Play recording **1.5**. Learners listen to Indra's friends organising her party and answer the questions.

> 1 Invitations and food
> 2 Decorations and a piñata (which can be seen in the picture). They decide against a badge.

3 a 👥 / 👥👥 *Presentation*. Learners read the conversation on the right and put the expressions 1–9 into groups according to their function.

Elicit learners' answers, writing the expressions up on the board in three groups.

> 1 1, 2, 3, 4, 6, 8
> 2 a 9   b 5, 7

b Learners look at the expressions in the box and add them to the same groups as in **a**. Again, elicit learners' answers and write the expressions in the correct groups.

> 1 and all that, and whatnot, and stuff, and so forth
> 2 a what's-her-name   b thingummy

Language note

Of the expressions in group 1:
- most mean 'and similar things', but 8 (*and all sorts of things*) is rather different. It means 'and many other things';
- most can be used in a range of different situations (formal/ neutral/informal), but *and all that* and *and stuff* are more informal. Some speakers regard *and what have you* and *and whatnot* as slightly old-fashioned.

Expressions like those in groups 2a and b are only appropriate in informal situations.

4   *Practice.* Learners choose expressions from **3** to complete the conversation. Point out that different answers are possible.

    / Learners compare their answers.

> *Suggested answers*
> 1 what's-his-name   2 and that kind of thing
> 3 and so on   4 and stuff   5 thingy   6 and things

5 a   Learners choose an event from the list or think of their own.

   b   Learners make a list of things they'll need for their event, thinking about the topics provided (food and drink, equipment, etc.) and any other areas they feel are relevant. Encourage them to use expressions from **3a** and **3b** where appropriate.

      Tell learners that they'll have to report to the class on what they've decided. Ask them to make notes of their decisions and decide which member(s) of their groups will present their ideas to the class.

6   Each group reports to the class on what kind of event they've planned, what things they've decided they'll need, and why.

Alternative

Voting for a proposal. At **5a**, ask all the groups to plan the same kind of event, something which you feel will appeal to your particular group of learners. Then at **6**, ask learners to vote for their favourite proposal (other than their own).

1 Look again

Review

VOCABULARY Skills

1 a   / Learners put the expressions in the box into two lists.

> be: good with numbers, physically fit, a good listener
> have: plenty of endurance, a lot of self-discipline, the ability to compromise

   b   / Learners add more expressions to the list from memory, then look back at VOCABULARY Skills on p9 to check and complete their answers.

> be: strong, able to think logically, focused, an effective communicator, able to delegate, able to manage groups, sensitive to people's feelings, well organised
> have: good eyesight, plenty of imagination, a good sense of balance, quick reflexes

Alternative

Grouping dictation. Instead of **1a** and **b**, read all the expressions (without *be* and *have*) aloud to the learners, pausing only briefly between each item. Learners listen and note down the expressions in two groups: a *be* group and a *have* group.

   c   Learners choose people to exemplify any five of the skills in **a** and **b**. These can be celebrities, family members, friends, colleagues, etc.

   d   / Learners listen to each other's ideas and ask questions to find out more.

      Round-up. Ask one person from each group to tell the class who they think is the most interesting or unusual-sounding person they've just heard about.

GRAMMAR Present perfect simple and progressive

2 a   Learners read the paragraph about Remi and choose the correct forms.

> 1 has released   2 has organised   3 has always had
> 4 has become   5 has been working

   b   Learners write a similar paragraph about someone they know.

   c   / Learners read each other's paragraphs and ask questions to find out more.

Extension

SPELLING AND SOUNDS /dʒ/

3 a   Write on the board /dʒ/. Ask learners what sound this represents (*j* as in *jump*). Write on the board: *j, g, dg*. Explain that these (combinations of) letters can all be used to represent a /dʒ/ sound in English words.

      Learners complete the spellings of the words.

> jail, manager, injure, gym, jigsaw, journal, budget, subject, logically

   b   / Learners find words in **a** to match each pattern 1–4.

> 1 jail, journal, injure
> 2 manager, logically, gym
> 3 subject, jigsaw
> 4 budget

      Tell learners that the first two statements are useful general rules to bear in mind. The last two statements cover exceptions to these general rules.

   c   *Books closed.* Play recording **1.6**. Learners listen and write down the 12 words, then look at script **1.6** on p142 to check their spelling.

NOTICE *good at, good with*

4 a Direct learners' attention to the two sentences or write them on the board. Answer the two questions as a class.

> 1 good at   2 good with

b 👥 / 👥👥 Learners put the expressions in the box into two lists, according to whether they follow *good at* or *good with*.

> *good at: cooking, explaining things, maths, music, sports, writing*
> *good with: children, computers, my hands, money, people, words*

c Learners move around the room and talk to different people, asking questions like *Are you good at maths? Would you say you're good with money?* Their task is to find at least one person who's good at/with each of the things in **b**.

👥 / 👥👥 Learners sit down and compare their findings.

Round-up. Quickly run through the list of things in **b** and ask learners to shout out people who are good at/ with each thing.

Self-assessment

To help focus learners on the self-assessment, you could read it through, giving a few examples of the language they have learned in each section (or asking learners to tell you). Then ask them to circle the numbers on each line.

Unit 1 Extra activities on the Teacher's DVD-ROM

Printable worksheets, activity instructions and answer keys are on your Teacher's DVD-ROM.

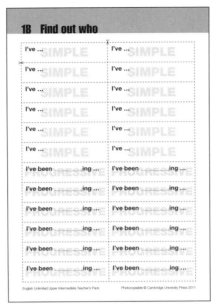

1A Netiquette

Activity type: Reading and speaking – Exchanging opinions – Individuals / Small groups

Aim: To practise using expressions for reacting to ideas

Language: Reacting to ideas – Use at any point from 1.1.

Preparation: Make one copy of the worksheet for each learner. Fold each worksheet along the line so the expressions at the bottom are hidden while learners read the 'Mind your netiquette' article.

Time: 25 minutes

1B Find out who

Activity type: Writing and speaking – Mingle and report back – Whole class / Pairs

Aim: To practise using the present perfect simple and progressive

Language: Present perfect simple and progressive – Use at any point from 1.2.

Preparation: Copy and cut up enough cards for each learner to have two Simple and two Progressive cards. Keep them in separate piles.

Time: 30 minutes

1C Skills for life

Activity type: Speaking – Pelmanism and guessing game – Pairs

Aim: To practise using expressions for describing transferable skills

Language: Skills – Use at any point from 1.2.

Preparation: Make one copy of the worksheet for every two learners. Cut up each worksheet to make a set of 36 cards.

Time: 25 minutes

Unit 1 Self-study Pack

In the Workbook

Unit 1 of the *English Unlimited Upper Intermediate Workbook* offers additional ways to practise the vocabulary and grammar taught in the Coursebook. There are also activities which build reading and writing skills and a whole page of listening and speaking tasks to use with the Interview video, giving your learners the opportunity to hear and react to authentic spoken English.

- **Vocabulary:** Routes to success; Reacting to ideas; Skills; Giving advice
- **Grammar:** Present perfect simple and progressive
- **Explore writing:** A covering letter
- **Interview:** Hidden talents – Clare and Carlos

On the DVD-ROM

Unit 1 of the *English Unlimited Upper Intermediate Self-study DVD-ROM* contains interactive games and activities for your learners to practise and improve their vocabulary, grammar and pronunciation, and also their speaking and listening, with the possibility for learners to record themselves, and a video of authentic spoken English to use with the Workbook.

- **Vocabulary and grammar:** Extra practice activities
- **Pronunciation:** Stress
- **Explore speaking:** *Yeah ..., Well ...*
- **Listening:** A job interview
- **Video:** Hidden talents

2 Misunderstandings

2.1

Goals: describe events in detail
deal with misunderstandings
describe experiences of things going wrong

Core language:

VOCABULARY	Dealing with misunderstandings
PRONUNCIATION	Contrastive stress
GRAMMAR	Past simple and past perfect simple

Not my day

LISTENING

1 *Pre-listening discussion.* To introduce the topic, write the word *misunderstandings* on the board. Ask learners what it means (*when someone doesn't understand something correctly*). Get the class to give one or two examples of things that are easy to misunderstand, e.g. *the time of a meeting, dates, places to meet, names.* Don't go into detail at this point about what misunderstandings learners have experienced. They will talk about this in *I was sure I'd ...* **3a**.

Now get learners to look at the pictures and discuss the two questions in pairs.

2 *Listening for main idea.* Learners read the questions. Check they know the meaning of *solution* (*the answer to a problem*).

Play recording **1.7**, pausing between the two conversations for learners to write notes.

> **Conversation 1**
> 1 Pauline thought the meeting was cancelled. It wasn't.
> 2 She'll get a taxi to Rainer's office and be there in 20 minutes.
> 3 Rainer, with his colleagues in the meeting
> **Conversation 2**
> 1 The plant's too big for the room (like a tree). Rainer can't return it, as it was on sale.
> 2 Rainer will take it to his office.
> 3 Rainer's mother

3 *Listening for detail.* Learners write *true* or *false* next to each statement. If necessary, play recording **1.7** again.

> 1 True   2 False   3 True   4 False   5 False   6 True

4 *Responding to the text.* Learners talk about what they'd say or do in the two situations.

VOCABULARY Dealing with misunderstandings

5 Learners complete the two groups of sentences. Note that each group of sentences has its own group of words for matching. Learners are not expected to sort through nine words for each sentence.

> 1 thought   2 told   3 said   4 meant   5 not   6 explains
> 7 if   8 logical   9 option

PRONUNCIATION Contrastive stress

6 **a** To introduce the idea of contrastive stress, ask *Is it [wrong day]?* Elicit *No, it's [correct day].* Then say, *Oh, right – [correct day].* Ask learners which words in the second and third sentences were stressed the most. Explain that we use this kind of stress to contrast something with previous information. We often use it to correct or clarify information. Play recording **1.8**. Learners listen and read an extract from the conversation.

b Learners underline the two words in each of the three sentences that they think are contrasted. Do not go through the answers, as this would pre-empt **c**.

c Play recording **1.9** or write the sentences on the board to check, eliciting which words to underline.

> 1 your; Chris's   2 plant; tree   3 normal; special

Learners say the sentences, pronouncing the contrasted words with an extra-strong stress but in a natural way. Note that learners will be using contrastive stress in **7b**.

SPEAKING

7 **a** *Preparation for role play.* Divide learners into A/B pairs. Learners read Situation 1, and think about what expressions from **5** they can use. Remind them to use contrastive stress if they need to correct anything.

b Learners have the first conversation. Monitor, give feedback and remind them to use contrastive stress if they haven't.

Repeat the steps in **a** for Situations 2 and 3, i.e. learners prepare, then have the conversations.

> You could use photocopiable activity 2A on the Teacher's DVD-ROM at this point.

I was sure I'd ...

GRAMMAR Past simple and past perfect simple

1 *Grammar presentation.* This section revises two past narrative tenses, both of which learners will have met at previous levels. As with other grammar sections in the course, this one makes use of sentences from the text which learners have just processed for meaning. This ensures that both the sentences and the context are clear. Learners choose which one of the two verb forms in each sentence describes the earlier action or event.

> 1 had spread   2 had texted   3 'd received   4 'd circled
> 5 had disappeared   6 had gone

Draw learners' attention to the note in the Grammar box about past simple verbs that are frequently followed by the past perfect simple, e.g. *I suddenly* **realised** *he had gone.* *I* **assumed** *he'd left.* *I* **was sure** *she'd told you.* These are useful to remember.

2 a 👤/👥 *Practice.* Learners choose the best options in the story.

b Play recording **1.10** to check the answers, pausing when necessary.

> 1 realised   2 had come   3 was   4 had told   5 got
> 6 had already left   7 noticed   8 had disappeared
> 9 remembered   10 had walked   11 'd taken
> 12 'd taken   13 had given   14 came   15 'd forgotten
> 16 'd lost

Alternative

Reading for detail. Learners read the paragraph and find out what problems Carl had.

> He went to the wrong station. He missed his train.
> Someone stole his bag with important possessions in it.
> Someone threw water in the window and soaked him.

Then learners read the paragraph again and choose the best options as in **2a**.

Note: Grammar practice

You could do the grammar practice on p132 at this point.

SPEAKING

3 a *Preparation for discussion.* Tell learners they are going to talk about a time in their life when something went wrong. They read the topics listed. Give them time to plan what to say, encouraging them to note down a few key words or ideas to help them organise their thoughts. Remind them to think about the order of events and where they can use the past perfect simple.

b 👥 *Discussion.* Learners tell each other what happened and ask follow-up questions.

4 👥 *Task repetition.* Learners get into new pairs and tell each other about the same incidents. This time, they should include any details that their first partner asked about in order to develop the story further.

Round-up. Ask a few learners to tell the class what they heard.

2.2

Goals: describe events in detail ♻
tell a story from your country

Core language:

VOCABULARY	Adverbs for describing actions
GRAMMAR	Past progressive and past perfect progressive

Sen no Rikyū

LISTENING

1 a *Prediction.* To introduce this topic, draw learners' attention to the pictures. Explain they're connected with a historical story about two people from Japan in the 1500s. Explain or elicit what a *warlord* is (*a military leader who controls a particular area of a country*). Ask if anyone knows about the Japanese tea ceremony. (*It's a slow, peaceful ceremony for the preparation, serving and drinking of tea. The ceremony is done step by step, using special objects*

and movements, and has a long history. A tea master is an expert in this ceremony and can be head of a style or school of tea ceremony.)

Pronounce *Hideyoshi* as four syllables: /hi de jɒ shi/ and *Rikyū* as two syllables: /ri kjuː/.

👥 Learners look at the pictures and read the items, guessing which of the two men does these things.

b *Listening for main idea.* Play recording **1.11**. Learners check their prediction ideas.

> 1 Hideyoshi   2 Rikyū   3 Rikyū   4 Hideyoshi
> 5 Hideyoshi

2 a *Listening for detail.* This activity can be done in pairs. Learners read a–h and try to recall the order of the main events of the story. They number them 1–8.

b Play recording **1.11** again to check the answers.

> a 4   b 3   c 6   d 2   e 8   f 5   g 1   h 7

Alternative for weaker classes

Give the learners time to read a–h, then play recording **2.5** without asking learners to recall the order first. Learners number the order of events.

3 a *Responding to the text.* Learners discuss what they think the meaning of the story is – that is, why Rikyū cut down the flowers and what Hideyoshi understood when he saw the single, perfect flower.

b Play recording **1.12**. Learners listen to Shiori's interpretation and compare their ideas.

VOCABULARY Adverbs for describing actions

4 👤/👥 Learners match the pairs of opposite adverbs.

> 1 carelessly   2 gradually   3 enthusiastically
> 4 accidentally   5 furiously

5 👥/👥👥 Explain that these adverbs all describe *how* something is done (adverbs of manner). They can go in different positions in the sentence. Learners read the sentences in **4** again to find out where the adverbs can go and match them to positions a–c.

> a 1, 4   b 3, 5   c 2

Optional extra

Learners practise saying one or two of the sentences in three different ways, each time moving the position of the adverbs, e.g.
– *Carefully* he would choose tea bowls and pots and so on.
– He would *carefully* choose tea bowls and pots and so on.
– He would choose tea bowls and pots and so on *carefully*.

SPEAKING

6 a *Preparation for story-telling.* Divide learners into two groups, A and B. They prepare in their groups how to tell the story of Rikyū and Hideyoshi from their particular character's point of view. Encourage them to add details (e.g. *One day, I was out riding my horse when I saw ...*) and to choose useful adverbs from **4**.

b 👥 *Story-telling.* Put learners in A/B pairs. They tell the story to their partner from their character's point of view.

Significant stories

GRAMMAR Past progressive and past perfect progressive

1   🔸 / 🔹 *Grammar presentation.* This section looks at two more past narrative tenses. Learners match the time lines and their descriptions with the sentences from the story, then write the name of the form underneath description a or b.

> a *past progressive*   b *past perfect progressive*

2 a   🔸 / 🔹 *Practice.* To introduce this story, say that it is a traditional Polish folk legend (or folk story) about the discovery of a famous salt mine – part of which is shown in the picture. Explain that because it's a legend, there are one or two magical elements to the story.

Learners write the correct form of the verb in brackets.

> **Alternative**
>
> *Reading for main idea.* Learners read the story to find out where Kinga threw away her ring and where it turned up again. Then learners complete the gaps with the correct form of the verb in brackets.

b   Play recording **1.13** to check the answers.

> 1 *was preparing*   2 *gave*   3 *was leaving*
> 4 *had been living*   5 *had been travelling*   6 *reached*
> 7 *was shining*   8 *recognised*

> **Note: Grammar practice**
>
> You could do the grammar practice on p132 at this point.

SPEAKING

3 a   *Preparation for story-telling.* Get learners to look at the types of story listed. For monolingual classes, learners brainstorm a list of stories from their country or region. Write them on the board. For multilingual classes, learners brainstorm in groups from the same culture and note down their ideas.

b   🔸 Learners choose a story and prepare their ideas. Remind them to think of the order of events and choose from the four narrative tenses in the unit: past simple, past perfect simple, past progressive and past perfect progressive. Encourage them to choose suitable adverbs for describing actions to add detail to their stories.

c   🔹 / 🔹 *Story-telling.* Learners tell their stories. The listeners ask follow-up questions. If they know the story someone's telling, they can add details afterwards.

Round-up. Ask a few learners to say what story they heard and whether they liked it.

> **Optional extra**
>
> *Task repetition and mingle.* At the Round-up stage, make a list of all the story topics and write the names of the people who told the story next to the topics. Learners then choose a story they're interested in, find the storyteller and ask them to tell the story.

 You could use photocopiable activity 2B on the Teacher's DVD-ROM at this point.

2.3 Target activity

Goals: describe events in detail ♻
                explain why you're not satisfied with a service

Core language:

TASK VOCABULARY	Explaining a complaint
2.1 VOCABULARY	Dealing with misunderstandings
2.1 PRONUNCIATION	Contrastive stress
2.1 GRAMMAR	Past simple and past perfect simple
2.2 GRAMMAR	Past progressive and past perfect progressive

Make a complaint

TASK LISTENING

1   To introduce the topic of making a complaint, tell the class the name of a company or organisation you've made a complaint to. Get learners to say which companies or organisations tend to receive a lot of complaints from the public. Don't go into detail at this point about learners' own experiences. They will talk about this in **8**.

🔹 / 🔹 Learners discuss the three questions.

2   *Listening for main idea.* Give learners the chance to read the task. Then play recording **1.14**.

> a *to find out why Maureen was unhappy*

3   *Listening for detail.* Give learners the chance to read Ian's notes quickly. Explain the answers are between one and three words long. Then play recording **1.14** again while learners complete the notes.

> 1 *7*   2 *just after 9*   3 *cold*   4 *wet*   5 *£20*   6 *£10*

4   *Responding to the text.* Learners answer the questions.

TASK VOCABULARY Explaining a complaint

5   🔸 / 🔹 Learners match the headings a–c with the groups of sentences 1–3.

> 1 *b*   2 *a*   3 *c*

TASK

6 a   *Preparation for role play.* Divide the class into two groups, A and B. The groups read their situations and plan together what they will say. This includes selecting useful expressions from **5**. Remind learners to use contrastive stress if they need to.

b   🔹 *Role play.* Put learners into A/B pairs. They talk together to resolve Situation 1.

c   🔹 Learners go back to their groups and report on the details of their conversation.

7   🔹 In their groups, learners repeat the preparation and speaking stages in **6a** and **6b** for Situation 2. Then they report to the group on the details of their second conversation.

8   *Personalisation.* In small groups, learners describe incidents in which they've made a complaint to a company or organisation. The listeners ask questions to find out more.

Round-up. Get a few learners to tell the class what incidents they heard about from their partners.

 You could use photocopiable activity 2C on the Teacher's DVD-ROM at this point.

2 Explore

Across cultures: Aspects of culture

Goal: to make learners aware of aspects of culture a visitor or new resident in a country might want to know about

Core language:

Generalising and talking about differences: *have a tendency to; most people won't; Generally speaking; tend to; can be; You will typically; There's a big difference between … and; vary from … to; do things in a slightly different way*

LISTENING

1 **a** To introduce this listening activity, get the class to tell you one or two things they'd like to know before they visited or moved to another country. Write them on the board.

In groups, learners brainstorm more topics they'd like to know about.

b Learners tell you their additional topics. Write them on the board so they have a class list to refer to in **2** and **6**.

2 *Listening for main idea.* Draw learners' attention to David's picture – pronounce *David* as /dævɪd/ – and ask them to read the instruction. Play recording **1.15**. Learners listen to David talk and note down the topics he mentions from the class list, as well as any other topics he mentions.

> David talks about: differences between the city and countryside, languages, attitude to foreigners (helping foreigners), relations between Portuguese people (talking, discussions), differences between regions (personality, traditions), weddings, food/meals, coffee.

3 **a** *Listening for detail.* Play recording **1.15** again, pausing when necessary for learners to write down one or two details in note form about each of David's topics. Learners compare their notes in pairs.

> Answers can include:
> – *differences between the city and countryside: people usually learn languages in the cities, but not so much in the countryside.*
> – *languages: you can use English in the cities; some city people speak English, French, Spanish, maybe Italian and German. Visitors should use simple Portuguese in the countryside.*
> – *attitude to foreigners (helping foreigners): everyone will try to help you.*
> – *relations between Portuguese people (talking, discussions): used to be friendlier, more open, but not now, especially in big cities.*
> – *differences between regions (personality, traditions): families and friends in the north talk a lot and loudly, can be opinionated; people in the south are quieter, calmer, maybe because it's sometimes too hot to talk much.*
> – *weddings: countryside weddings are big, all the family comes, they always have singing; city weddings are more expensive, have smaller groups, sometimes no music.*
> – *food/meals: the food's good, it's important in daily life, people have 3–6 meals a day, lunch breaks are 30 minutes–2 hours, people go home or to restaurants for lunch.*
> – *coffee: it's important in daily life, it's like espresso, it keeps you awake after big lunches, people have 3–4 coffees every day.*

> **Alternative for weaker classes**
>
> Do the first example together and check it. Then play the rest of recording **1.15**, pausing between each topic.

b Learners read script **1.15** on pp143–4 to check their ideas.

4 *Responding to the text.* Learners discuss the questions. Emphasise that this is just one man's opinion on his culture and that Portuguese learners, if there are any in the class, are free to disagree and contribute their own ideas.

VOCABULARY Generalising and talking about differences

5 **a** Learners complete the highlighted expressions in the sentences from David's talk.

> 1 tendency   2 people   3 speaking   4 tend   5 can
> 6 typically   7 difference   8 vary   9 different

b Learners choose five or six of the target language expressions and write sentences about a few aspects of their culture.

SPEAKING

6 *Preparation for talk.* Learners prepare an informal talk like David's, but not as long as his. First of all, they decide what type of audience their talk is for (what are their interests?), then choose three or four aspects of culture from the class list on the board that they'd like to talk about. Remind them to choose expressions from **5a** to generalise and talk about differences.

7 *Talk.* First, learners agree in their groups whether they'd like to accept questions during or at the end of their talks. Then they give their informal talks and answer questions from their listeners.

8 Learners discuss the questions, reflecting on what they've heard.

Round-up. Ask each group to describe one or two of the points they heard about in **7** or discussed in this activity.

Explore writing

Goal: write a dramatic story

Core language:

Introducing and finishing a story: *I've always ...; One day ...*
Finishing a story: *I still can't believe ...; ... since then.*
Expressing thoughts and feelings: *I realised that ...; I remember feeling ...*
Describing a period of time: *Up till then; All the time; For the first few minutes*
Sequencing events: *Next thing I knew; Finally; Then*

1   To introduce the story, get learners to look at the picture and answer the questions.

2   *Reading for main idea.* Learners read and match the topics with the paragraphs.

> *a 3   b 4   c 1   d 2*

3   *Reading and responding to the text.* Learners read the text again and think of answers to the questions. They compare their ideas with a partner.

> *Possible answers*
> *realistic, brave, practical, calm, clear-thinking*

4   👤 / 👥 Learners look at ways in which Charlie makes his story more dramatic in paragraph 3.

> *1 "Right, I'm dead."*
> *2 All the time I <u>was falling and turning</u>, with no control.*
> *3 I briefly saw the ground and a little shack. Then I hit the roof of the shack. I bounced off it, hit a wall and then the ground. I never lost consciousness.*

5   👤 / 👥 Learners match expressions for introducing and finishing a story. Then they check in the article to see where Charlie uses them.

> *1 one day, I've always ...*
> *2 I still can't believe ..., since then*

6   👤 / 👥 Learners sort the highlighted expressions in Charlie's story into the three categories.

> *1 I realised that, I remember feeling*
> *2 Up till then, All the time, For the first few minutes*
> *3 Next thing I knew, Finally, Then*

7 a 👤 / 👥 *Preparation for writing.* Learners choose one of the topics provided, or think of their own, on the theme 'What it feels like to ...'. They can be true or invented stories.

 b 👤 / 👥 The preparation stages 1–3 can be done individually or in pairs. Each person has their own story topic, but the pair could discuss and prepare together, sharing ideas and giving each other suggestions about details to include. They consider how to organise their stories into paragraphs, choose suitable language and decide how to add drama to their stories. Encourage them to make notes.

8   👤 *Writing.* Learners write their stories alone.

> **Alternatives**
>
> • Get learners to do the preparation stages in **7a** and **b**. They then write the first paragraph in class, while you monitor and correct, ensuring that they're on the right track. Learners do the rest at home and hand it in for correction.
> • In class, learners write a number of key sentences from their story describing main events or thoughts. Encourage them to use ideas or expressions from **4**, **5** and **6**. Monitor and correct before they take the sentences home to complete the story. They hand it in for correction the next day.

9   👥 Learners read a partner's story and ask follow-up questions before deciding whether the story is real or invented.

> **Alternative**
>
> *Reading and mingling.* Post the stories around the room. Learners read one or two, then go and ask the writers questions to find out more before secretly (they don't say yet) deciding whether the stories are real or invented.
> *Round-up.* Find out who read the different stories and ask them if they think they're real or invented. The writers confirm. You can also ask for opinions about the various stories.

2 Look again

Review

VOCABULARY Adverbs for describing actions

1 a 👤 Learners think of something for each cue 1–5.

 b 👥 / 👥 Learners compare answers and ask each other follow-up questions.

> **Alternative**
>
> *Guessing game.* Learners write down a short note (a few words) for each point 1–5 in mixed-up order. They exchange papers with a partner and guess which notes match which points. Then they ask follow-up questions.

GRAMMAR Past verb forms

2 a Learners read the paragraph about Patti's important day and answer the question.

> *She's working as a landscape gardener.*

 b 👤 / 👥 Learners match the highlighted past forms a–c in the description with the definitions 1–3.

> *1 a   2 c   3 b*

 c 👤 Explain that learners should choose two important days from their life that could involve, for example, an education or work choice, a decision about a friend or relative, or a new hobby or interest they started. Learners write a few sentences using different past forms to describe the important days and the background to them.

 d 👥 / 👥 Learners tell each other about their important days and ask follow-up questions.

> **Extension**
>
> Get a few learners to summarise what a partner said. They can start like this, for example: *This is what Constanza told me. A few years ago when she was looking through a magazine, she found ...*

CAN YOU REMEMBER? Unit 1 – Routes to success

3 a 👤/👥 Learners complete the questions. They can either write them out, or just say the sentences.

> 1 goals 2 training 3 feedback 4 practice
> 5 experience 6 results 7 talent

b 👤 Learners choose a topic and think of answers to the questions in **a** about their chosen topic. 👥 They then tell each other the topic they chose and ask and answer the questions about it.

Extension

SPELLING AND SOUNDS /n/

4 a 👤/👥 Learners underline the letters that make an /n/ sound. This includes silent letters, as in the first example *resign*.

> resig<u>n</u>, ca<u>n</u>opy, reig<u>n</u>, fu<u>nn</u>iest, <u>kn</u>ow, pla<u>nn</u>ed, sig<u>n</u>, te<u>n</u>dency, begi<u>nn</u>ing, grou<u>nd</u>

b 👤/👥 Learners match the words in **a** with the spelling patterns.

> 1 canopy, tendency, ground
> 2 funniest, planned, beginning
> 3 know
> 4 resign, reign, sign

c 👤/👥 Learners complete the spelling of the words, then check in a dictionary. Alternatively, elicit the spelling of each word and write it on the board.

> design, funnier, ceremony, knife, foreign, runner, knee, reluctantly

NOTICE Verbs with two objects

5 a 👤/👥 Learners look at a pattern in sentences from a few texts in this unit. They underline both objects of the highlighted verb and answer the question.

> 1 sent <u>me</u> <u>a text</u>
> 2 wish <u>her</u> <u>'Happy Birthday'</u>
> 3 cost <u>me</u> <u>another 20 pounds</u>
> 4 give <u>you</u> <u>some vouchers</u>
> Of the two objects, a person comes first.

b 👤/👥 Learners put the words of each sentence in order. They can either write them out or just say the sentences.

> 1 Could you get me some chocolate?
> 2 I left you a message on your voice mail.
> 3 Would you lend me 50 euros?
> 4 He didn't even offer me a seat.
> 5 I owe you a big favour.
> 6 But you promised me a surprise!

c 👥 Learners write a conversation between two people, using their own ideas but trying to include three or four of the verbs with two objects from **a** and **b** (just the highlighted verbs, not the whole sentences).

d Learners listen and pick out the verbs with two objects.

Optional extra

Learners work in two teams. They take turns to give each other one of the highlighted verbs in **5a** and **b**. The other team has to make two different sentences with it as quickly as possible. The team with the most correct sentences wins. For example, *send: I sent my friend an email the other day. You'd better send them your application form as soon as possible.*

Self-assessment

To help focus learners on the self-assessment, read it through and get learners to give you a few examples of the language they have learned in each section. Give an example to start them off if necessary. Then learners circle the numbers on each line.

Unit 2 Extra activities on the Teacher's DVD-ROM

Printable worksheets, activity instructions and answer keys are on your Teacher's DVD-ROM.

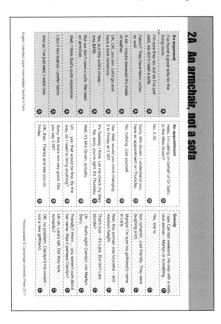

2A An armchair, not a sofa

Activity type: Speaking and Pronunciation – Re-ordering – Pairs

Aim: To contrast and correct information using contrastive stress

Language: Contrastive stress – Use at any point from 2.1.

Preparation: Make one copy of the worksheet for every two learners. Cut up each worksheet to make three conversations with ten strips in each conversation. Keep the conversations separate. (Note that the conversations are not printed in the right order on the worksheet.)

Time: 30 minutes

2B The case of the roasted chicken

Activity type: Speaking – Game – Pairs / Whole class

Aim: To complete the sentences in a story with the correct verb forms

Language: Past simple and past perfect / Past progressive and past perfect progressive – Use at any point from 2.2.

Preparation: Make one copy of the worksheet for every two learners and fold it along the line.

Time: 35 minutes

2C Wait till you hear this

Activity type: Reading and speaking – Role play – Groups/Pairs

Aim: To describe an incident in which you had problems and made a complaint

Language: Explaining a complaint – Use at any point from 2.3.

Preparation: Make one copy of the worksheet for each learner. Cut up each worksheet to make one tent advert and one email for each learner. Keep one copy of the role-play cards for every two learners.

Time: 40 minutes

Unit 2 Self-study Pack

In the Workbook

Unit 2 of the *English Unlimited Upper Intermediate Workbook* offers additional ways to practise the vocabulary and grammar taught in the Coursebook. There are also activities which build reading and writing skills and a whole page of listening and speaking tasks to use with the Interview video, giving your learners the opportunity to hear and react to authentic spoken English.

- **Vocabulary:** Dealing with misunderstandings; Adverbs for describing actions; Explaining a complaint
- **Grammar:** Past simple and past perfect simple; Past progressive and past perfect progressive
- **Explore reading:** Describing a problem
- **Interview:** A holiday to forget – Emma

On the DVD-ROM

Unit 2 of the *English Unlimited Upper Intermediate Self-study DVD-ROM* contains interactive games and activities for your learners to practise and improve their vocabulary, grammar and pronunciation, and also their speaking and listening, with the possibility for learners to record themselves, and a video of authentic spoken English to use with the Workbook.

- **Vocabulary and grammar:** Extra practice activities
- **Pronunciation:** Contrastive stress
- **Explore speaking:** Using strong stress to show surprise or disbelief
- **Listening:** Making a complaint
- **Video:** A holiday to forget

Learners and teachers

3.1

Goals: express views about different options
talk about education and training

Core language:

VOCABULARY	Discussing options
PRONUNCIATION	Fluent speech 1 – leaving out /t/
VOCABULARY	Education and training

Doing a course

READING AND LISTENING

1   👥 / 👥👥 *Pre-reading discussion.* To focus on the topic of the reading and listening, learners discuss the three questions.

Round-up. Ask a few learners to tell the class about their answers. In a multilingual class, focus on questions 1 and 3 and find out if there are any differences from country to country.

Alternative

Introduction with books closed. Put the questions on the board for learners to discuss.

---

2   *Reading for detail.* Learners read the brochure and find at least one course which they think could help someone do each of the things listed.

👥 / 👥👥 Learners compare their ideas.

Suggested answers
- *communicate more effectively: Creative writing, Psychology*
- *understand part of another culture: Bollywood workout, Malaysian cookery*
- *entertain guests: Malaysian cookery*
- *save money: Car maintenance*
- *help other people: First aid, Psychology*
- *be more creative: Creative writing, Malaysian cookery*
- *get fit: Bollywood workout*
- *understand people: Psychology*

---

3   *Listening for main ideas.* Play recording **1.16**. Learners listen and answer the questions.

---
1 So they can support each other. They feel slightly lonely because their children have recently left home.
2 They discuss five courses: Bollywood workout, Creative writing, First aid, Malaysian cookery, Psychology.
They manage to choose one course: Malaysian cookery.

---

4   *Listening for detail.* Play recording **1.16** again. Learners listen and make notes about the questions. Suggest that learners organise their notes under five headings, one for each of the five courses which Don and Carrie discuss.

Alternative

Listening worksheet. Give learners a blank version of the table below to write their notes in, or write it on the board for learners to copy down.

Course	Wants to do it	Doesn't want to / isn't sure	Reasons why not
Bollywood workout	Don	Carrie	She can't dance. She thinks she'll look foolish.
Creative writing	Don	Carrie	She's not sure she'll have enough time for homework.
First aid	Carrie	Don	He thinks it sounds boring.
Malaysian cookery	Both	–	–
Psychology	Carrie	Don	It might be too much of a time commitment.

VOCABULARY Discussing options

5   *Presentation.* Learners find two sentences from 1–8 to match the meaning of each sentence A–D.

A 2, 5   **B** 3, 6   **C** 4, 8   **D** 1, 7

Focus on the B sentences and ask: *Which of the three expressions is the strongest?* (3 *There's no way I'm doing that!*) and *Who could you use this expression with?* (*close friends and family*).

Optional extra

Disappearing drill. While going through the answers to **5**, write all 12 sentences up on the board, scattered about at random. Draw a speech bubble round each sentence. Then drill, pointing at different sentences and asking learners to repeat as a class. Rub out some words from the sentences and continue the drill, asking learners to remember the complete sentences. Slowly rub out more and more words as you drill. Find out if the learners can remember the sentences once they've disappeared completely, leaving only the empty speech bubbles.

---

6   👥 *Memorisation.* Learners cover sentences 1–8 in **5** and try to remember the two expressions which go with A–D. After a minute or so, they uncover 1–8 to check their answers and remind themselves of any expressions they'd forgotten. They repeat until they feel able to remember all the sentences comfortably.

PRONUNCIATION Fluent speech 1 – leaving out /t/

7   **a**   *Presentation.* Play recording **1.17** while the learners look at the four example sentences. Point out how the highlighted /t/ sounds disappear.

👥 / 👥👥 Learners choose the correct options in the two statements.

---
1 the end   2 consonant

---

b *Practice.* Learners practise saying the four sentences rapidly and without the /t/ sound, repeating after you or the recording.

👥 / 👥👥 Then learners practise in pairs or groups.

SPEAKING

8 a 🔖 *Preparation for discussion.* Learners look through the brochure again and prepare to have a discussion to choose a course to do together. Encourage them to choose some expressions from **5** which might be useful in the discussion.

b 👥👥 *Discussion.* Learners tell each other how they feel about the different courses. Their goal is to find, if possible, one course they'd all like to do together.

Round-up. Ask each group to tell the class whether they found a course they'd all like to do and, if so, which one.

 You could use photocopiable activity 3A on the Teacher's DVD-ROM at this point.

Learning choices

VOCABULARY Education and training

1 👥 / 👥👥 *Presentation.* Learners discuss the meanings of the expressions in each group a–d.

> **a** distance learning – *a way of studying where you learn mostly at home, receiving and sending off work by post or Internet*
> online learning – *studying over the Internet; a type of distance learning*
> face-to-face learning – *studying in the traditional way, in a room with a teacher and/or fellow students*
> **b** postgraduate courses – *courses for students who have a first degree; such courses can be academic (e.g. a doctorate) or practical (e.g. teaching)*
> evening courses – *part-time courses for students who work or have other studies during the day*
> full-time courses – *courses which take roughly the same amount of time every week as a regular job*
> **c** vocational training – *training which prepares you for a specific job, e.g. accountancy, nursing*
> apprenticeships – *long periods of time when someone does paid work for a skilled person in order to learn that person's skills and become a professional*
> work experience – *a short period of time when someone (often a student) does unpaid work to gain experience*
> **d** lectures – *formal talks on a serious or specialist subject given to a group of people*
> seminars – *occasions when a teacher and a group of people meet to study and discuss something*
> coursework – *work done at regular times as part of an educational course*
> dissertations – *long pieces of writing on a specific subject, done as part of a course at college or university*

2 *Practice.* Learners cover the expressions in **1** and try to complete the statements 1–8, using the first letters to help them remember. Then they look back at **1** to check.

> 1 *apprenticeships* 2 *vocational training* 3 *Seminars; lectures* 4 *Distance learning; face-to-face learning* 5 *coursework* 6 *work experience* 7 *postgraduate courses* 8 *Evening courses*

SPEAKING

3 a 🔖 *Preparation for discussion.* Learners think about whether they agree with the statements 1–8 in **2** and mark each with a symbol accordingly.

b 👥 / 👥👥 *Discussion.* Learners compare and express their opinions about each statement.

Round-up. Ask some learners to tell you one or two statements they totally agree (++) or disagree (– –) with. See if the rest of the class feels the same.

3.2

Goals: talk about experiences of education and training
describe habits and tendencies in the past and present

Core language:

VOCABULARY	Work and commitment
GRAMMAR	Habits and tendencies – past and present

Head teacher

READING

1 a 👥👥 *Prediction.* Learners look at the pictures of Babur Ali and his school, and read the first paragraph of the article. They tell each other what they'd like to find out in the rest of the article.

b *Reading for main ideas.* Learners read the rest of the article and try to find out about the things they mentioned in **a**.

👥👥 Learners tell each other whether they found what they were looking for in the article.

2 *Reading for detail.* Learners read and find out about 1–8.

> 1 Because their parents couldn't afford to send them to school (and/or they'd dropped out).
> 2 Eight
> 3 Ten teachers and 650 pupils
> 4 Teachers are not paid. Things like books and furniture are donated.
> 5 Three
> 6 Mostly other pupils from Babur's fee-paying school
> 7 Proud of his son, reassured that his teaching won't have a bad effect on his studies
> 8 So he can continue teaching while doing his degree.

3 👥 / 👥👥 *Responding to text.* Learners discuss the questions.

Round-up. On the board, write the things which Babur says teachers need to be/do in order to be successful: *dedicated, determined, create a positive environment, create goodwill between teachers and students.* Elicit further ideas from the learners to create a class list.

VOCABULARY Work and commitment

4 a *Presentation.* Learners complete 1–8 with the verbs in the boxes.

b Learners look back in the article to check their answers.

> 1 work on   2 work towards   3 keep up   4 carry on
> 5 take on   6 sign up   7 give up   8 drop out

Point out how:
- *sign up* is often followed by the preposition *for*;
- *drop out* is often followed by the preposition *of*;
- *give up* is often followed by an *-ing* form.

Language note

You *work on* a task; you *work towards* a particular goal.
Carry on means *continue*; *keep up* specifically means
continue something at a high level.
If you *sign up*, you agree to attend or participate in an
organised activity; if you *take* something *on*, you agree to be
responsible for it.
If you *drop out* of something, you stop attending or
participating in it; if you *give up* an activity, you stop doing it
permanently.

---

5   *Practice.* Play recording **1.18**, which consists of eight
spoken instructions. Learners listen to the instructions
and write down their answers, but *not* in order. Pause
the recording briefly between each instruction to allow
learners some thinking and writing time.

Alternative for weaker classes

Instead of playing the recording **1.18**, give out or display a
copy of the script on p144.

SPEAKING

6   / Learners look at each other's written answers
from **5** and try to guess what they mean, using the
verbs from **4**. Once they've found out what an answer
means, they ask questions to find out more.

Alternative

Demonstration. Before learners begin **6**, write down your
own answers to the instructions in **5** on the board, scattered
about at random. Then ask learners to guess what they
mean, encouraging them to use the verbs from **4** and to ask
follow-up questions.

They were always asking questions

GRAMMAR Habits and tendencies – past and present

1 a *Presentation.* Direct learners' attention to the
sentences 1–7. Ask: *Which are about the present?*

> 2, 4, 7

Then ask: *Which are about the past?*

> 1, 3, 5, 6

b / Learners match the forms A–D with the
descriptions 1–4.

> 1 D   2 C   3 B   4 A

2 a / *Practice.* Learners complete Brianna's
description. Tell them that, in some cases, more than
one answer is possible. Do not go through the answers
at this stage, as this will pre-empt **b**.

b / Learners compare their answers. If their
answers differ, they decide whether both answers
could be correct or one of them is wrong. Be ready to
deal with any queries learners may have at this stage.

Round-up. Go through the answers with the class,
establishing the range of possible right answers and
discussing what might be the most natural-sounding
answers in each case.

Suggested answers
The most natural-sounding answers are <u>underlined</u> –
see the Language note below.
1 <u>used to meet</u> / would ('d) meet
2 used to do / <u>would ('d) do</u>
3 used to push / would ('d) push / <u>was always pushing</u>
4 used to suggest / would ('d) suggest / <u>was always
  suggesting</u>
5 write
6 read / will ('ll) read
7 tell

Language note

When talking about habits in the past, you often use *used to*
to start with, followed by a chain of *would*s. Using *used to* all
the time sounds rather unnatural. This is why the suggestions
for the most natural-sounding answers for 1, 2, 5 and 6 are
used to ..., *would ...*, *would ...*, *would ....*
In 3 and 4, the best answers are probably with *was always
-ing*, as Brianna is clearly trying to emphasise how good
(demanding, inspirational) her tutor was.

Note: Grammar practice

You could do the grammar practice on p133 at this point.

SPEAKING

3 a *Preparation for discussion.* Learners write two or
three sentences about each of the three topics. Monitor
closely to help the learners and make sure they are
using the grammar forms correctly.

b / *Discussion.* Learners put away their
sentences and discuss the three topics together.

 You could use photocopiable activity 3B on the
Teacher's DVD-ROM at this point.

3.3 Target activity

Goals: express views about different options ♻
talk about experiences of education and training ♻
describe habits and tendencies in the past and present ♻
describe important mentors in your life

Core language:

TASK VOCABULARY	Describing a mentor
3.1 VOCABULARY	Discussing options
3.2 VOCABULARY	Work and commitment
3.2 GRAMMAR	Habits and tendencies – past and present

Decide who to nominate for an award

TASK LISTENING

> **Option: Lead-in**
>
> *Books closed.* Write this definition, adapted from the *Cambridge Advanced Learner's Dictionary*, on the board: *an experienced person who gives help and advice to someone with less experience.* Tell learners this is a dictionary definition, and ask: *Which word does it define?* If necessary, give learners the first few letters to help them guess (*mentor*). Then ask: *Think about your own lives. What kinds of people can be mentors?* (Possible answers: *teachers, sports coaches, bosses at work, parents, grandparents, (usually older) brothers or sisters,* etc.)

1   *Pre-listening discussion.* To introduce the context of the listening, learners read the notice from a local newspaper. Ask them if they know or have heard of any organisations that offer awards like this.

2 a   *Prediction.* Refer learners to the pictures of Alex and Bill. Tell them they're going to listen to Alex talking about Bill, his old driving instructor, who he's thinking of nominating for a 'Great Mentor' award. Learners think of skills and characteristics you probably need to be a good driving instructor.

Elicit each pair/group's ideas onto the board. Make a class list.

b   *Listening for main ideas.* Play recording **1.19**. Learners make a note of the skills and characteristics Alex mentions.

Go back to the list on the board and ask: *Did Alex mention any of the things on our list? Which ones? What else did he mention?*

> *Alex says that Bill was: patient, calm, quiet, encouraging, motivating, inspiring.*

3 a   *Listening for detail.* Play recording **1.19** again. Learners listen and answer the questions.

b   Learners read script **1.19** on pp144–5 to check their answers.

> 1 Alex's parents paid for his lessons as a 17th birthday present.
> 2 He had about 60 lessons and didn't pass until he was 18.
> 3 'Terrible'. He made a lot of mistakes, sometimes dangerous ones.
> 4 Bill would calmly persuade him to continue with his lessons.

TASK VOCABULARY Describing a mentor

4 a   *Presentation.* Learners use the words in the box to complete Alex's sentences from the listening.

> 1 impression   2 so   3 ever   4 never   5 those
> 6 always   7 positive   8 taught   9 owe

> **Alternative for weaker classes**
>
> Learners look once again at script **1.19** on pp144–5 to check their answers and review the vocabulary expressions in context.

b   To consolidate meaning, learners put the sentences from **a** into three groups.

> 1 Sentences 2, 3, 5
> 2 Sentences 4, 6
> 3 Sentences 1, 7, 8, 9

TASK

5 a   *Preparation for description.* Learners choose a mentor from their lives to nominate for a 'Great Mentor' award. Then they think about the six points listed and prepare to talk about their mentor. Encourage learners to choose expressions from **4a** to use in their descriptions. Remind them that they can also use language from VOCABULARY Work and commitment and GRAMMAR Habits and tendencies – past and present.

b   *Description.* Learners tell each other about their mentors and ask questions to find out more.

6 a   Give each learner in a pair the label A or B, then put the learners into two big groups: all the As together and all the Bs together. Learners tell their groups about their *partner's* mentor from **5b**, then choose one mentor to nominate for the award. Remind learners that they can use expressions from VOCABULARY Discussing options.

> **Alternative for large classes**
>
> Give half the pairs in your class the labels A and B, and the other half C and D. Then put the learners into four groups: A, B, C and D.

b   Ask one learner from each group to explain who they chose to nominate, and why.

3 Explore

Keyword: *use*

Goals: use expressions with the verb *use* and the noun *use*
use *be used to* and *get used to* to talk about being and becoming accustomed to things

Core language:
The verb *use*: use *something to/as/for …*
The noun *use*: *the use of, be in use, make use of, …*
be used to, get used to

The verb *use*

1 a   *Prediction.* Draw learners' attention to the picture of Karen and Niklas, and read through the caption with the class. Elicit a few ways in which a tennis ball or a number of tennis balls could be used creatively, e.g. they could be painted to make decorations, or stuck together on a board to make a mattress. Then put learners in groups to generate more ideas.

b *Listening for detail.* Play recording **1.20** for learners to listen to Karen and Niklas. Elicit the ideas Karen and Niklas had, then ask the learners if any of their ideas were the same ideas, and what other ideas they had.

> *Karen and Niklas come up with eight ideas: ball games, a cup, a rainwater catcher, a stress ball, a ball for hand exercises, a toy for a cat, a door protector, packing material.*

2 a 👥 / 👥👥 *Presentation.* Learners match the sentence halves to make three complete sentences from the recording.

> 1 c 2 a 3 b

Language note

You use *use as* + noun to talk about the <u>identity</u> of something. You use *use for* + an expression describing an action (often an *-ing* form) to talk about the <u>purpose</u> of something. Compare:
*I **use** my mobile phone **as** a music player.*
*I **use** it **for** listening to music.*

---

b *Pronunciation.* Say a sentence from **a**, e.g. *You could use it as a cup.* Ask learners whether *use* has a /s/ or a /z/ sound.

> a /z/ sound

Ask learners to repeat the sentence a few times, making sure they use the correct sound.

3 a 👥👥 *Practice.* Learners think of as many ways as possible for using a bottle. Set a time limit (e.g. five minutes). Encourage them to use the three expressions with the verb *use*.

b Ask each group to tell the class about their ideas. Make a list of all the ideas on the board.

Round-up. Go through the ideas on the board one by one, asking learners to vote for their favourite ideas. Each learner can vote twice, for two different ideas. Count the number of votes for each idea and find out which are the class's favourites.

The noun *use*

Optional lead-in

Gap-fill. Put the questions in **4a** on a worksheet, putting gaps in place of the following words in the highlighted expressions:
1 *of*
2 *in, into, out of*
3 *of, of*
With books closed, learners complete the expressions. Then they open their books to check their answers.

---

4 a 👤 *Noticing.* Learners read through the questions and decide how they'd answer them.

Note

The language aim of this stage is to bring the highlighted expressions with the noun *use* to the learners' attention as they read through the questions. The meanings of the expressions should be clear from the words which make them up.

---

b *Pronunciation.* Say a question from **a**, e.g. *Do you think you made good use of your time at school or college?*. Ask learners whether *use* has a /s/ or a /z/ sound.

> a /s/ sound

Ask learners to repeat the question a few times, making sure they use the correct sound.

5 👥 *Practice.* Learners take turns to ask and answer the questions.

Round-up. Ask a few pairs to tell the class about an issue on which they disagreed. Ask the rest of the class what they think about these issues.

be used to, get used to

6 👥 / 👥👥 *Presentation.* Learners answer the questions.

> 1 The present. The time reference is shown by the form of the verb 'be' (= 'is') and not by 'used'.
> 2 It's normal for him. He doesn't feel it's unusual.
> 3 /s/

Alternative: Jumbled sentence

Books closed. Dictate the following eight words one by one for learners to write down:
working Babur hours is long to remarkably used
Learners put the words in order to make a sentence from earlier in the unit. Then they open their books and look at **6** to check.

Language note

The different pronunciations of *use(d)* can be summarised as follows:
- /z/: *u<u>s</u>e* (verb), *u<u>s</u>ed* (adjective, as in *a used car*)
- /s/: *u<u>s</u>e* (noun), *I'm / I get u<u>s</u>ed to* + noun / *-ing* form, *I u<u>s</u>ed to* + infinitive

---

7 a 👤 *Practice.* Learners write two or three of their own *Do you know anyone who ... ?* questions to add to the list. While learners are writing, monitor closely to make sure they're using the expressions *be used to* and *get used to* correctly.

b 👥 / 👥👥 Learners ask and answer all the questions.

 You could use photocopiable activity 3C on the Teacher's DVD-ROM at this point.

Explore speaking

Goal: show different attitudes and feelings

Core language:
Common adverbial expressions in spoken English:
apparently, thankfully, to be honest, ...

---

1 a *Listening for main ideas.* Read through the four questions. Check that learners remember who Babur Ali (from the article on p24) is.

Ask learners to cover the scripts of the two conversations on the right and play recording **1.21**. Learners listen and answer the questions.

b 👥 / 👥👥 Learners compare their answers, then read the scripts to check.

> 1 He's amazed, impressed.
> 2 That they should make a donation to his school.
> 3 A tree branch fell through a neighbour's living-room window.
> 4 They weren't at home because they'd got stuck in traffic.

2 a 👥 / 👥👥 *Presentation.* Learners find the highlighted expressions in the scripts which match the paraphrases 1–9.

> 1 Funnily enough 2 Apparently 3 Obviously
> 4 Frankly 5 Basically 6 Surprisingly 7 Personally
> 8 Thankfully 9 Seriously

b 👥 / 👥👥 Learners look at the five expressions in the box and write a meaning for each one in the same style as those in **a**.

> Suggested answers
> unfortunately: "I'm not pleased/happy about this."
> hopefully: "I hope (but am not sure) this is true."
> to tell you the truth: "This is the truth / my honest opinion." (similar to 'Frankly')
> actually: "This may be unexpected for you, but …", "What you said/think is not quite correct."
> between you and me: "This is a secret.", "Don't tell anyone, but …"

3 👥 / 👥👥 *Practice.* Learners choose expressions from **2** to complete the conversation. Point out that different answers are possible.

Play recording **1.22**, emphasising that it demonstrates just one possible set of answers.

> 1 unfortunately 2 between you and me 3 hopefully
> 4 To tell you the truth 5 Personally 6 basically

Ask learners if any of their answers were different, and discuss with them how this affects the meaning of what the people say.

4 a 👥 *Practice.* Give each pair a sheet of paper and guide them through the instructions 1–5.

To make sure that all pairs are ready to pass on their sheets of paper at roughly the same time, set a time limit (e.g. two minutes) for writing each line of the conversation.

At the end of the activity, ask learners to write one or two lines to conclude the conversation on their sheet of paper.

b Pairs perform the conversations on their pieces of paper while the class listens. To conclude, ask learners which was their favourite conversation, and why.

3 Look again

Review

VOCABULARY Discussing options

1 a 👥 / 👥👥 Learners read and find alternative expressions to complete the conversation.

> 1 I like the sound of Silks Nightclub.
>   I wouldn't mind going to Silks Nightclub.
> 2 Silks doesn't really appeal to me.
>   Silks isn't really my thing.
> 3 For me, it's a choice between Silks or Terence's Café.
>   I've narrowed it down to Silks or Terence's Café.
> 4 I can't make up my mind about Terence's Café.
>   I've got mixed feelings about Terence's Café.

b Tell learners that they're going to plan a class party. Ask them to make three lists: possible places to go, things to eat and drink, and things to do. Work with the class to make the three lists on the board.

c Help learners plan the party, discussing and choosing options from each list. Each group explains its decisions to the class.

GRAMMAR Habits and tendencies – past and present

2 a 👥 / 👥👥 Learners read through the paragraph, underlining the verb forms which describe habits and tendencies. Ask learners to explain why these particular forms are used.

> When I was 21, I had a Volkswagen camper van. I <u>was</u> extremely proud of it, and I <u>was always polishing</u> it. I <u>used to go travelling</u> in it every summer. Sometimes my friends <u>would come</u> with me, and we'<u>d have</u> a great time. But I'm 'green' nowadays, so I'<u>m always thinking</u> of ways to help the environment. I <u>go</u> most places by bicycle, and for long-distance journeys I'<u>ll take</u> the bus or train. But to tell you the truth, I still miss my old van.

b 👤 Learners read and think about the task, making notes if they wish. Encourage them to think about how they can use the grammar from this section.

👥 / 👥👥 Learners discuss their topics together.

CAN YOU REMEMBER? Unit 2 – Misunderstandings

3 👥 / 👥👥 Learners complete the conversation. Encourage them to do this without looking back at the expressions on p14 until they've finished. You could ask them to compare their answers in pairs before checking against the Coursebook.

> 1 thought 2 meant 3 said 4 explains
> 5 if 6 thing 7 option

> **Optional extra**
>
> *Whole class.* Ask pairs of learners to perform the conversation for the whole class. At the end, ask the learners if they've ever been involved in misunderstandings similar to those in the conversation.

Extension

SPELLING AND SOUNDS /ʃ/

4 a Write on the board /ʃ/. Ask learners what sound this represents (*sh* as in *ship*). Write on the board: *sh*, *ch*, *che*, *s*. Explain that these (combinations of) letters can all be used to represent a /ʃ/ sound in English words.

👥 / 👪 Learners complete the spellings of the words.

> *shout, mushroom, rush, champagne, brochure, crèche, sure, championship, selfish*

b Elicit answers to the questions.

> *1 sh, ch, s*
> *2 sh, ch*
> *3 sh, che*
> *The most common spelling is 'sh'.*

c Play recording **1.23**. Learners write the words, then check their answers on p145.

NOTICE *provide, include, cover, ...*

5 a Learners match 1–6 with a–f. Then they check their answers by looking back and finding the sentences in the Markham College brochure on p23.

> *1d 2a 3b 4f 5c 6e*

Point out the highlighted verbs in 1–6, and ask learners to find two pairs which, in the context of the brochure, have similar meanings (*provide/offer* and *include/cover*).

b 👥 / 👪 Learners follow the instructions to write a description of a course on a piece of paper. Tell them that their description will be read by other learners in the class and so should be clearly legible. Encourage them to use the verbs from **a** and monitor for correct use.

c Display the descriptions around the room on walls or desks. Learners walk around the room and read all the descriptions.

👥 / 👪 Learners go back to their pairs/groups from **b** and tell each other which course (not their own) they'd most like to do, and why.

Round-up. Have a class vote to find out which is the most popular course.

Self-assessment

To help focus learners on the self-assessment, you could read it through, giving a few examples of the language they have learned in each section (or asking learners to tell you). Then ask them to circle the numbers on each line.

Unit 3 Extra activities on the Teacher's DVD-ROM

Printable worksheets, activity instructions and answer keys are on your Teacher's DVD-ROM.

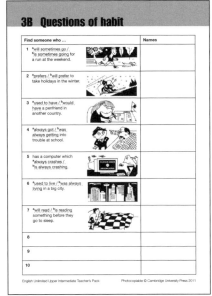

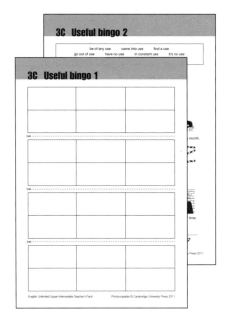

3A Decisions, decisions

Activity type: Reading, writing, speaking and listening – Dominoes / Writing and performing a conversation – Pairs / Whole class

Aim: To practise expressions for discussing and choosing options

Language: Discussing options – Use at any point from 3.1.

Preparation: Make one copy of the worksheet for every four learners. (To reduce the amount of printing or photocopying required, there are two sets of dominoes on the sheet.) Cut up the worksheet to make two sets of dominoes. Prepare one slip of paper with a situation for conversation-writing if you are going to do the Extension activity.

Time: 40 minutes

3B Questions of habit

Activity type: Writing and speaking – Find someone who – Individuals / Class mingle / Groups

Aim: To practise using a variety of forms for describing present and past states and habits

Language: Habits and tendencies – Past and present – Use at any point from 3.2.

Preparation: Make one copy of the worksheet for every learner.

Time: 25 minutes

3C Useful bingo

Activity type: Listening and speaking – Bingo / Sentence completion – Whole class / Pairs

Aim: To practise common expressions with the noun *use*

Language: Expressions with the noun *use* – Use at any point from Keyword *use*, p27.

Preparation: Make enough copies of Worksheet 1 to ensure each learner has one bingo card. (Each copy can be cut up to make four bingo cards.) Make one copy of Worksheet 2 for each learner.

Time: 20 minutes

Unit 3 Self-study Pack

In the Workbook

Unit 3 of the *English Unlimited Upper Intermediate Workbook* offers additional ways to practise the vocabulary and grammar taught in the Coursebook. There are also activities which build reading and writing skills and a whole page of listening and speaking tasks to use with the Interview video, giving your learners the opportunity to hear and react to authentic spoken English.

- **Vocabulary:** Discussing options; Work and commitment; Education and training; Describing a mentor
- **Grammar:** Habits and tendencies – past and present
- **Explore writing:** A letter to a newspaper
- **Interview:** Pass it on – Carlos and Liu

On the DVD-ROM

Unit 3 of the *English Unlimited Upper Intermediate Self-study DVD-ROM* contains interactive games and activities for your learners to practise and improve their vocabulary, grammar and pronunciation, and also their speaking and listening, with the possibility for learners to record themselves, and a video of authentic spoken English to use with the Workbook.

- **Vocabulary and grammar:** Extra practice activities
- **Pronunciation:** Fluent speech – leaving out /t/
- **Explore speaking:** Question tags
- **Listening:** A radio phone-in
- **Video:** Pass it on

Local knowledge

4.1

Goals: describe landmarks
talk about landmarks where you live

Core language:

VOCABULARY	Describing landmarks
VOCABULARY	History of a landmark
PRONUNCIATION	Weak forms

Landmarks

VOCABULARY Describing landmarks

1 a To introduce the topic, write *landmark* on the board.
Get learners to tell you what it means (*a building
or structure that's striking and easily recognised,
especially one that helps you know where you are*).
Get them to name a famous landmark in the town or
city you're in, then in a few other major cities, e.g.
Paris, New York, Sydney and Cairo.

   👥 *Prediction.* Learners look at the pictures and
   discuss where they think the landmarks are, how big
   they are, and what they're made of.

   b 👤 Learners match pictures A–D with descriptions 1–4,
   and check their predictions.

> A 3 a) Tokyo (Ueno Park) b) 3.7m high c) bronze
> B 4 a) Warsaw, Poland b) 15m high c) steel, plastic
>   and natural bark
> C 1 a) Dublin, Ireland b) 120m high, 3m wide at base,
>   15cm at top c) steel
> D 2 a) Gateshead, England b) 20m high, 54m wingspan
>   c) steel

2 👥 Learners answer the questions and compare ideas.
Allow flexibility for different interpretations of some
of the highlighted expressions.

> *Suggested answers, with definitions*
> 1 C, D (monument = a building or other structure that is
>   built to make people remember an event in history or
>   a famous person)
> 2 D and possibly A (statue = a figure that looks like a
>   person or animal, usually made from stone or metal)
> 3 all of them (sculpture = a piece of art that is made
>   from stone, wood, clay, etc.)
>   Note: The Millennium Spire is one of the tallest
>   sculptures in the world.
> 4 modern: A, B, C   traditional: D
> 5 abstract: C   realistic: B and D
>   A is partly realistic.
> 6 a D   b C   c D   d A, B   e B   f B

3 👥 *Practice.* Learners describe the pictures using the
new language. There's no need for a personal reaction
to the sculptures, as they'll do that in **6**.

LISTENING

4 *Listening for main idea.* Play recording **1.24**. Learners
identify which landmark each person talks about (one
is not mentioned) and identify the speakers' feelings.
Pronounce Cian /ˈkiːən/.

> *Cian: C (The Millennium Spire): He didn't like it at first,
> but is used to it now.*
> *Beryl: A (The Angel of the North): She doesn't think it's a
> wonderful sculpture, but likes it.*
> *Dominika: B (Greetings from Jerusalem Avenue): She
> likes it.*
> *D (Saigō Takamori) is not talked about.*

5 *Listening for detail.* Learners listen to recording **1.24**
again and take notes on the four topics for each of the
three monuments.

> Millennium Spire
> 1 on O'Connell Street (main street) in the middle of
>   Dublin, Ireland
> 2 unveiled at the end of 1999
> 3 to celebrate the Millennium
> 4 Controversial and criticised at first, but people are
>   beginning to like it, are more used to it.
> Angel of the North
> 1 on a hill by the side of the A1 road, near the city of
>   Gateshead in the north of England
> 2 during the 1990s
> 3 to signify an arrival somewhere
> 4 Everyone says, 'Look!' when going past it.
> Greetings from Jerusalem Avenue (palm tree)
> 1 on a main street in Warsaw, Poland
> 2 a few years ago
> 3 to brighten up a bleak part of the city, surprise people,
>   show them something unexpected
> 4 Puzzled at first, controversial, but now they love it,
>   look forward to seeing it.

6 👥 *Responding to the text.* Learners express their
feelings about the four landmarks.

A big impression

VOCABULARY History of a landmark

1 👥 / 👥 Learners discuss the meaning of the
highlighted expressions.

> 1 similar meanings
> 2 different meanings: 'unveiled' = uncovered or shown
>   to the public; 'opened to the public' = letting people
>   go inside (e.g. a building, a park)
> 3 similar meanings
> 4 different meanings: 'controversy' = a lot of
>   disagreement and argument; 'a big impression' = a
>   strong feeling, usually favourable
> 5 similar meanings
> 6 similar meanings (though 'warmed to' has more of an
>   idea of 'liking' than 'love')
> 7 different meanings: 'a landmark' = see VOCABULARY
>   1a above; 'a tourist attraction' = a place many tourists
>   want to go to
> 8 different meanings: 'part of the landscape' =
>   something accepted as normal in its surroundings;
>   'an eyesore' = something that looks ugly compared to
>   the things around it

2 a 👤 / 👥 *Practice.* Learners complete the paragraph,
choosing from the highlighted expressions in **1**.
Explain that because some expressions have similar
meanings, sometimes more than one answer is
possible. Do the first one together to illustrate this.

> 1 was put up / was erected

b 👥 Learners compare their ideas. Then confirm the answers.

> 1 was put up / was erected
> 2 was opened to the public
> 3 caused a lot of controversy / was heavily criticised / was badly received
> 4 an eyesore
> 5 didn't know what to make of / were baffled by
> 6 grew to love / warmed to
> 7 a landmark / a tourist attraction
> 8 a tourist attraction / a landmark

PRONUNCIATION Weak forms

3 a 👥 This section focuses on weak forms, said with a schwa /ə/ sound. If learners are not familiar with the /ə/ sound, say in fast natural speech: *I'm going to the bank.* Ask them how you pronounced *to*: /tə/ or /tuː/. In fast natural speech, we say /tə/. Ask them which other word in that sentence has the same sound (*the*).

Play recording **1.25** while learners listen, then say the sentence, focusing on the /ə/ sounds.

b Learners read about categories of words which commonly have /ə/ sounds.

👤 They mark the words they think would have a weak form in the rest of the sentences in **1**. Answers to both columns are provided in script **1.26**. Alternatively, you can divide learners into A/B pairs and ask the As to mark the column A sentences and the Bs to mark the column B sentences. They then exchange ideas.

c Play recording **1.26**. Learners listen and read the script on p146 to check their answers. Note: there are, of course, other schwa sounds in the sentences, e.g. *celebrate*. However, only those occurring in weak forms are highlighted in the key below.

> *The underlined sounds are weak forms pronounced as /ə/.*
> 1 It w<u>a</u>s erected t<u>o</u> celebr<u>a</u>te th<u>e</u> Millennium. It w<u>a</u>s put up during th<u>e</u> 1990s.
> 2 It w<u>a</u>s unveiled <u>a</u>t th<u>e</u> very end <u>o</u>f 1999. It w<u>a</u>s opened t<u>o</u> th<u>e</u> public in 2006.
> 3 It w<u>a</u>s heavily criticised <u>a</u>t first. It w<u>a</u>s badly received.
> 4 It caused <u>a</u> lot <u>o</u>f controversy. It made <u>a</u> big impression on people.
> 5 People didn't know what t<u>o</u> make <u>o</u>f it. People w<u>e</u>re baffled by it.
> 6 People grew t<u>o</u> love it. People warmed to it after <u>a</u> while.
> 7 It became <u>a</u> landmark. It became <u>a</u> tourist attraction.
> 8 People see it <u>a</u>s part <u>o</u>f th<u>e</u> landscape. People regard it <u>a</u>s <u>a</u>n eyesore.

Pronunciation note

In the second sentence in item 6 (*People warmed to it after a while*), *to* is not pronounced with an /ə/ because it's followed by a vowel. There's an intruded /w/ sound between *to* and *it*: /tuːwɪt/.

SPEAKING

4 a 👤 *Preparation for discussion.* Learners choose two or three landmarks in their region or country, or landmarks they're familiar with in other countries. They prepare answers for questions 1–5. Encourage them to choose useful expressions

from VOCABULARY Describing landmarks and VOCABULARY History of a landmark. Remind them to use /ə/ when appropriate.

b 👥 *Discussion.* In small groups, learners tell each other about their landmarks. They listen and ask questions, contributing more details if they can. Then they answer the follow-up question about which landmarks they'd like to see.

Round-up. Get a few learners to tell you what they heard from the other members of their group.

Optional extension

Learners write a paragraph at home describing one of the landmarks they talked about and hand it in the next day for correction. They can gather extra information or details about it from the Internet, and include a picture.

 You could use photocopiable activity 4A on the Teacher's DVD-ROM at this point.

4.2

Goals: talk about well-known people where you live
describe someone's life and work

Core language:

VOCABULARY — Talking about well-known people
GRAMMAR — Using the passive

Two voices

READING

1 a 👤 *Prediction.* Learners look at the photos and read the captions. Clarify the meaning of any of the things listed if necessary. Learners guess which expressions might appear in an article about the singer or the writer.

b 👥 *Reading for main idea.* Divide learners into A/B groups; each group reads quickly through its particular article for the expressions in **a**.

> Umm Kulthum
> *Cairo, radio concerts, a huge funeral, lyrics, records, up to six hours*
> Bohumil Hrabal
> *Prague, an accident or suicide, real events, an Oscar, a single sentence, banned books*

2 a 👥 *Reading for detail, Preparation for discussion.* This task is preparation for **b**. Learners, still in their groups, note down one or two details about the six things in **1a** from their article. Answers depend on learner choice of details.

> *Possible answers*
> Umm Kulthum
> – *Cairo: went there at 16, invited by famous musician, met a poet who wrote 137 songs for her, first success at Arabic Theatre Palace*
> – *radio concerts: on first Thursday of every month, everyone rushed home to listen to them*
> – *a huge funeral: over 4 million people attended, one of the largest gatherings in history*
> – *lyrics: about love and loss, universal themes*
> – *records: a million copies sold every year since her death*
> – *up to six hours: duration of her concerts, usually two or three songs only*

> **Bohumil Hrabal**
> – *Prague: lived and died in Prague, had a flat there*
> – *an accident or suicide: fell from fifth-floor hospital window in 1997, trying to feed pigeons, had a phobia about falling from fifth floor, wrote about it several times*
> – *real events: everything he wrote was based on real events, nothing was invented*
> – *an Oscar: a film based on his book (Closely Watched Trains) won the Oscar for Best Foreign Film in 1967*
> – *a single sentence: One of his books is one sentence long (Dancing Lessons for the Advanced in Age); it had more editions than his other works.*
> – *banned books: His work was banned in his country 1968 to 1975. In 1975, many of his works were published again, but some only published abroad. In 1989, more of the banned books were published.*

b 👥 *Discussion*. Learners get into A/B pairs and tell each other about their articles, using their notes from **a** to help them.

Responding to the text. Learners answer the follow-up question in their pairs, or as a class.

VOCABULARY Talking about well-known people

3 👤/👥 Learners match the halves of the sentences.

> 1 d   2 g   3 a   4 h   5 c   6 f   7 b   8 e

SPEAKING

4 👤 *Preparation for discussion*. Learners choose two or three famous writers or performers (singers, musicians) to talk about. They plan what to say, using the highlighted expressions in **3** as a guide, adding to and adapting them as necessary, e.g. *One of his most famous works is …* → *One of her most famous songs was …*

👥 *Discussion*. In small groups, learners talk about their chosen writers or performers and ask questions to find out more.

Round-up. Ask one learner from each group to say who their group talked about. Find out from a few people who they found the most interesting.

> **Alternative**
>
> *Mingle*. In **4**, just before the *Discussion* stage, ask learners to write the names of the people they're going to talk about on pieces of paper, with their own name at the top. Post them around the room. Learners go round and read them, choose two or three writers or performers they want to hear about, then talk to the learners whose names are at the top. To round up, ask a few learners who they heard about, who was most interesting, and why.

She's known as …

GRAMMAR Using the passive

1 👤 *Grammar presentation*. In a guided discovery activity, learners read the information in the Grammar box, then look at sentences 1–6 in the box and match a–d with the four passive sentences.

> a 1   b 5   c 6   d 2

The key to the usage of the passive is that the speaker (or writer) wishes to keep the focus on the main topic:

the person, their experiences, their abilities, facts about them, etc. So the speaker or writer naturally makes these things the subjects of sentences, choosing either active or passive to do so.

2 👤/👥 Learners complete the five expressions from the Umm Kulthum article.

> 1 based   2 said   3 attended   4 regarded   5 estimated

3 a 👤/👥 *Practice*. Learners read the profile about Jang Nara and decide which sentences should be left active and which should be rewritten with passives. Do the first bullet point with them:
* *Jang Nara was born in Seoul in March 1981. (OK. The focus is on her.)*
* *People consider her one of the best entertainers in South Korea. ('People' is vague and not important, so put the focus on Jang Nara. Elicit: She is considered one of the best entertainers in South Korea.)*

Learners continue through the rest of the profile.

b Play recording **1.27** for learners to compare their ideas. In each case underlined below, Jang Nara or something related to her has become the subject of a sentence.

> * *Jang Nara was born in Seoul in March 1981. <u>She is considered</u> one of the best entertainers in South Korea.*
> * *She started out as an actress in her primary school days, when <u>she was invited</u> to appear in the play, Les Misérables. Later, in high school, she modelled in a number of television ads.*
> * *Jang had her first real success as a singer in 2001, when <u>her debut album was released</u>. <u>300,000 copies of the album were sold</u>, and <u>she was awarded</u> Best New Singer of that year.*
> * *At the same time, her acting career continued to develop. <u>She was hired</u> to star in popular sitcoms and dramas, and <u>she was also invited by</u> a Chinese television station to star in the successful drama My Bratty Princess. She is very popular in China, where <u>she is known as</u> 'Zhang Na La'.*
> * *In addition, <u>she has been recognised for</u> her charity work in different countries. <u>She was appointed</u> a goodwill ambassador by one Chinese charity, the first foreigner to receive this honour.*

> **Note: Grammar practice**
>
> You could do the grammar practice on p133 at this point.

WRITING AND SPEAKING

4 a 👤 *Writing*. Learners choose a person to include on a website about their own country like the one Jang Nara is featured on. They prepare a profile like the Jang Nara one, using bullet points. Remind them to choose useful expressions from VOCABULARY Talking about well-known people, and from the highlighted passive expressions in **1** and **2**.

b 👥/👥 *Reading and speaking*. Learners exchange profiles and ask questions about them. If they know about the people in other learners' profiles, they can contribute extra information.

 You could use photocopiable activity 4B on the Teacher's DVD-ROM at this point.

4.3 Target activity

Goals: talk about landmarks where you live ♻
talk about well-known people where you live ♻
give information about interesting or important sights

Core language:

TASK VOCABULARY	Recalling details
4.1 VOCABULARY	History of a landmark
4.2 VOCABULARY	Talking about well-known people
4.2 GRAMMAR	Using the passive

Describe well-known sights to a visitor

TASK LISTENING

1   As a warmer, learners answer the question in pairs or as a class.

> **Alternative**
>
> *Using pictures.* Bring in pictures of the five places listed in **2** (e.g. from the Internet). Tell learners they're all places to see in or around Beijing, China. Write the names of the places on the board. Learners guess which names go with which pictures. Ask them which they'd want to visit if they went to Beijing.

2   *Listening for main idea.* Play recording **1.28**. Learners listen and circle the one place that's not mentioned.

> The Summer Palace

3   *Listening for detail.* Play recording **1.28** again. Learners write the names of the places next to each question.

> 1 The Forbidden City, The Temple of Heaven
> 2 The Temple of Heaven, The Great Wall
> 3 The Forbidden City
> 4 The Great Wall
> 5 The Temple of Heaven

TASK VOCABULARY Recalling details

4 **a**   The goal of the target activity is 'give information about interesting or important sights'. In this vocabulary section, learners focus on the language of recalling details because these expressions often precede the giving of information, especially when the speaker is not totally sure of some details or of where they got the information.

👤/👥 Learners complete the six sentences from the recording with the words.

> 2 say   3 think   4 heard/read   5 read/heard
> 6 remember

b   Learners read script **1.28** on p146 to check, getting further exposure to the language as well as possible ideas for their own role-play conversation in **5**.

TASK

5 **a**   👤 *Preparation for role play.* This is a two-stage preparation. In **a**, learners make a list of interesting places to see in an area (town, city, region) they know well in their country. Alternatively, they can choose an area in another country which they know about.

> **Alternative**
>
> *Online research.* Learners can do some online research in advance of the Task. Monolingual classes can even be assigned different cities or regions in their country to research. They just need enough information about each sight in their chosen area to answer the questions in **5b**.

b   👤 In the second preparation stage, learners focus on what to say and how to say it. Remind them to choose useful expressions from TASK VOCABULARY Recalling details, VOCABULARY History of a landmark and VOCABULARY Talking about well-known people. Point out that the passive will be useful. Give an example or two: *The Blue Mosque can be seen from quite far away. Cape Town is known as the jewel of South Africa. The Taj Mahal was built by the emperor Shah Jahan to commemorate his wife.*

c   👥 *Role play.* Learners take turns being the host (giving information) and being the visitor (asking questions). Learner A gives information first.

> **Optional extra**
>
> Learners can change pairs after the first role play. Get the Bs to move to the next pair so they can give information to new A partners.

6   👥 Learners answer the follow-up question.

Round-up. Ask a few learners what city or region they heard about and which sights they'd like to visit if they had the chance to go there.

4 Explore

Across cultures: Special occasions

Goal: to make learners aware of special occasions in different cultures

Core language:

VOCABULARY	Describing a special occasion: *Nowadays; In the old days; Traditionally; The reason we … is because; It's quite normal to; There's a lot of; There will be; It can be anywhere between … and; turn out; go on for*

LISTENING

1   👥👥 To introduce this topic, ask learners to name a few special occasions. Choose one of them and ask them what kind of atmosphere it has, e.g. cheerful, serious, mysterious.

👥 Then get learners to look at the two pictures in pairs and describe the atmosphere of each occasion. Ask for their ideas and get them to explain why they chose that description.

2   *Listening for main idea.* Tell learners they're going to listen to two people describing those special occasions. Beryl will be the first speaker. Give learners time to read the expressions listed. Tell them the speakers might use slightly different expressions from these, so they should be alert. Then play recording **1.29**. Learners put *B* for Beryl, *D* for Dominika or both initials next to the topics they talk about.

> Beryl: *fireworks, a kind of doll, government buildings, the community*
> Dominika: *food, borrowed items, the community, dancing*

3 *Listening for detail.* Give learners time to read items 1–6. Play recording **1.29** again. Learners mark the statements true or false according to what the speakers say.

> 1 True   2 False   3 False   4 True   5 True   6 False

4 *Responding to the text.* Learners answer the question in pairs or as a class. As a follow-up question, ask them how they'd describe the atmosphere of the two occasions now that they've heard a bit more about them.

VOCABULARY Describing a special occasion

5 a Learners recall the descriptions, writing *B* next to sentences describing Bonfire Night and *W* next to sentences describing weddings in Poland.

b Learners read script **1.29** on pp146–7 to check.

> 1 B   2 B   3 W   4 B   5 W   6 B   7 B   8 W   9 B   10 W

Alternative for weaker classes

If learners have trouble with recollection tasks, let them look at the script (or even listen again) and mark the sentences as indicated: *B* for Bonfire Night, *W* for weddings in Poland.

SPEAKING

6 *Preparation for discussion.* Learners work alone and gather their ideas. Encourage them to note down their ideas, along with useful expressions from **5a**. They can write out a few key sentences using the expressions if they wish.

7 *Discussion.* Learners talk about their special occasions in groups. There are interactions for both monolingual and multilingual classes suggested in the Coursebook.

Optional extra

Learners write out their talk in a paragraph at home and hand it in for correction the next day. Remind them to make use of the expressions in **5a**. They also might want to include pictures of their special occasion (e.g. from the Internet).

Explore writing

Goal: write an email or letter recommending places to see

Core language:

Recommending: *Be sure to; It's advisable to; Check out; Don't miss; You should; I recommend you; Make sure you; Don't forget to; Try out; It's well worth*
Adjectives of description: *enormous; charming; jammed; fascinating; well-stocked; impressive; ancient; historic; refreshing; traditional*

1 *Reading for main idea.* To introduce the topic, ask learners if they have ever given travel advice to someone. Ask them if they gave the advice face to face, in a letter or email, by text, etc. Find out what kind of things they recommended, e.g. places to go, ways to get there, things to see and do when they get

there, how to behave, etc. Then explain that this page focuses on recommending things to see and do when they get to a place.

Learners read Gareth's email to answer the two questions, then compare their ideas.

> *They're going to Japan.*
> *Gareth and his wife are interested in culture, history and art. Their son Dylan is interested in Disneyland.*

2 *Responding to the text.* This is a personal opinion question, as learners read Ellie's email and decide which things they personally would find most interesting if they went to Japan. Learners can compare their ideas afterwards in pairs. Ask a few learners what they chose and why.

3 Learners match the paragraphs 1–5 in Ellie's email with the topics a–e.

> a 5   b 1   c 4   d 2   e 3

4 Learners complete the expressions with two or three words, as in the example.

> 2 It's advisable to   3 check out   4 don't miss
> 5 You should   6 I recommend you   7 Make sure you
> 8 Don't forget to   9 try out   10 It's well worth

5 Learners quickly read through Ellie's email, looking for useful adjectives to describe places.

> a enormous   b charming   c jammed   d fascinating
> e well-stocked   f impressive   g ancient   h historic
> i refreshing   j traditional

6 a *Preparation for writing.* Learners read the context and begin preparing their ideas, making sure to use points 1–3 as a guideline.

b *Writing.* This can be done either in class or at home. If you wish, learners can start writing in class, for example just the first paragraph, while you monitor and correct. This reassures them that they have made a good start, and they can then finish the email or letter at home and bring it in the next day.

7 Learners exchange emails or letters with a partner and ask questions about it.

> You could use photocopiable activity 4C on the Teacher's DVD-ROM at this point.

4 Look again

Review

VOCABULARY Talking about landmarks

1 a Learners try to recall as many expressions as they can for each category 1–6. If they need help after a while, they can look at VOCABULARY Describing landmarks and VOCABULARY History of a landmark on p30 and p31 respectively.

b Learners say what they can remember about the three landmarks. They can use the pictures on p30, but get them to cover the rest of the page.

GRAMMAR Using the passive

2 a 👤/👥 Learners read the mini-biography and choose the correct options.

> 1 graduated 2 has been employed 3 moved
> 4 was published 5 have been translated
> 6 have been adapted 7 was awarded 8 lives

b 👤 *Writing.* Learners prepare to write a mini-biography about themselves, of a similar length to the one in **a**. Remind learners to include one or two imaginary details in their biography for the guessing activity in **c**. If you wish, you can give them a list of useful verbs, such as: *appoint, attend, award, employ, graduate, grow up, introduce, live, meet, move, offer, promote, recruit, start, travel, win, work.* Remind them to choose the active or passive as necessary.

> **Alternative**
>
> You may wish to set the actual writing in stage **2b** as homework.

c 👥 Divide learners into small groups to read all the mini-biographies. When they've finished reading, they guess which details are true and which are imaginary in each person's biography. The writer confirms which are imaginary.

CAN YOU REMEMBER? Unit 3 – Work and commitment

3 a 👤/👥 Learners choose the best options in each person's hope or plan.

> 1 carry on 2 take on 3 give up 4 work on

b 👤 Learners think of similar sentences regarding their hopes and plans for the next year or so. They can select from any of the verb options in **a**.

SPELLING AND SOUNDS /m/

4 a 👤/👥 Learners underline the /m/ sound in each word. That includes double and silent letters.

> cli<u>mb</u>, colu<u>mn</u>, co<u>mm</u>on, i<u>mm</u>ediately, <u>m</u>ille<u>nn</u>iu<u>m</u>, <u>m</u>onu<u>m</u>ent, pa<u>lm</u>, su<u>mm</u>on

b 👤/👥 Learners match each word with the rules 1–3.

> 1 millennium, monument
> 2 common, immediately, summon
> 3 climb, column, palm

c Play recording **1.30**. Learners listen and write the words, then check their spelling in script **1.30** on p147. Alternatively, you can elicit the spelling and write it on the board.

> autumn, calm, community, impression, estimated, immigration, mummy, summary, thumb, demonstration, recommend, enormous

> **Optional extra**
>
> Ask learners to match the words they've just spelled in **4c** with the rules in **4b**.

NOTICE *very, the very*

5 a 👤/👥 Learners look at the difference between *very* and *the very* as illustrated in Cian's sentences and answer the questions on meaning and usage.

> 1 a2 b1,3
> 2 a2 b1,3

b 👤 Learners complete questions 1–4. Explain there is more than one possibility for each question, so they can choose whichever word they think makes the most interesting question – and is correct in terms of usage.

> **Possible answers**
> 1 beginning/end
> 2 first/last/best/worst
> 3 top/bottom
> 4 best/worst

c 👥 Learners ask and answer the questions. Afterwards, ask a few learners what answers they got from the people they talked to.

> **Alternative**
>
> You can do **5c** as a mingle, where learners move freely around the class asking the questions. Then ask a few of them what answers they got from the people they talked to.

Self-assessment

To help focus learners on the self-assessment, read it through and get learners to give you a few examples of the language they have learned in each section. Give an example to start them off if necessary. Then learners circle the numbers on each line.

Unit 4 Extra activities on the Teacher's DVD-ROM

Printable worksheets, activity instructions and answer keys are on your Teacher's DVD-ROM.

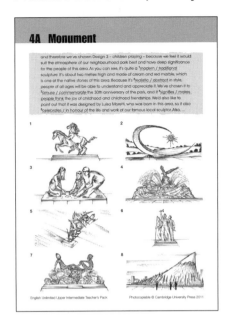

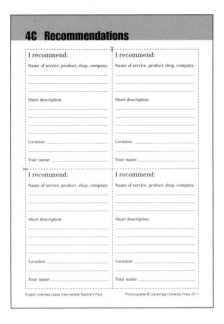

4A Monument

Activity type: Speaking – Proposal – Small groups / Whole class

Aim: To choose a monument for a particular part of your town or city and explain your choice

Language: Describing landmarks – Use at any point from 4.1.

Preparation: Make one copy of the worksheet for every learner.

Time: 40 minutes

4B Tunisia and Patagonia

Activity type: Speaking – Gap-fill quiz / Information gap – Pairs/Groups

Aim: To revise the passive and do a quiz about a country and a region

Language: Using the passive – Use at any point from 4.2.

Preparation: Make one copy of the worksheet for every four learners. Cut each worksheet up to make one Tunisia quiz and one Patagonia quiz. Cut off the answer-key strips and keep the two sets separate.

Time: 40 minutes

4C Recommendations

Activity type: Speaking – Making recommendations – Individuals/ Mingle

Aim: To recommend a particular product, service, shop, etc.

Language: Expressions of recommendation – Use any time after Explore writing.

Preparation: Make one copy of the worksheet for every four learners. Cut each worksheet up to make a set of four forms.

Time: 40 minutes

Unit 4 Self-study Pack

In the Workbook

Unit 4 of the *English Unlimited Upper Intermediate Workbook* offers additional ways to practise the vocabulary and grammar taught in the Coursebook. There are also activities which build reading and writing skills and a whole page of listening and speaking tasks to use with the Interview video, giving your learners the opportunity to hear and react to authentic spoken English.

- **Vocabulary:** Describing landmarks; History of a landmark; Talking about well-known people; Recalling details; Describing a special occasion
- **Grammar:** Using the passive
- **Explore reading:** Article: Machu Picchu
- **Interview:** Come to my country – Rezarta and Liu

On the DVD-ROM

Unit 4 of the *English Unlimited Upper Intermediate Self-study DVD-ROM* contains interactive games and activities for your learners to practise and improve their vocabulary, grammar and pronunciation, and also their speaking and listening, with the possibility for learners to record themselves, and a video of authentic spoken English to use with the Workbook.

- **Vocabulary and grammar:** Extra practice activities
- **Pronunciation:** Weak forms
- **Explore speaking:** Being vague with *sort of*
- **Listening:** Places to see
- **Video:** Come to my country

Images

5.1

Goals: describe and give opinions about images
choose something for a room

Core language:

VOCABULARY	Describing an image
VOCABULARY	Choosing something for a room

Picture story

LISTENING

1 a 👥 / 👪 *Prediction.* Learners look at the painting and make guesses about the questions 1–3.

Then ask each pair/group to tell the class about their guesses.

b *Listening for main ideas.* Tell learners that they are going to listen to an introduction to the painting from an audio guide on an art-gallery website. Play recording **2.1**. Learners listen to find the answers to the questions.

> 1 There are two groups of people: a family and soldiers.
> 2 The two groups are on opposing sides in a civil war.
> 3 The soldiers have occupied the family's house.
>   They're questioning the little boy about the
>   whereabouts of his father.
> (Learners may have made further speculations in 1a
> which they will be able to check when they listen to
> recording 2.2.)

2 *Listening for main ideas.* Tell learners that they will now listen to another part of the audio guide, a commentary of the various people in the painting. Play recording **2.2**. Learners listen to find out in what order the people in the painting 1–6 are described.

> 4, 2, 1, 6, 3, 5

3 a 👥 / 👪 *Listening for details.* Learners read 1–6 and try to remember what the audio guide said about each point.

Then play recording **2.2** again. Learners listen and complete their answers.

b 👥 / 👪 Learners compare their answers, then read script **2.2** on p147 to check any details as necessary.

> 1 His small size, the colour of his hair and his blue suit
>   highlight his (dangerous) innocence.
> 2 She may be worried about what her brother will say or
>   the prospect of being questioned.
> 3 They emphasise the fact that the family is helpless.
> 4 He may be genuinely friendly or trying to trick the boy.
> 5 It suggests that he feels sorry for the little girl.
> 6 It suggests that the soldiers are stealing the family's
>   possessions.

4 👥 / 👪 *Responding to the text.* Learners tell each other how they feel about the painting, using the questions to guide their discussion.

VOCABULARY Describing an image

5 👥 / 👪 *Presentation.* Learners look at the sentences from the audio guide, focusing on the highlighted expressions. They find five pairs of expressions which have a similar meaning.

> 1 shows – 6 portrays
> 2 highlight – 5 emphasises
> 3 can be seen – 4 are visible
> 7 seems to – 9 appears to
> 8 implies – 10 suggest

Ask: *Which expressions are more for giving a physical description of an image?* (1/6, 3/4) *Which are more for giving a personal opinion or interpretation?* (2/5, 8/10). (Expressions 7/9 could be used for both purposes.)

Optional extra: Peer testing

Learners test each other in pairs. Learner A says sentences 1–10 in random order. Learner B (book closed) listens and reformulates the sentences using the other expression from the pair. For example: *More soldiers are visible.* → *More soldiers can be seen.* Then they swap roles.

SPEAKING

6 a 🧍 *Preparation for description.* Learners turn to p122 and look at the paintings. They each choose one painting and prepare to describe what it shows, and how they interpret it. Encourage learners to choose expressions from **5** to use in their descriptions.

b 👥 / 👪 *Description.* Learners listen to each other's descriptions of the paintings, and say what they think about each other's interpretations.

Round-up. As a class, briefly discuss each of the paintings in turn. Elicit different learners' interpretations.

Alternative

Learners bring to the lesson an image of their choice (a painting, a drawing, a photograph) which they'd like to talk about. Use these images for **6a** and **6b** instead of the paintings on p122.

I can imagine it in the kitchen

LISTENING

Optional extra: Personalised lead-in

Books closed. To focus on the topic of the listening, tell the class about: 1) different kinds of pictures you have in different rooms in your home (original paintings or drawings, reproductions, posters, photographs including family photos etc.); 2) how you got them (bought them, received them as gifts, made them yourself, etc.). Then learners discuss the same two topics in pairs/groups.

---

1 *Listening for main ideas.* Look at the picture of Paloma and James and read through the caption together. Play recording **2.3**. Learners listen and identify which posters on p122 James and Paloma decide to buy.

2 *Listening for details.* Play recording **2.3** again. Learners listen and make notes on Paloma and James's opinions about all four of the posters.

👥 / 👥👥 Then learners compare their notes. If there are any differences, resolve them during class feedback or ask learners to check for themselves in script **2.3** on p147.

> B Interesting, but too dark and depressing, and the shape is wrong: it's too wide and needs to be squarer.
> C James suggests the painting is a good size, that it's cheerful and that the horse is 'nice'; Paloma hates it.
> D Strong colours, but style doesn't suit living room; it would suit the kitchen, though.
> A Bright, they like the sunlight coming down through clouds, and the shape is OK; it will suit the living room and make it look bigger.

VOCABULARY Choosing something for a room

3 👥 / 👥👥 *Presentation.* Learners use the words in the boxes to complete the sentences from the conversation.

> 2 put   3 suit   4 see   5 go   6 look
> 8 wrong   9 good   10 sure   11 bright/cheerful
> 12 bigger

> **Language note**
>
> Point out that we use:
> - *suit* to talk about style, *fit* to talk about size/shape, and *go* to talk about either style or size/shape:
>   *It wouldn't **go in** / **suit** the living room.* (= It's the wrong style.)
>   *It wouldn't **go on** / **fit on** that wall.* (= It's the wrong size or shape.)
> - the expression *nice and ...* to emphasise a positive characteristic:
>   *It's nice and cheerful.*
>   We also use it to show that we see a characteristic of something as positive:
>   *It's nice and big.* (= It's big and this is a good thing.)

4 a 🧍 *Practice.* Learners look again at the paintings on p122 and think about the questions. They choose expressions from **3** to help explain their answers, making notes if they wish.

b 👥 / 👥👥 Learners compare their answers. Get feedback from the whole class to find out which were the most and least popular posters.

SPEAKING

5 a 👥 *Decision-making.* Learners imagine they've been given the task of brightening up the classroom. One of the things they'd like to do is put up a picture. Learners choose a picture to put up in the classroom and decide exactly where it should go. They can choose any picture from the lesson, from the Coursebook, or another picture they know of. Tell learners they must be ready to give reasons for their decisions. Remind them to use the expressions from **3**.

b 👥👥 Put pairs together to make groups of four. They compare and explain ideas, then decide on one picture and location to propose to the whole class.

c Each group from **b** explains its proposal. Learners vote for their favourite proposal.

 You could use photocopiable activity 5A on the Teacher's DVD-ROM at this point.

5.2

Goals: discuss what makes a good design
describe designs and designed objects

Core language:

VOCABULARY	Discussing design
GRAMMAR	Describing objects – past participle clauses
PRONUNCIATION	Groups of words 1

Design classics

VOCABULARY Discussing design

1 a Look at the pictures of the two products and discuss the questions with the class. Elicit a range of suggested answers, but do not comment on which are right or wrong at this stage.

b Learners read the paragraph about Dieter Rams and find answers to the questions in **a**.

> The Braun T3 radio is from 1958. The Apple iPod is from 2001.
> Dieter Rams, designer of the T3, was an important influence on Jonathan Ive, designer of the iPod.

2 👥 / 👥👥 *Presentation.* Learners match each expression 1–7 in the paragraph with a similar-meaning expression a–g.

> 1c   2a   3e   4b   5d   6f   7g

Check learners' understanding of a few of the more difficult words:
- Elicit some possible opposites of *innovative/novel* (*possible answers: old-fashioned, traditional*).
- Elicit the meaning of *obtrusive* (*too noticeable, difficult to ignore*); and hence *unobtrusive*.
- Elicit which words, in the context of Rams's principles, suggest that everything in a design should be connected, that everything should have the same style (*consequent/consistent*).

> **Alternative for stronger classes**
>
> Learners think of words and expressions which can be used to describe *bad* design, i.e. which mean the opposite of the target items in **2**. They write 'ten principles of bad design', a mirror-image of Rams's principles. Possible words and expressions: *unoriginal, tired, ugly, unattractive, obtrusive, distracting, complicated, confusing, goes out of date quickly, inconsistent, bad for the environment.*

3 🧍 *Practice.* Learners make two short lists: 1) things they own which they think are well designed; 2) things which they think are badly designed. They think about how to describe the things in their lists and explain why they're well/badly designed. Encourage learners to use words from **2**.

👥 / 👥👥 Learners tell each other about the things in their two lists.

READING

4 Check that learners know what is meant by a *design classic* (*a design which is well known and regarded as high quality or special in some way*) and elicit a few examples of design classics (e.g. company logos).

Reading for main ideas, responding to the text. Learners read and decide whether the paperclip deserves to be called a design classic.

👥 / 👥👥 Then they compare and explain their opinions.

5 *Reading for details.* Learners read again and gather information on the four topics.

> 1 Norwegian; an inventor; the first man to patent the paperclip, though it didn't make him any money; there's a statue of a giant paperclip in memory of him outside Oslo.
> 2 As a tool; to make into miniature animals and buildings; to clean fingernails, pipes and teeth; as something to fiddle with when stressed; as poker chips; to hold clothes together; as a national symbol.
> 3 The well-known 'Gem' paperclip was first made by Gem Manufacturing Ltd, a British company, though they didn't patent the idea. A few years later, in 1899, Johan Vaaler took out a patent for his own version of the paperclip in Germany.
> 4 During the Second World War, Norwegians were forbidden from wearing national symbols, so they used the paperclip as an 'unofficial' national symbol. The paperclip suggests the idea of togetherness, of people sticking together.

A survey conducted by ...

GRAMMAR Describing objects – past participle clauses

1 👥 / 👥👥 *Presentation.* Learners read the grammar box, then answer the two questions below it.

> 1 a Defining   b Non-defining
> 2 a Defining   b Non-defining   c Non-defining

Alternative

Books-closed presentation. Write on the board:
1 Of (every 100,000 paperclips) which are made in the United States, 17,200 hold clothing together.
2 (The humble paperclip), which was first patented by Johan Vaaler, remains indispensable.
Ask:
- *What are the underlined parts called?* (relative clauses)
- *Which relative clause could you delete without changing the meaning? Why?* (2, because it only adds an extra detail about the paperclip. In 1, the relative clause is necessary because it tells us that the sentence is specifically about paperclips made in the USA.)
- *What do we call the two kinds of relative clause?* (1 defining, 2 non-defining)
Now write equivalent sentences with past participle clauses.
1 Of (every 100,000 paperclips) made in the United States, 17,200 hold clothing together.
2 (The humble paperclip), first patented by Johan Vaaler, remains indispensable. (non-defining)
   or
   First patented by Johan Vaaler, (the humble paperclip) remains indispensable.
Point out how:
- defining participle clauses are simple: they always go straight after the noun (and in writing have no commas);
- non-defining participle clauses can go before or after the noun (and in writing are separated by commas).

---

2 👤 *Practice.* Learners combine the pairs of sentences into single sentences using past participle clauses. Tell learners that in some sentences, the participle clause can go in two places (because it's non-defining).

> 1 The famous soy sauce bottle made by the Kikkoman Company was designed by Kenji Ekuan in 1961.
> 2 The Boeing 747, first flown in 1969, was chosen by architect Norman Foster as his favourite 'building'. / First flown in 1969, the Boeing 747 was chosen by architect Norman Foster as his favourite 'building'.
> 3 More than five million cigarette lighters made by Bic are sold every day.
> 4 Zhang Xiaoquan scissors, first produced in 1663, are made in Hangzhou, China. / First produced in 1663, Zhang Xiaoquan scissors are made in Hangzhou, China.
> 5 A Swiss Army knife known as The Giant features 85 tools and weighs a kilo.

Note: Grammar practice

You could do the grammar practice on p134 at this point.

PRONUNCIATION Groups of words 1

3 a Play recording **2.4** a few times. Learners listen and at the same time read the two sentences. Point out how the speaker says the words in groups to make the sentences easier to understand.

Then focus on the participle clauses in each sentence and elicit answers to the question.

> 1 Defining   2 Non-defining

Alternative for stronger classes

Books closed. Write the sentences on the board (if you wrote them up while looking at the answers to **2**, you can use these) and play recording **2.4**. Ask learners to:
- identify the groups of words and say where the // symbols should go;
- explain why the participle clause is sometimes in the same group as the noun it describes, and sometimes separate.

---

b Learners repeat the sentences together as a class. Listen carefully to make sure they say the words in the groups as shown.

Optional extra

Peer drill. For more practice, learners say the other sentences in **2**. In pairs, they take turns to point to sentences and say them in groups of words.

> **Suggested answers**
> // The famous soy sauce bottle made by the Kikkoman Company // was designed by Kenjo Ekuan // in 1961. //
> // Zhang Xiaoquan scissors, // first produced in 1663, // are made in Hangzhou, // China. //
> // First produced in 1663, // Zhang Xiaoquan scissors // are made in Hangzhou, // China. //
> // A Swiss Army knife known as The Giant // features 85 tools // and weighs a kilo. //

SPEAKING

4 a 👥 *Decision-making.* Learners think of objects or designs to include in an exhibition of design classics. They write a list similar to the example, using past participle clauses. Each learner should make their own copy of the list.

b 👥 / 👥 *Report.* Put learners into new groups. Learners tell each other which objects and designs they chose in **a**, and why.

> **Optional extra**
>
> *Class discussion.* As a class, listen to each group's ideas from **4a** and write them on the board. Discuss the various ideas and have a class vote to choose the final six objects or designs.

 You could use photocopiable activity 5B on the Teacher's DVD-ROM at this point.

5.3 Target activity

Goals: describe and give opinions about images ♻
describe designs and designed objects ♻
participate in a decision-making discussion

Core language:

TASK VOCABULARY	Getting a consensus
5.1 VOCABULARY	Describing an image
5.2 GRAMMAR	Describing objects – past participle clauses

Choose a logo

TASK LISTENING

1 *Pre-listening discussion.* To introduce the topic of the listening, ask learners to look at the picture of Callie, Brett and Kim.

👥 / 👥 Then learners look at logos 1–3 and tell each other which they think is best, and why.

Round off with a quick class discussion. Ask learners to summarise what they see as the strengths and weaknesses of each logo.

2 *Listening for main ideas.* Play recording **2.5**. Learners listen and answer the questions.

> 1 Design 2
> 2 They'll ask for the colours to be toned down (made less bright).

3 *Listening for details.* Play recording **2.5** again. Learners listen and match each statement a–e with one of the designs.

> a1 b1 c2 d3 e3

TASK VOCABULARY Getting a consensus

4 a 👥 / 👥 *Presentation.* Learners put expressions from the listening into three groups a–c.

> a 1, 2, 4, 7
> b 6, 8
> c 3, 5

b Play recording **2.6**. Learners listen to the three groups of sentences and check their answers. Then practise saying the sentences with the class.

TASK

5 a 👥 *Preparation for meeting.* Tell learners they're going to have a meeting to choose a logo for a business called From Nature To You. Learners read the description of the business and underline points which might be important to bear in mind for someone designing a logo for this business.

Then compare key points as a class.

> **Suggested answers**
> organic food, in your town and city (= local), vegetables and fruit, nuts, seeds and oil, baskets, courier

b 👤 Learners prepare for the meeting. They look at the three logos, A–C, and think about the questions 1–4 individually. Remind learners that they can talk about the logos using expressions from VOCABULARY Describing an image and GRAMMAR Describing objects – past participle clauses.

c 👥 *Meeting.* Learners discuss and choose the most suitable logo. They also decide if they'd like to ask the designer to make any changes to their chosen logo. Tell learners they'll need to describe and explain their decisions to the class. Encourage them to make use of the expressions in **4a** to manage their meeting.

6 👥 *Report.* Each group explains its decisions to the class.

Round-up. The class votes to find the most popular logo. Each learner can give two votes to their favourite design (two hands up) and one vote to their second favourite design (one hand up).

---

5 Explore

Keyword: *as*

Goals: use *as* to describe the identity or purpose of something
use common referring expressions with *as*

Core language:

as, like, such as
as you know, as promised, as you suggested, ...

as compared with *like*

1 a 👥 / 👥 *Presentation.* Explain that the sentences 1–5 are extracts from texts which learners have already seen earlier on in the course. Learners complete the sentences with *as, such as* or *like.* Two answers are possible in two of the sentences.

> 1 as   2 such as / like   3 as   4 such as / like   5 like

> **Optional extra**
>
> Learners check their answers by finding and looking in the relevant texts from earlier in the course. Point out the unit numbers given at the end of each sentence.

b 👥 / 👥👥 Learners identify the functions of *as*, *such as* and *like*.

> *1 as   2 like   3 such as, like*

To further clarify the difference between *as* and *like*, put these sentences on the board:
1 I work as a waiter in a local café.
2 I look like a waiter in these clothes.

For each sentence, ask: *Is the speaker a waiter?* (*In 1, yes. In 2, the speaker is not a waiter, but is similar to a waiter in one way, i.e. in his appearance.*)

Ask learners to translate these sentences into their first languages, and find out whether the words for *as* and *like* would be the same or different.

Language note

This section focuses exclusively on *as* and *like* as prepositions (= followed by noun phrases). Both words can also be used as conjunctions (= followed by clauses), but in this case, *as* and *like* are <u>both</u> used to describe sameness or similarity:
It was a great party – exactly as/like I imagined it!
However, the use of *like* as a conjunction is less formal and some people consider it wrong.

The conjunction *as* can also be used in a similar way to *when/while* and *because*:
As I came out of the shop, I saw my car pulling away.
As we're so busy, perhaps we should delay the meeting until next week?

---

2 a 🧍 *Practice.* Learners complete the sentences with *as / like / such as* + their own ideas to make six sentences, four true and two false. Monitor closely during this stage to check correct use of the target expressions and provide assistance as necessary.

> *Possible answers*
> *I once worked as a teacher.*
> *I really don't like films such as / like 'The Ring'.*
> *I know someone who looks a bit like Angela Merkel.*
> *At school, I was known as 'Brainbox'.*
> *I think my friends see me as a reliable person.*
> *I wouldn't mind a career as a translator.*

b 👥 / 👥👥 Learners listen to each other's sentences and ask questions to find out more about them. They then try to guess which sentences are true and which are false.

Referring expressions with *as*

3 a 🧍 *Reading for main ideas.* Learners read and put the chain of emails between Keith and Leona in order. Then they compare their answers.

> *A, C, D, B, F, E*

b 👥 / 👥👥 *Presentation.* Learners find eight expressions with *as* in the emails and put them into three groups according to their function.

> *1 as you know, as you probably remember*
> *2 as you suggested, as agreed (last time), as I mentioned (last week), as promised, as planned*
> *3 as you'll see*

c 👥 / 👥👥 Learners look at four more common expressions with *as* and decide which expression in the emails each one could replace.

> *as arranged: as planned, as agreed*
> *as I said: as I mentioned*
> *as you proposed: as you suggested*
> *as you're aware: as you know*

4 👥 / 👥👥 *Practice.* Divide the class into two groups, A and B. Group A learners (as a single big group or as a number of sub-groups) look at Leona's emails on p120 and reconstruct Keith's emails from memory. Group B learners look at Keith's emails on p123 and reconstruct Leona's emails. Learners' emails do *not* have to be exactly the same as the originals, but they should have roughly the same meaning (i.e. they need to fit into the chain of correspondence) and include some expressions with *as*.

Round-up. Elicit the learners' emails onto the board in order (Group B, Group A, Group B, etc.) or ask members from each group to come and write their emails up on the board.

Learners read the complete sequence of emails. They suggest corrections and, if necessary, changes to make the sequence of emails coherent. Work with the class to perfect the emails, focusing in particular on use of expressions with *as*.

Option for weaker classes

Provide each group with a few key expressions, and/or the relevant expressions with *as*, to help them write their emails.

Explore speaking

Goals: express disagreement in different situations
make concessions and counter-arguments

Core language:
Are you joking? I see what you mean. But even if that's the case, …

1 *Listening for main ideas.* Tell learners they're going to listen to extracts from two conversations they've already heard in this unit. Play recording **2.7**. Learners listen and answer the questions.

👥 / 👥👥 Learners check their answers together.

> Conversation 1
> *1 In a shop*
> *2 They're choosing posters for their home.*
> *3 They live together (probably as a couple).*
> Conversation 2
> *1 In a meeting at work*
> *2 They're choosing a logo for their company.*
> *3 They're colleagues.*

2 a 👥 / 👥👥 *Presentation.* Learners complete the conversation scripts on the right-hand side of the page using the expressions a–h.

b Play recording **2.7** again. Learners listen to check their answers.

> *1 a   2 d   3 c   4 f   5 g   6 b   7 h   8 e*

3 a 👥/👥👥 Point out that the expressions in **2a** are arranged in three groups according to their function. Learners add the expressions from the box to the correct groups.

> Group 1: *Are you serious?; How can you say that?; I have to disagree with you there; I wonder about that.*
> Group 2: *I'd go along with you there; Maybe you're right about that.*
> Group 3: *That may be so, but ...; I take your point, but ...*

b Play recording **2.8**, in which learners hear all the expressions in each group. Learners listen and check their answers. Alternatively, learners look at script **2.8** on p147.

Optional extra: Focus on form and pronunciation

Write these three expressions on the board: *the cost, it's expensive, what's the alternative?*
Play recording **5.8** again, pausing between each sentence so that learners can repeat. Where a sentence is 'unfinished' (e.g. *I wouldn't exactly say*), learners complete it using one of the expressions on the board. Check that learners stress the sentences correctly and choose the correct expressions to complete the 'unfinished' ones.

> 1
> *Are you joking?*
> *I wouldn't exactly say it's expensive.*
> *I'm not so sure about the cost.*
> *Oh, come on.*
> *Are you serious?*
> *How can you say that?*
> *I have to disagree with you there.*
> *I wonder about that.*
> 2
> *I have to admit that it's expensive.*
> *I see what you mean.*
> *I'd go along with that.*
> *Maybe you're right about that.*
> 3
> *It's true that it's expensive but what's the alternative?*
> *But even if that's the case, what's the alternative?*
> *That may be so, but what's the alternative?*
> *I take your point, but what's the alternative?*

---

4 👥/👥👥 Learners look through all the expressions and answer the questions about appropriacy.

> 1 *Are you joking?; Oh, come on; Are you serious?; How can you say that?*
> 2 *The rest*

5 a 👥/👥👥 *Practice.* Tell learners they're going to prepare for four discussions. Divide learners into two groups, A and B. Learners in Group A read the four situations on the page. Learners in Group B read the four corresponding situations on p121. In their groups (or in smaller sub-groups or pairs), they brainstorm reasons to support their opinions, making notes if they wish.

b 👥 Put learners into pairs, one person from Group A with one person from Group B. They have the four discussions in turn and try to persuade their partner of their opinion. Encourage them to use expressions from **2a** and **3a**.

Set a time limit for each discussion (e.g. four minutes).

6 👥/👥👥 Learners go back to their pairs/groups from **5a**. They tell each other about the discussions they had and what conclusions, if any, they reached.

 You could use photocopiable activity 5C on the Teacher's DVD-ROM at this point.

5 Look again

Review

VOCABULARY Choosing something for a room

1 a 👥/👥👥 Learners choose the correct verbs in 1–6. Then they look back at VOCABULARY Choosing something for a room on p39 to check their answers.

> *1 look   2 put   3 go   4 see   5 suit   6 feel*

Alternative: Gapped dictation

Books closed. Write these verbs on the board: *feel, go, look, put, see, suit.* Read the sentences 1–6 aloud, saying *gap 1, gap 2,* etc. in place of the verbs. Learners listen and write down the verb which goes in each gap, then check in pairs/groups.

---

b 👤 Learners think of one or two specific items they'd like to have in their homes. They think about how to describe their appearance and where they would put them, using highlighted expressions from **a**.
👥/👥👥 Learners tell each other about their ideas.

GRAMMAR Past participle clauses

2 a 👥 Learners change 1–6 into questions with past participle clauses. To demonstrate, do the first one as a class.

> *Possible answers*
> *1 Do you live in a house <u>built more than a century ago</u>?*
> *2 Do you eat fruit <u>grown in your own garden</u>?*
> *3 Have you still got any presents <u>given to you when you were very young</u>?*
> *4 Have you recently seen a film <u>based on a true story</u>?*
> *5 Are you wearing shoes <u>made in Italy</u>?*
> *6 Do you like raisins <u>covered in chocolate</u>?*

Then they think of two more questions for the people in their class with past participle clauses.

b Learners move around the room talking to different people. They try to find at least one person who answers 'yes' to each question, and ask follow-up questions to get more details.

c 👥 Learners return to their pairs from **a** and compare their findings.

CAN YOU REMEMBER? Unit 4 – Recalling details

3 a 👥/👥👥 Learners look at 1–6 and unscramble the anagrammed words in the <u>underlined</u> expressions. Then they look back at TASK VOCABULARY Recalling details on p34 to check their answers.

> *1 If I remember rightly   2 I think I'm right in saying that*
> *3 As far as I can remember   4 I read somewhere that*
> *5 I've heard that   6 They say that*

b Learners think of someone who's very well known (for good or bad reasons) in their country at the moment. They get ready to say what they know about the person, choosing expressions from **a** to help them.

c 👥/👥👥 Learners tell each other what they know about the people.

Alternatives: Mono- and multilingual classes

- With a monolingual group, brainstorm a list of well-known people at the board. Then learners work alone to think about what they know about the people before talking together and sharing/correcting each other's ideas.
- With a multilingual group, put learners of the same nationalities in the same groups. In their groups, they think of some well-known people from their countries and share what they know about them. Then put the learners into new, mixed-nationality groups so they can find out about well-known people from each other's countries.

Extension

SPELLING AND SOUNDS /g/

4 a 👥/👥👥 Learners find and underline the letters or combinations of letters in each group which make the /g/ sound.

> *guide, ghost, bigger, guard, colleague, fog, degree,*
> *hugged, dialogue, blogger, global, digging, guarantee,*
> *logo, guest, vague*
> *The following letters make the /g/ sound: gu, gg, gh,*
> *gue, g.*

b 👥/👥👥 Learners find words in **a** to exemplify each statement 1–4.

> *1 fog, degree, global, logo*
> *2 bigger, hugged, blogger, digging*
> *3 guide, guard, guarantee, guest; colleague, dialogue,*
> * vague*
> *4 ghost*

c 👥 *Spellcheck.* Learners take turns to choose and read aloud any eight words from **a** and **b**, while their partner listens (book closed) and writes them down. Then they check their spellings and correct any mistakes.

NOTICE *the* with times and places

5 a Write three headings on the board: *a) decades or centuries, b) important historical events, c) places in a picture or document.* With the class, go through the sentences 1–4 and ask learners to identify expressions with *the* to go under each heading a–c.

> *a the early 1960s*
> *b the English Civil War*
> *c the far left, the foreground*

b 👥/👥👥 Learners think of a few more expressions which could go in each group a–c.

Then elicit and write learners' ideas up on the board, adding suggestions of your own.

> *Possible answers*
> *a the First World War (but: the World War One),*
> * the Mexican Revolution, the Renaissance, …*
> *b the twentieth century, the mid-seventies, the late*
> * nineties, …*
> *c the right, the bottom, the background, the side, …*

c 👤 Learners think about how to answer the four questions, including expressions with *the* like those in **a** and **b**.

👥/👥👥 Learners ask and answer the questions.

Round-up. For each question, ask a few pairs/groups to tell the class about their answers.

Self-assessment

To help focus learners on the self-assessment, you could read it through, giving a few examples of the language they have learned in each section (or asking learners to tell you). Then ask them to circle the numbers on each line.

Unit 5 Extra activities on the Teacher's DVD-ROM

Printable worksheets, activity instructions and answer keys are on your Teacher's DVD-ROM.

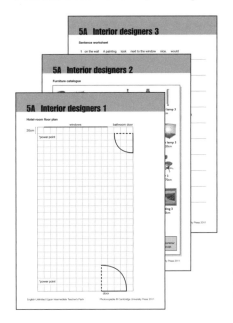

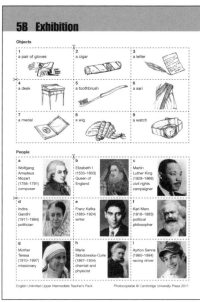

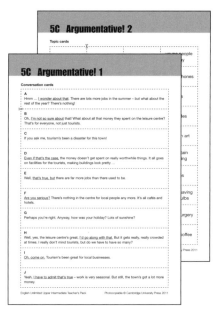

5A Interior designers

Activity type: Reading and speaking – Decision-making and presentation – Pairs / Small groups

Aim: To practise expressions for choosing things for a room

Language: Choosing something for a room – Use at any point from 5.1.

Preparation: Make one copy each of Worksheets 1–3 for each pair.

Time: 30 minutes

5B Exhibition

Activity type: Writing and speaking – Generating and presenting ideas – Small groups

Aim: To practise describing objects with past participle clauses

Language: Describing objects – past participle clauses – Use at any point from 5.2.

Preparation: Make one copy of the worksheet for every group of learners. Cut up the worksheet to make a set of nine Object cards and nine People cards.

Time: 25 minutes

5C Argumentative!

Activity type: Reading and speaking – Mingle / Forced debate – Pairs / Whole class

Aim: To practise expressing disagreement, making concessions and making counter-arguments

Language: Expressions for the above – Use at any point from Explore speaking.

Preparation: Make one copy of Worksheet 1 for every pair of learners. Cut up the worksheet to make a set of ten Conversation cards. (Note: the Conversation cards are prejumbled, so needn't be cut up at all if time is short.) Make one copy of Worksheet 2 for the class. Cut up the worksheet to make a set of 40 Topic cards.

Time: 30 minutes

Unit 5 Self-study Pack

In the Workbook

Unit 5 of the *English Unlimited Upper Intermediate Workbook* offers additional ways to practise the vocabulary and grammar taught in the Coursebook. There are also activities which build reading and writing skills and two whole pages of listening and speaking tasks to use with the Documentary video, giving your learners the opportunity to hear and react to authentic spoken English.

- **Vocabulary:** Describing an image; Choosing something for a room; Discussing design; Getting a consensus
- **Grammar:** Describing objects – past participle clauses
- **Explore writing:** Posting on a website
- **Documentary:** The sculptors

On the DVD-ROM

Unit 5 of the *English Unlimited Upper Intermediate Self-study DVD-ROM* contains interactive games and activities for your learners to practise and improve their vocabulary, grammar and pronunciation, and also their speaking and listening, with the possibility for learners to record themselves, and a video of authentic spoken English to use with the Workbook.

- **Vocabulary and grammar:** Extra practice activities
- **Pronunciation:** Groups of words
- **Explore speaking:** Agreeing and disagreeing
- **Listening:** An evening-class lecture
- **Video:** Documentary – The sculptors

6.1

Goals: talk about crimes and justice
justify your point of view

Core language:

VOCABULARY   Crimes and justice
VOCABULARY   Justifying your point of view

Is it a crime?

READING

1   👥 / 👥👥 Get learners to look at the picture and answer the questions. Then ask for a few of their ideas afterwards.

> **Alternative lead-in**
>
> To introduce the topic of 'virtual reality', ask learners if they know of or have played any virtual-reality games, such as *Second Life, MapleStory*, or any game that's popular where they live. If anyone has, elicit a short description of what such a game is (e.g. a game played online where you create a character who is 'you' and you then move through different parts of the online world, meeting others, doing tasks, building a home, etc.). You might like to bring in pictures of *MapleStory, Second Life*, etc. to show what a 'world' can look like, and what 'digital' characters can look like. Then get learners to answer the second question in **1**: *Why do you think people enjoy playing games like this?*

2 **a** 👥 / 👥👥 *Prediction.* Learners read the headline of the article and try to predict what the article may be about.

   b *Reading for main idea.* Learners read again to check their ideas from **a**, and to identify the actual crime.

> **a** breaking into someone's computer

3   *Reading for detail.* Learners read and correct the sentences. Explain that in some cases, the correction may be one word and in others, it may be a few words or part of a sentence. Learners can either write their answers down or say them.

> 1 The man and woman were married to each other *virtually*.
> 2 *They lived far from each other and* never met in real life.
> 3 The man divorced the woman *without warning*. (She thought everything was fine.)
> 4 MapleStory has millions of members *and long-term relationships are not uncommon*.
> 5 In the Netherlands, two young people were *sentenced to 360 hours of community service* for virtual theft.

4   👥 / 👥👥 *Responding to the text.* Learners discuss the question.

   Round-up. Ask a few learners to tell you what they discussed. Find out how many others agree.

VOCABULARY Crimes and justice

5   👤 / 👥 Learners complete a summary of the article *It was a virtual murder* with the words in the box. By doing this, they're completing ten highlighted expressions for talking about crimes and justice.

> 1 arrested   2 accused   3 crime   4 sentence   5 fine
> 6 suspected   7 prison   8 sentenced   9 community
> 10 law

SPEAKING

6 **a** 👤 *Preparation for discussion.* Learners think of a crime they've heard or read about from one of the categories listed. To practise their new vocabulary and help them to prepare for the next stage, they may wish to write a few key sentences about the crime, choosing suitable expressions from **5**. Monitor and correct as they write.

> **Optional extra**
>
> In **6a**, learners can do some research on the Internet to find out more details about the crime they've chosen to discuss. They can write practice sentences at home, which you can correct before they do **6b**.

   b 👥👥 *Discussion.* Learners talk about the crimes. They can ask questions to find out more, then answer the follow-up questions about the sentences for the crimes and how they feel about them.

   Round-up. Find out about the crimes learners discussed, one from each group at least, and ask if they agreed with the sentences – or what they think appropriate sentences would be.

Consequences

VOCABULARY Justifying your point of view

1   Learners read the web postings people have written in response to the article *It was a virtual murder* and answer the question.

> Sue756 and Mortimer think the woman should go to prison.

2 **a** Draw learners' attention to the highlighted expressions 1–3 in the postings. They match those expressions with a–c that have a similar meaning.

> **a** 1 ('Otherwise' and 'If not' typically begin sentences and are capitalised.)
> **b** 3 ('or' and 'or not' typically link sentences and are not capitalised.)
> **c** 2 ('That way' and 'Then' typically begin sentences and are capitalised (unless they follow a conjunction like 'and' or 'but').)

   b Learners choose the correct option in each sentence.

> 1 or else   2 then   3 Otherwise   4 If not

SPEAKING

3   *Discussion.* In groups, learners read and discuss each situation on p123 one by one. Remind them to use expressions from **1** and **2**, along with expressions from VOCABULARY Crimes and justice. After the discussion, find out if the groups agree about a suitable punishment for each situation.

Alternative for weaker classes

Give learners time to think about the situations and perhaps make a few notes before they begin the discussion in groups. You can even do the first situation as a class to get them started, then they can continue in groups.

💿 You could use photocopiable activity 6A on the Teacher's DVD-ROM at this point.

6.2

Goals: talk about media and the Internet
report different points of view
describe possible consequences of actions

Core language:

VOCABULARY	Reporting points of view
GRAMMAR	Conditional clauses – present and future
PRONUNCIATION	Groups of words 2

Sharing or stealing?

LISTENING

1   👥 As a warmer, learners answer questions 1–3. Afterwards, find out from a few what they discussed and check if other groups felt roughly the same.

2   *Listening for main idea.* Play recording **2.9** for learners to listen to the radio interview about file sharing. They should mark statements 1–4 *True* or *False*.

| 1 True   2 False   3 True   4 False |

3   a   *Listening for detail.* Play recording **2.9** again. Learners listen and note down two or three arguments on each point 1–3. You may need to play the recording twice and/or stop it once or twice to give learners time to catch up.

> *Possible answers*
> 1 – It's stealing / illegal.
>   – The music industry has lost money because of it.
>   – If people like someone's music, they should pay for it.
> 2 – People often download things that you can't buy anyway.
>   – It's a form of advertising. People use it to listen to something and decide whether to buy it or not.
>   – Music prices are too high, and that's damaging sales, not file sharing.
>   – There's legal file sharing, too. It's not all illegal.
> 3 – It's not their job to police the web.
>   – They don't want to cut off their own customers.
>   – It takes lots of time and money to find out who's sharing files illegally.
>   – They don't want to lose their customers to rivals.

b   Learners read script **2.9** on p148 to check. Tell them to add more details to their notes if possible. They will use these notes in **4a**. Note that they will have a chance to express their opinions on the issue of file sharing in **5**, so it's not necessary to have a personal-response task at this point.

VOCABULARY Reporting points of view

4   a   👥 Learners use their notes from **3b** (the main arguments on file sharing) as a basis for this activity. In pairs, learners orally summarise the main arguments in the interview with Robin Bland. They begin the arguments with suitable expressions from the box. Draw learners' attention to the speech-bubble examples so they can see what to do.

Alternative for weaker classes

In pairs, learners can write out the sentences instead of doing them as controlled oral practice. Then they can compare their ideas with another pair, taking turns to read their sentences aloud.

b   👥 *Practice.* Having prepared with one partner in **a**, learners now change partners and try summarising the interview orally, using the expressions in **a** but trying not to look at their books.

SPEAKING

5   *Responding to the text.* Learners round off this topic by expressing their opinions about file sharing.

Round-up. Find out what the general consensus is in the class.

 You could use photocopiable activity 6B on the Teacher's DVD-ROM at this point.

Making a case

GRAMMAR Conditional clauses – present and future

1   👥 This is a revision of real and unreal conditionals, which learners will have done at previous levels. They look at the six sentences in the grammar box and discuss the distinction between real and unreal conditionals.

> *All six conditional sentences give the consequences of situations. In the real conditional sentences, 1–4, these are situations which are realistic or likely to happen. In sentences 5 and 6, the unreal conditional shows that a situation is imaginary, unlikely or impossible.*

2   a   👤/👥 Draw learners' attention to the highlighted clauses beginning *as long as*, *unless*, *even if* and *provided* in sentences 3–6 in the grammar box. Ask them to choose the correct option in each sentence so that each conditional clause still has the same meaning as in 3–6.

> Sentence 3: but only if
> Sentence 4: doesn't happen
> Sentence 5: Whether or not
> Sentence 6: but only if

b   Learners answer the question as a class.

> as long as, provided

3   👤 *Practice.* Learners work alone at this stage – they'll use these sentences as a basis for speaking in **5**. They choose one of the options for each sentence beginning and complete the sentences with their own ideas. Explain that their choice of sentence beginning depends on their own opinion or experience, i.e. what's true for them. Encourage them to use present

and future conditional clauses with *if, as long as, unless, even if* and *provided*. Monitor and correct their sentences before they go on to **4** and **5**.

> **Note: Grammar practice**
> You could do the grammar practice on p135 at this point.

PRONUNCIATION Groups of words 2

4 a Play recording **2.10**. Learners read and listen to two ways of dividing a sentence into groups and choose the one that flows more naturally and is easier to follow.

> *The first grouping is more natural and is easier to follow because it separates the main ideas into clear groups. In this case, the groups are divided where the comma is, and also just before the conjunction 'and'.*

b Learners go back to the sentences they wrote in **3** and divide them into groups of words. They might find it useful to read their sentences aloud quietly so they can see if they sound and feel natural.

SPEAKING

5 *Discussion.* Learners read their sentences to each other, being careful to pronounce them in groups of words. They compare and explain their ideas.

> **Alternative**
> Learners do **5** in pairs. Then they get into new pairs for task repetition. This helps them to improve their fluency and confidence, and they can also try adding more details the second time round.

Round-up. Find out which topic most learners agreed about, and which most of them disagreed about.

> You could use photocopiable activity 6C on the Teacher's DVD-ROM at this point.

6.3 Target activity

Goals: justify your point of view ♻
    describe possible consequences of actions ♻
    suggest changes to a plan or document

Core language:

TASK VOCABULARY	Describing changes
6.1 VOCABULARY	Justifying your point of view
6.2 GRAMMAR	Conditional clauses – present and future

Design a site map

TASK LISTENING

1 Learners discuss the three questions together. Afterwards, find out from a few what they said.

2 Learners look at the site map and the photo of the two men, and read the caption. They give their opinions about the organisation of the site map. Even if they are unfamiliar with site maps as such, they can make a judgement about the layout and organisation from a common-sense point of view. Most people are familiar with organisational charts, flow charts or filing systems – and a site map has the same underlying idea: logical organisation with main groups leading to sub-groups.

3 *Listening for main idea.* Play recording **2.11**. Learners identify the pages the two men mention.

> Portrait advice, Portraits, About us, homepage, Contact us, How to find us, Lanscapes, Weddings

4 *Listening for detail.* Play recording **2.11**. This time, learners mark the suggested changes on the site map, then say whether they think the new site map is better.

- *'About us' moved to the Home page*
- *'How to find us' as a new sub-heading/branch of 'Contact us'*
- *'Weddings' as third branch off 'Gallery'*
- *'Landscapes' as fourth branch off 'Gallery'*
- *'Portrait advice (preparing for a portrait)' as new sub-heading of 'Portraits']*

TASK VOCABULARY Describing changes

5 Learners match the five words in the box with words of the same meaning in sentences 1–6. Explain that one of the sentences doesn't have a match.

> 1 connect 2 drop 3 – 4 shift 5 add 6 switch

> **Language note**
> *Stick* and *place* in this context have a similar meaning to *put*. *Move* and *shift* mean 'move something from one place to another'. *Swap* and *switch* mean two things change places with each other.

TASK

6 a Divide learners into small groups. They choose one of the ideas listed, or think of one of their own, to design a site map for. Then they need to decide together what kind of shop or band (etc.) it is.

b Each group member prepares their ideas individually (though they can stay in their group from **a**) about what kinds of information their chosen site would feature. For example, a shop might have practical pages (*location, contact,* etc.) as well as pages devoted to their products (e.g. for a gift store: cards, toys, candles, ornaments …). Then each learner draws a quick site map to present to the others in their group. At this stage, they should choose useful expressions from **5** to use in **c**, and also from VOCABULARY Justifying your point of view on p47. Remind them to use conditionals when possible.

c In their groups from **a**, learners present and compare their site-map designs. They discuss and justify their ideas and consider what changes to make and what the consequences would be. Their project is to make one final site map as a group, based on their discussion about what's best. They can draw it on a large piece of paper; encourage them to use different colours.

7 👥 Each group presents their site map to the others and explains their reasoning. The other groups can suggest further improvements or changes, which the first group can accept or not as they wish.

6 Explore

Across cultures: Ways of communicating

Goal: to make learners aware of ways of communicating in various situations in different cultures

Core language:

VOCABULARY   Habits and customs: *If you …, it's really important that you; It's increasingly common for; If …; I wouldn't dream of; If it's … , then I'll probably; If it's …, then I'll definitely; the proper thing to do; There's no way I'd; It's unheard of to; You're expected to; I'd always*

LISTENING

1 👥 / 👥 Learners discuss the two questions. Find out from a few learners what they discussed.

2 *Listening for main idea.* Play recording **2.12**. Learners number the topics in the order they're mentioned. Note that one is *not* mentioned.

> *1 being offered a job*
> *2 applying for a job*
> *3 thanking someone for a gift*
> They don't discuss *'inviting someone to a party'*.

3 a *Listening for detail.* Give learners time to read the instructions. Explain that they need to answer the questions for each of the three situations mentioned in **2**. Then play recording **2.12** again while learners make notes. You can pause at intervals to give them time to catch up.

   b Learners read script **2.12** on pp148–9 to check.

> Most appropriate ways of communicating
> – *being offered a job: Liesbeth: in writing / on a piece of paper. Hugo: agrees with Liesbeth, also says a phone call beforehand is common.*
> – *applying for a job: Hugo and Liesbeth: online applications.*
> – *thanking someone for a gift: Hugo: a phone call or text to a friend. Hugo and Liesbeth: a handwritten letter to older people.*
> Reasons for their ideas
> – *a written job offer: very useful if you're discussing contracts, you need official documents*
> – *job applications online: easier, quicker, especially for sending similar messages to many companies*
> – *thanking someone for a gift: older people expect handwritten letters, but for younger people, that custom has almost disappeared*

4 👥 / 👥 *Responding to the text.* Learners discuss what people where they live would say about these ways of communicating.

VOCABULARY Habits and customs

5 a 👤 / 👥 Learners read the sentences from the recording

and sort the highlighted expressions into two groups.

> *a 3, 4, 5*
> *b 1, 2 (Note: 'you' in sentence 1 is the general 'you', not the personal one.)*

   b Learners add more expressions to the two categories in **a**.

> *a 7, 10*
> *b 6, 8, 9 (Note: 'you' in sentence 9 is the general 'you', not the personal one.)*

SPEAKING

6 a 👤 *Preparation for discussion.* Learners choose four or five of the ten bullet-pointed situations and think about how to answer questions 1–4 about each of their chosen situations. Remind them to choose useful expressions from **5**. They can note down their ideas if they wish.

   b 👥 Learners discuss their chosen situations.

7 👥 Learners share their experiences of different ways of communicating in other cultures. This can be through personal experience or from what they've read or heard about.

Optional extra

In groups, learners write a guide about how to communicate where they live. The intended audience would be new residents in their country. The guide can be in point form and would deal with all the bullet-pointed situations listed under **6a**, which would form headings. Remind learners to use the 'general customs' expressions from **5**.
Example:
Inviting someone to a wedding
1 If you receive a wedding invitation, it's really important that you answer in writing.
2 It's unheard of to respond by text. It's too informal.
3 You're expected to respond immediately, as they need to plan the seating, amount of food, etc.
Learners then exchange guides with another group, or post them around the room. They read and compare ideas.

Explore writing

Goal: put forward an argument in a web posting

Core language:

Stating your intention: *This is in response to; I'd like to present; I'd like to reply to; I'd like to have my say about this.*
Stating your main arguments: *It's important to remember that; Another benefit is; But consider this for a moment; What you might not know is that; Don't forget that*
Referring to other people's views: *Psychologists have long recognised that; Many gamers have claimed that; Experts say that; A lot of people have found that*
Stating your conclusion or final thought: *All in all, you have to admit; At the end of the day; To sum up, I believe that*

1 *Reading for main idea.* To introduce the topic, ask if anyone writes or reads web postings and if so, what kind. Learners then read the short posting by RealGuy about virtual gaming (the theme echoes the article on virtual games at the beginning of the unit). Learners discuss the two questions in groups.

2 Learners read Merlynda's response to RealGuy's posting and find out how many of her arguments are the same as the ones they discussed for question 2 in **1**.

3   *Reading for detail.* Learners read Merlynda's posting again and answer questions 1–3, which focus on her different arguments.

> 1 There are many kinds of 'experience', and virtual-reality gaming is one of them. People in virtual worlds interact with people around the world, learn new skills and work together to tackle challenges. All this affects their real life.
> 2 You won't be judged on the basis of your real-world age, health, appearance, job or financial status.
> 3 People present the image they want – an image of their own choice – so they often feel free to express themselves better, make decisions more confidently and become more independent.

4   ▲ / ▲▲ Learners identify the purpose or theme of each paragraph.

> Paragraph 1: to give the reason for her posting and state her attitude.
> Paragraph 2: first set of benefits of virtual-reality games, focusing on how they contribute to your life experience and what you can learn.
> Paragraph 3: second set of benefits, focusing on how these games allow you to be yourself and become stronger.

5   a   ▲ / ▲▲ Learners sort the seven highlighted expressions in the posting into four groups.

> a 1, 2   b 4, 5   c 3, 6   d 7

   b   ▲ / ▲▲ They now add more expressions to the four groups in **a**.

> a 4, 8   b 1, 3, 6   c 5, 9   d 2, 7

   c   ▲▲▲ Learners can add more useful expressions to the four groups if they wish, e.g. *In conclusion, I'd like to say ...; One important point is ...; Another point is ...* .

6   a   ▲ *Preparation for writing.* Learners choose one of the three web postings on the right to make an argument against.

   b   ▲▲ They find someone who has chosen the same posting, then plan their responses together. This would include planning their arguments, organising their response into paragraphs, and choosing useful language from **5**. Both learners should make notes.

   c   ▲ They work alone and write their posting. Alternatively, the writing can be started in class (e.g. the first paragraph) while you monitor and correct, ensuring they're off to a good start. Then they complete the posting at home and hand it in for correction later. They may want to type it out like a real posting.

7   ▲▲▲ Put learners into groups. Ideally, each group would have responses to each of the three postings in **6a**. Learners read each other's postings, discuss the arguments and express their opinions.

6 Look again

Review

VOCABULARY Reporting points of view

1   a   Play recording **2.13**. Learners complete the sentence beginnings, then check script **2.13** on p148.

> 1 As <u>far as</u> they're <u>concerned</u>, ...
> 2 You <u>have people who say</u> that ...
> 3 There's also <u>the argument</u> that ...
> 4 The music companies <u>will tell you</u> that ...
> 5 A <u>lot of people think</u> that ...
> 6 What <u>they say</u> is that ...
> 7 Many musicians <u>will say</u> that ...

> **Alternative**
>
> Let learners try completing the sentence beginnings from memory, then play recording **2.13** to check.

   b   ▲▲ *Preparation for discussion.* Each pair looks at the four questions and prepares arguments for and against each question, using the expressions in **a**. They can note down key ideas.

   c   ▲▲ *Discussion.* Learners get into new pairs and tell their new partner all their arguments from **b**, adding their own opinions at the end.

GRAMMAR Conditional clauses – present and future

2   a   Explain that learners should underline the most *likely* option in each sentence. In some cases, both answers are possible, but one is more likely and makes more sense.

> 1 as long as   2 Unless   3 provided   4 Even if

   b   ▲▲▲ Learners look at the bullet-pointed situations and answer the two questions for each situation.
   Round-up. Find out the majority opinion on each of the situations.

CAN YOU REMEMBER? Unit 5 – Discussing design

3   a   ▲▲ / ▲▲▲ Learners try to remember the synonyms for the highlighted words 1–5. Then they try to remember Rams's other five principles. They can check afterwards on p40.

> 1 novel   2 attractive   3 low-key   4 straightforward
> 5 long-lasting
> The other principles are:
> Good design makes a product useful.
> Good design helps us to understand a product.
> Good design is purposeful in every detail.
> Good design is environmentally friendly.
> Good design is as little design as possible.

   b   ▲▲ *Discussion.* In pairs, learners choose two or three objects in the room and decide if they meet Dieter Rams's principles of good design. Note: objects can include classroom tools and machines, pencils, pens, bags, clothes, shoes, etc. Learners explain their ideas and find out if their partner agrees.

SPELLING AND SOUNDS /ʌ/

4 a 👤/👥 In this exercise, learners underline the letters that make an /ʌ/ sound. Encourage them to say the words aloud.

> *otherwise, abrupt, onion, luxury, discuss, government, husband, justice, punishment, sometimes, hunt, suddenly*

They then complete the spelling patterns 1–3.

> *1 /ʌ/ can be spelled u or o.*
> *2 u is the most common spelling.*
> *3 o is most often found before the letters m, n, th and v.*

b 👤 Learners read the words spelled with *ou* that also make this sound.

c 👤/👥 Learners complete the spelling of the words with *o*, *u* or *ou* and then check in a dictionary. Alternatively, you can elicit the spelling and write it on the board.

> *tough, sponge, puzzled, double, muscle, youngster, glove, humble, cousin, among, southern, stomach*

NOTICE Compound adjectives

5 a 👤/👥 Learners match the compound adjectives with expressions 1–8 from the article *It was a virtual murder*, then check in the article on p46.

> *2 low-quality science-fiction movies*
> *3 a middle-aged piano teacher*
> *4 a face-to-face meeting*
> *5 a flesh-and-blood crime*
> *6 a role-playing game*
> *7 long-term commitments*
> *8 real-world justice*

b 👥 Learners test each other in pairs, taking turns to say 1–8 while their partner says the compound adjectives that go with each one:
A: *a game*
B: *a role-playing game*

Self-assessment

To help focus learners on the self-assessment, read it through and get learners to give you a few examples of the language they have learned in each section. Give an example to start them off if necessary. Then learners circle the numbers on each line.

Unit 6 Extra activities on the Teacher's DVD-ROM

Printable worksheets, activity instructions and answer keys are on your Teacher's DVD-ROM.

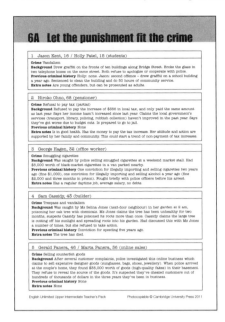

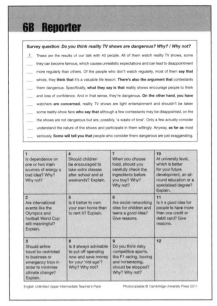

6A Let the punishment fit the crime

Activity type: Reading and speaking – Role play – Small groups / Whole class

Aim: To discuss and make decisions about legal cases as members of a panel of judges

Language: Crimes and justice / Justifying your point of view – Use at any point from 6.1.

Preparation: Make one copy of the worksheet for each learner.

Time: 40 minutes

6B Reporter

Activity type: Reading and speaking – Reordering a paragraph – Pairs/Mingle

Aim: To get people's opinions on a survey question and report the results

Language: Reporting points of view – Use at any point from 6.2.

Preparation: Make one copy of the worksheet for every pair of learners.

Time: 40 minutes

6C It's OK if …

Activity type: Speaking – Gap-fill – Individuals/Groups

Aim: To talk about conditions under which you will or would do certain things

Language: Conditional clauses – present and future – Use at any point from 6.2.

Preparation: Make one copy of the worksheet for every learner.

Time: 40 minutes

Unit 6 Self-study Pack

In the Workbook

Unit 6 of the *English Unlimited Upper Intermediate Workbook* offers additional ways to practise the vocabulary and grammar taught in the Coursebook. There are also activities which build reading and writing skills and a whole page of listening and speaking tasks to use with the Interview video, giving your learners the opportunity to hear and react to authentic spoken English.

- **Vocabulary:** Crimes and justice; Justifying your point of view; Reporting points of view; Describing changes; Habits and customs
- **Grammar:** Conditional clauses – present and future
- **Explore reading:** Article: Ethical hacking
- **Interview:** Virtual world – Qusay and Ekapop

On the DVD-ROM

Unit 6 of the *English Unlimited Upper Intermediate Self-study DVD-ROM* contains interactive games and activities for your learners to practise and improve their vocabulary, grammar and pronunciation, and also their speaking and listening, with the possibility for learners to record themselves, and a video of authentic spoken English to use with the Workbook.

- **Vocabulary and grammar:** Extra practice activities
- **Pronunciation:** Groups of words
- **Explore speaking:** *whatever*
- **Listening:** Talking about different points of view
- **Video:** Virtual world

7 Inspiration

7.1

Goals: talk about how you deal with problems
describe experiences of problem-solving

Core language:

VOCABULARY	Problems and solutions
VOCABULARY	Problem-solving experiences

Working it out

READING

1 *Books closed.* Tell the class about two or three things which help you when you're thinking about problems, e.g. getting some sleep, listening to music. Then ask the class to tell you a few things which they, or people they know, do to help them think about problems.

👥 / 👥👥 Learners open their books, look at the list of activities and discuss the questions.

2 *Reading for main idea.* Learners read the article to find out which of the activities listed in **1** can help you when trying to solve problems.

> The most important answer is: thinking about something else for a while.
> The article also gives three examples of activities to help us do this: having a bath, meditating, going out for a walk.

3 *Reading for detail.* Learners read again and answer the questions.

👥 / 👥👥 They compare their answers, then check as a class.

> 1 Because distractions can make it easier to solve a problem when you come back to it.
> 2 Both groups did a word-association test, but one of the groups did another test in the middle of this.
> 3 The group which had to do another test
> 4 These are forms of distraction.
> 5 Giving their staff time to relax rather than expecting them to work continuously

4 👥 / 👥👥 *Responding to the text.* Learners tell each other what they think about the ideas in the article.

VOCABULARY Problems and solutions

5 a 👥 / 👥👥 *Presentation.* Learners look at the pairs of expressions from the article and say whether they mean similar or different things. If they have different meanings, learners explain the difference.

Check answers as a class.

> 1 Different: <u>concentrate on</u> = think very hard about; <u>sort out</u> = solve (similar to the expressions in 2)
> 2 The same
> 3 Different: <u>give up on</u> = stop trying to solve, because it's too difficult; <u>come up with</u> = think of, create

b 👥 / 👥👥 Learners do the same with three more pairs of expressions. Check answers as a class.

> 4 Different: <u>mull over</u> = think slowly and carefully about; <u>tackle</u> = attack in an energetic way
> 5 Different: <u>ignore</u> = behave as if it doesn't exist; <u>put off</u> = decide to think about it later
> 6 The same

6 👤 *Practice.* Learners cover the six pairs of expressions in **5a** and **5b** and try to complete the questions, using the first letters given to help them.

👥 / 👥👥 Learners compare, then uncover **5a** and **5b** to check.

> 2 find out 3 concentrate on; tackle 4 put off; sort out
> 5 come up with 6 ignore

SPEAKING

7 👥 / 👥👥 *Discussion.* Learners ask and answer the questions in **6**.

Round-up. Ask some pairs/groups to tell the class their answers to questions 2 and 5, about times and places where they find it easiest to solve problems and come up with ideas.

What we decided to do was …

LISTENING

1 a To lead in to the topic of the listening, look as a class at the cover of the magazine *Polyglossia*, the picture of Hugo and the caption. Encourage learners to think about the magazine title and images on the cover, and ask them to suggest what the magazine might be about and what kind of articles it might include.

b *Listening for main idea.* Play recording **2.14**. Learners listen to Hugo and find out what kind of magazine *Polyglossia* is and what is unusual about it.

> It's a magazine with articles in different languages.

2 *Listening for details.* Give learners time to read questions 1 and 2, then play recording **2.14** again. Learners listen and answer the questions.

Learners read script **2.14** on p149 to check and complete their answers.

> 1 Hugo talks about two of the problems:
> a finding people to work with him. (Solution: He interviewed different people.)
> c finding a way to make it appeal to more people. (Solution: They decided to include English-language summaries of each article.)
> 2 Hugo says he learned two skills:
> b seeing things from other people's point of view ('what I really learned was to <u>put myself in other people's shoes</u> …')
> c being ready to think in new and creative ways ('… and also <u>thinking outside the box</u>')

Point out the idioms in the script (<u>underlined</u> above) which give the answers to question 2.

3 *Responding to the text.* Round off the listening by briefly discussing the two questions with the class.

VOCABULARY Problem-solving experiences

4 👥 / 👥👥 *Presentation.* Learners reorder the highlighted text to form key expressions from the interview.

> 1 The biggest problem was that
> 2 I found it difficult to
> 3 It presented us with a problem because
> 4 What we decided to do was
> 5 My way of solving this problem was to
> 6 What I learned was to

SPEAKING

5 👤 *Preparation for discussion.* Read through the extract from the application form with the class. Learners then plan answers to the questions, choosing useful expressions from **4**.

6 a 👥👥 *Discussion.* Learners tell each other how they'd answer the questions on the application form.

b Each group chooses one problem with a particularly interesting solution to tell the class about.

7.2

Goals: talk about where you get ideas
describe a scene

Core language:

VOCABULARY	Inspiration
PRONUNCIATION	Fluent speech 2 – *the* with linking /j/
GRAMMAR	Describing scenes – present and past participle clauses

Dreamers

LISTENING

1 👥 / 👥👥 To focus on the topic of dreams and dreaming, learners discuss the two questions.

2 As a class, look at the pictures of Shelley, Ramanujan and Kekulé and read through the captions. Ask learners which of these people they've heard of, and what (if anything) they know about them.

3 *Listening for main ideas.* Tell learners that they are going to listen to a radio programme about the role of dreams in these three people's lives. Play recording **2.15**. Learners listen and say whether the descriptions of the dreams mention just images, just sounds, or both images and sounds.

> Images only

4 a 👥 / 👥👥 *Listening for details.* Before learners listen for a second time, they look at the list of 15 items and try to match five of them to each person's story.

Play recording **2.15** again. Learners listen to check their answers and make changes as necessary.

> Mary Shelley: *Switzerland, Byron, storms, ghost stories, a monster*
> Srinivasa Ramanujan: *Namagiri, a screen, blood, a hand, equations*
> August Kekulé: *a chair, a fire, atoms, a snake, a circle*

b 👥 / 👥👥 Learners use the items in **a** to retell each story.

> **Alternative**
>
> Put learners into groups of three for this stage. Each learner tells one of the stories, while the others listen, make corrections and add details as necessary.

VOCABULARY Inspiration

5 a 👥 / 👥👥 *Presentation.* Learners think of possible ways to complete the six sentences from the radio programme. They do not necessarily have to be the same words used in the recording.

> **Alternative for weaker classes**
>
> Give learners the first letter of each word in **5a**:
> 1 c...   2 g...   3 i...   4 g...   5 r...   6 g... .

b Learners look in script **2.15** on pp149–50 to compare their answers.

> 1 came   2 got   3 inspired   4 get   5 realised   6 give

PRONUNCIATION Fluent speech 2 – *the* with linking /j/

6 a *Presentation.* Play recording **2.16**. Learners listen while reading the three example expressions.

Ask learners to repeat the three expressions, pointing out how, in the third one, 1) *the* has a long /iː/ sound, 2) a /j/ sound can be heard between *the* and the following word *idea*. Ask learners why this happens. (In expression 3, the word following *the* (*idea*) starts with a vowel sound. In the other two expressions, the words following *the* (*famous* and *shape*) start with a consonant, so *the* is pronounced in the usual way with a schwa /ə/ and there is no linking /j/ sound.)

b 👥 / 👥👥 *Practice.* Learners decide how to say the expressions and practise saying them. In each pair, one expression is pronounced with a long /iː/ in *the* and a linking /j/, while the other is pronounced with the usual schwa /ə/ and no linking /j/. Practise saying the expressions as a class.

> the *with* /iː/ *and linking* /j/
> 1 the eighties   2 the east   3 the end   4 the English
> 5 the inspiration   6 the artist
> the *with* /ə/ *and no linking* /j/
> 1 the nineties   2 the west   3 the beginning
> 4 the Japanese   5 the solution   6 the writer

SPEAKING

7 a 👤 *Preparation.* Learners prepare to talk about good ideas they've had and where the ideas came from. Encourage them to choose language from **5a** to describe their experiences.

> **Optional extra**
>
> Before learners start their preparation, tell them about some good ideas you've had in different aspects of your life: your work (e.g. an idea for encouraging learners to use less L1 in class), your free time (e.g. an idea for a holiday), your interests (e.g. an idea for something you cooked recently). Be sure to include a few expressions from **5a**. Invite learners to ask you questions to find out more details.

b 👥/👥👥 *Discussion.* Learners tell each other about their experiences, listening and asking questions about aspects which interest them.

I saw atoms dancing ...

GRAMMAR Describing scenes – present and past participle clauses

1 👥/👥👥 *Presentation.* Learners read the grammar box, then answer the two questions below it.

> *1 a 1, 3 b 2, 4*
> *2 a present participle b past participle*

Alternative: Presentation

Books closed. Write on the board:
1 *I saw (atoms) which were dancing before my eyes.*
2 *There was (a red screen) which was formed by flowing blood.*
Ask:
- *What are the underlined parts called?* (relative clauses)
- *Which words could we delete from the sentences without changing their meaning?* (**1** *which were,* **2** *which was*)

Rub out the words and ask: *What do we call the underlined parts now?* (**1** a present participle clause, **2** a past participle clause)
Ask: *Which clause has an active/passive meaning?* (**1** active meaning, **2** passive meaning)
Write the above descriptions next to each sentence.

---

2 a 👥/👥👥 *Practice.* Learners read the story quickly and tell each other whether they think Coleridge's story is true or not.

b 👤 Learners read again, choosing the correct participles in 1–7.

👥/👥👥 Learners compare their answers, then check as a class.

> *1 inspired   2 connected   3 told   4 written   5 visiting*
> *6 lasting   7 writing   8 used*

Note: Grammar practice

You could do the grammar practice on p136 at this point.

SPEAKING

3 a 👤 *Preparation.* Put learners into pairs, Learner A and Learner B. Learner As look at the pictures on p121; Bs look at the pictures on p124. They plan how to describe the pictures with present and past participle clauses, using the participles in the box to help them.

Alternative for weaker classes

Instead of learners preparing descriptions on their own, divide the class into two groups, A and B. The learners in each group work together to prepare. Then, for **3b**, put the learners into A/B pairs.

---

b 👥 *Describing images.* Learners describe their pictures to each other.

4 Learners look at each other's pictures and discuss the questions.

Round-up. As a class, discuss learners' ideas as to what the pictures might mean, whether or not they like the pictures, and why.

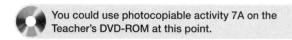
You could use photocopiable activity 7A on the Teacher's DVD-ROM at this point.

7.3 Target activity

Goals: describe experiences of problem-solving ♻
describe a scene ♻
participate in a problem-solving discussion

Core language:

TASK VOCABULARY	Discussing possible solutions
7.1 VOCABULARY	Problem-solving experiences
7.2 GRAMMAR	Describing scenes – present and past participle clauses

Come up with solutions

TASK LISTENING

Optional lead-in / review of participle clauses

Picture dictation. Put learners into pairs, Learner A and Learner B. Learner A (book open) describes the picture at the top of p58, using participle clauses where possible. Learner B (book closed) listens and draws the picture on a piece of paper according to A's description, asking questions to get more details and clarify any points which are unclear. When A has finished the description, they compare B's drawing with the original.

---

1 👥/👥👥 Learners look at the picture, read Case study 1, and answer the questions.

Check answers as a class to ensure that learners have grasped the context for the listening that follows.

> *Equipment is disappearing from Chen's lab. He suspects two workers whom he saw carrying something out of the building and heard talking about selling something. He hasn't taken any action because he's not completely sure of his suspicions.*

2 *Listening for main ideas.* Tell learners that they're going to listen to three students discussing Chen's problem as part of a course in problem-solving. Give learners time to read through the seven possible solutions to Chen's problem a–g.

Then play recording **2.17**. Learners listen and find out which solution the three students decide would be best.

> *b tell his boss about the missing items*

3 👥/👥👥 *Listening for details.* Learners tell each other what they can remember about the students' reasons for rejecting the other six possible solutions in **2**.

Then play recording **2.17** again. Learners listen to check the students' reasons for rejecting solutions a and c–g.

> *a Other people need access to the lab.*
> *c Supervising the lab is Chen's job.*
> *d It might be illegal.*
> *e He can't be sure who's responsible for the disappearances.*
> *f They could be very upset.*
> *g It would take too long.*

4 👥/👥👥 *Responding to the text.* Learners say what they think about solution b. Is it the best solution? Would they prefer one of the other solutions? Can they suggest an alternative solution?

Round-up. Ask some pairs/groups to tell the class their opinions.

TASK VOCABULARY Discussing possible solutions

5   *Presentation.* Learners try to complete the expressions for discussing possible solutions in 1–10.

  They compare answers, then check script **2.17** on page p150.

> 1 *worth*   2 *Alternatively*   3 *option*   4 *approach*
> 5 *something*   6 *feasible*   7 *considering*   8 *tricky*
> 9 *practical*   10 *recommend*

TASK

6 a   *Problem-solving.* Learners read Case study 2 on p123 and follow the instructions. They think of possible solutions, discuss the pros and cons of each, and decide which would be best. Encourage learners to use expressions from **5**.

b Learners do the same with Case study 3 on p123.

7 a   *Report.* In the same groups, learners plan how to tell another group about their discussions in **6a** and **6b**, using the three questions to guide them. Remind them that they can use expressions from VOCABULARY Problem-solving experiences and GRAMMAR Describing scenes – present and past participle clauses.

They decide who will give the report.

b Put groups together. Groups listen to each other's reports and find out whether they had similar or different ideas.

> **Alternative**
>
> For **7b**, make new groups of one person from each old group. With this alternative, every learner will have to speak as they tell their new group about their old group's discussions.

 You could use photocopiable activity 7B on the Teacher's DVD-ROM at this point.

7 Explore

Keyword: *come*

Goal: use expressions and multi-word verbs with *come*

Core language:

Expressions with *come: come in handy; come first; come as a shock; come along well; come to an agreement; …*
Multi-word verbs with *come: come into; come down with; come across; …*

Expressions with *come*

1   *Reading.* Learners read the three extracts and decide where they're from / what the situation is. Compare ideas as a class.

> *Suggested answers*
> A *an advertisement for an international food magazine*
> B *the politics section of a newspaper*
> C *a work email: a negotiator reporting back to his company headquarters*

2 a *Presentation.* Write the partial expressions with *come* 1–5 on the board. Ask learners to scan the three texts in **1** and find the words for you to complete the five expressions on the board.

> 1 *come in useful*   2 *came second*   3 *come as a shock*
> 4 *coming along slowly*   5 *come to an agreement*

b   Learners use the words to make more expressions with the patterns 1–5. Then check as a class.

> 1 *come in handy*
> 2 *came first/last*
> 3 *come as a disappointment/relief/surprise*
> 4 *coming along nicely/quickly/well*
> 5 *come to a conclusion / a decision / an end*

3 a   *Practice.* To set up the sentence-writing and provide learners with ideas for topics to write about, demonstrate by writing some sentences about yourself on the board and inviting learners to ask you questions about them. For example:

- *Last year, I did a course in First Aid because I thought it might come in useful some day.*
- *When I was at school, I always came last in geography.*
- *When England got knocked out of the World Cup, it came as a disappointment but not a surprise.*
- *Although I try to study every day, my German is coming along quite slowly.*
- *I always feel a bit depressed when my holidays come to an end.*

Learners write four or five sentences about their lives now or in the past. Each sentence should include one of the expressions with *come*. Monitor closely while learners are writing to check that they are using the expressions correctly and provide help as necessary.

b   Learners listen to each other's sentences and ask questions to find out more about any details which interest them.

Round-up. Learners get into new pairs/groups and tell their new partners about their conversations with their old partners.

> **Alternative: True / false game**
>
> In **3a**, learners write five sentences, three true and two false. Then at **3b**, learners listen to each other's sentences and ask questions to try and determine which are the false sentences. If you use this alternative, adapt your demonstration in **3a** accordingly.

Multi-word verbs with *come*

4   *Presentation.* Learners look at the seven extracts and try to work out the meanings of the multi-word verbs from the contexts. Then they check in a dictionary and/or as a class.

> *Possible answers*
> 1 *came out = was published (books, music, films)*
> 2 *the bill came to = the cost was*
> 3 *come up with = create, think of*
> 4 *come up = happened (unexpectedly)*
> 5 *came across = found (by accident)*
> 6 *comes across as = appears to be*
> 7 *come round = visit (someone's home)*
> 8 *came into = inherited (money)*
> 9 *come down with = caught (an illness)*

5 a 👤 *Practice.* Learners complete the five questions.

> 1 come across   2 come out   3 come into
> 4 come round   5 came to

Then they write two more questions of their own using multi-word verbs from **4**.

b 👥 / 👥👥 Learners ask and answer all the questions.

Round-up. Ask learners to tell the class about any particularly interesting questions created by the people in their pair/group. Ask other learners how they'd answer the questions.

Explore speaking

Goal: speak tactfully in different situations

Core language:

Expressions for:
- prefacing sensitive questions: *Maybe it's none of my business, but*; ...
- signalling sensitive topics: *It's a difficult situation*; ...
- avoiding topics: *I'd prefer not to answer that*; ...

Alternative for weaker classes

Books closed. Write two questions on the board: *1 Where are the people? 2 What's their relationship?* Play recording **2.18**. Learners listen and answer the questions for each of the three conversations.

> Conversation 1: *At work, in an office; colleagues*
> Conversation 2: *In a pub or café; probably friends*
> Conversation 3: *On the street; probably friends*

---

1 a *Listening for detail.* Give learners time to read the questions about the three conversations. Then play recording **2.18**. Learners listen and answer the questions.

b Learners check their answers by reading the extracts from the conversations on the page.

> Conversation 1: *Kelly's not happy in the Finance department. She used to be in a relationship with Ken, who also works in the department.*
> Conversation 2: *Rajeev looks tired. He doesn't want to say why, but it's something 'personal'.*
> Conversation 3: *Lucia asks the way to Paul's home. She won't say why she's in a hurry.*

2 *Presentation.* Divide the board into three columns and write an expression a–c at the top of each column:
a Maybe it's none of my business, but ...
b It's a difficult situation.
c I'd prefer not to answer that.

👥 / 👥👥 Learners read the conversations and say if the highlighted expressions 1–8 have a similar function to a, b or c.

Go through the answers as a class, writing each expression in the appropriate column on the board as you proceed.

> a 1, 3, 6   b 2, 5, 8   c 4, 7

Optional extra: Memorisation

Books closed. Rub out one word from each of the expressions on the board and replace it with a gap: _____. In pairs or groups, learners try to remember the whole expressions. Then rub out one more word in each expression, learners try to remember again; rub out one more word, etc. Rub out as many words as you can. To finish, ask learners to tell you the whole expressions and write them up on the board again.

---

3 a 👤 *Practice.* Learners complete the conversations with expressions from **2**. Explain that various answers are possible, although with weaker classes, you may want to tell them which group of expressions corresponds to each gap.

👥 / 👥👥 Learners compare their possible answers.

b Play recording **2.19**. Emphasise that the recording represents just one possible set of answers. Learners listen and compare their answers with the recording. If necessary, learners can also look at script **2.19** on p150.

4 a 👥👥 *Role plays.* Divide the class into two groups, A and B. Learners in Group A look at the role card on p122. Learners in Group B look at the role card on p126.

Working together, either as a single group or as a number of smaller sub-groups, learners decide how to approach each situation and plan what to say. Encourage them to choose language from **2**.

b 👥 Learners get into A/B pairs. They do the six role plays. Learner A should start conversations 1, 3 and 5. Learner B should start conversations 2, 4 and 6.

5 👥👥 *Round-up.* Learners return to their groups in **4a** and report on their conversations.

7 Look again

Review

VOCABULARY Problems and solutions

1 a 👥 / 👥👥 Learners add the missing words to the sentences using the words in the box.

Then learners look back at VOCABULARY Problems and solutions on p54 to check their answers.

Alternative: Dictation activity

Books closed. Write the words in the box on the board and dictate sentences 1–7. Learners listen and write down the sentences, adding words from the board to make them complete. Learners then compare sentences before checking as a class.

> 2 I spent a long time mulling it <u>over</u>.
> 3 I couldn't figure <u>out</u> what to do.
> 4 I couldn't concentrate <u>on</u> my work.
> 5 I thought it was best to put <u>off</u> the decision till later.
>   (or: put the decision <u>off</u>)
> 6 It was so frustrating that I just gave up <u>on</u> it.
> 7 They promised to sort <u>out</u> the problem straight away.
>   (or: sort the problem <u>out</u>)

Language note

In sentences 5 and 7, the missing words can go in two possible places. See the Grammar reference for Unit 9, *Verbs with adverbs and prepositions 1*, for an explanation.

b Learners choose two comments which remind them of experiences they've had and write brief notes in preparation for talking about them.

Learners tell each other about their experiences. Encourage learners to develop conversations by asking follow-up questions.

GRAMMAR Describing scenes – present and past participle clauses

2 a Learners choose the correct participles.

> 1 asking 2 designed 3 discovered 4 leaving; carrying

b Tell learners that 1–4 are descriptions of images or text from the unit. Learners look through the unit to find the images.

> 1 p55 2 p55 3 p56 4 p58

c Divide the class into three teams. Each team finds four images from anywhere in the book and writes descriptions of them using participle clauses. Monitor to ensure that learners are using participle clauses correctly.

d Teams take turns to read aloud one of their sentences. The other two teams listen and try to find the image being described. The first team to find the image wins a point. When all 12 sentences have been read out and all the images located, the team with the most points is the winner.

CAN YOU REMEMBER? Unit 6 – Describing consequences

3 a Learners complete the sentences 1–6 with their own ideas about health and fitness.

b Learners get into new pairs/groups and say whether or not they agree with each other's sentences.

Extension

SPELLING AND SOUNDS /ɒ/

4 a Learners read through the words together and underline the letters in each word which correspond to the sound /ɒ/.

Then check as a class, writing the words up on the board and underlining the appropriate parts.

> Australia, because, cauliflower, conscious, problem, psychology, quality, solve, squash, swap, volunteer, watch

b Learners read the patterns 1–3. For each pattern, they find example words from **a**.

Then check as a class, crossing out the words on the board as you match them to the descriptions.

> 1 conscious, problem, psychology, solve, volunteer
> 2 quality, squash, swap, watch
> 3 Australia, because, cauliflower

c *Spellcheck.* Play recording **2.20**. Learners listen to the ten words and write them down.

They compare their spelling of the ten words, then look at script **2.20** on p150 to check.

NOTICE *he, she* and *they*

5 a Learners read the extract and think of words or expressions which could go in the gap.

Ask learners for their suggestions and write them on the board.

> **Possible answers**
> *he / he or she / they*

Then learners look at script **2.14** on p149 to find out which word or expression was in fact used (*they*). Explain that, while in this case the speaker chose to use *they*, any of the above answers could have been used.

b Learners complete the explanation with the words and expressions in the box.

> 1 He 2 He or she 3 They 4 He/she / S(he)
> 5 s(he) / he/she

c Learners discuss the questions.

Round-up. Discuss the questions as a class. If you are teaching a multilingual class, ask learners with different first languages to comment on the second question.

Self-assessment

To help focus learners on the self-assessment, you could read it through, giving a few examples of the language they have learned in each section (or asking learners to tell you). Then ask them to circle the numbers on each line.

 You could use photocopiable activity 7C on the Teacher's DVD-ROM at this point.

Unit 7 Extra activities on the Teacher's DVD-ROM

Printable worksheets, activity instructions and answer keys are on your Teacher's DVD-ROM.

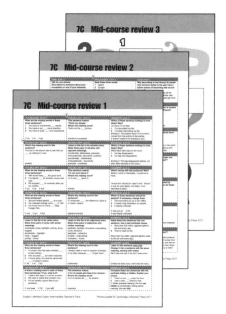

7A Would you make a good eyewitness?

Activity type: Writing and reading – Picture memory game – Individuals/Pairs

Aim: To practise describing a scene using participle clauses

Language: Describing scenes – present and past participle clauses – Use at any point from 7.2.

Preparation: Make one copy of Worksheet 1 and one copy of Worksheet 2 for each pair of learners.

Time: 20 minutes

7B What should I do?

Activity type: Speaking – Discussing problems – Groups of three or more

Aim: To practise proposing and reacting to possible solutions to problems

Language: Discussing possible solutions – Use at any point from 7.3.

Preparation: Make one copy of the worksheet for each group. Cut up the worksheet to make a set of 18 cards.

Time: 30 minutes

7C Mid-course review

Activity type: Speaking – Card quiz – Groups

Aim: To review vocabulary, grammar, spelling and topics from Units 1–7

Language: Various – Use at any point from the end of Unit 7.

Preparation: Make one copy each of Worksheets 1, 2 and 3 for each group of learners. Cut up Worksheets 1 and 2 to make a set of 42 cards. Shuffle each set of cards.

Time: 45 minutes

Unit 7 Self-study Pack

In the Workbook

Unit 7 of the *English Unlimited Upper Intermediate Workbook* offers additional ways to practise the vocabulary and grammar taught in the Coursebook. There are also activities which build reading and writing skills and a whole page of listening and speaking tasks to use with the Interview video, giving your learners the opportunity to hear and react to authentic spoken English.

- **Vocabulary:** Problems and solutions; Problem-solving experiences; Inspiration; Discussing possible solutions
- **Grammar:** Describing scenes: present and past participle clauses
- **Explore writing:** Giving advice
- **Interview:** An inspired blog – Valerie

On the DVD-ROM

Unit 7 of the *English Unlimited Upper Intermediate Self-study DVD-ROM* contains interactive games and activities for your learners to practise and improve their vocabulary, grammar and pronunciation, and also their speaking and listening, with the possibility for learners to record themselves, and a video of authentic spoken English to use with the Workbook.

- **Vocabulary and grammar:** Extra practice activities
- **Pronunciation:** Fluent speech – *the* with linking /j/
- **Explore speaking:** Repeating questions to gain time to think
- **Listening:** An interview with an author
- **Video:** An inspired blog

8.1

Goals: make deductions about the past
describe strong feelings

Core language:

GRAMMAR	Making deductions about the past
VOCABULARY	Describing strong feelings

One side of the story ...

LISTENING

1 / *Listening for main idea.* Draw learners' attention to the three pictures and let them talk for a minute or so about what they think is going on in each picture and how they think the people are feeling.

Play recording **2.21** while learners identify which of the people in each picture is talking.

> 1 Vic   2 Madison   3 Haneul

2 *Listening for detail.* Give learners time to read 1–6, then play recording **2.21** again. Learners note down their answers. They can compare with a partner before you check the answers.

> 1 To thank him for being a good host
> 2 When Vic paid the bill, Neil looked embarrassed and the waiter seemed angry.
> 3 A barbecue; people walking in and out of the house talking and eating
> 4 She sat with a group of people looking bored, then left early.
> 5 She looked uncomfortable and tried to smile.
> 6 She was fine.

This is the first part of the story. Learners will find out what was really going on later (Reading), but first they'll do some speculation about the three stories in the Grammar section.

GRAMMAR Making deductions about the past

3 a / In order to speculate about what was going on in the three stories from recording **2.21**, learners look at the language of deduction about past events. They read the sentences and add the four highlighted expressions to the diagram.

> I'm sure it's not true: 1 can't have
> It's possible: 3 might have
> It's very possible: 6 may well have
> I'm sure it's true: 7 must have

b / Learners complete the remaining gaps in the diagram with three more expressions.

> I'm sure it's not true: 2 couldn't have
> It's possible: 4 may have, 5 could have

c / Learners look at the form after *have*.

> past participle
> (so the complete form is modal + 'have' + past participle)

Language note

The use of *couldn't have* + past participle to speculate about the past was regarded as grammatically incorrect in the past, and *can't have* + past participle was taught as the correct form. However, *couldn't have* + past participle is increasingly used and accepted.

4 / *Practice.* Learners rewrite the underlined parts of the sentences using expressions from **3** which have the same meaning. Tell them there is more than one correct answer for some of the sentences (see below).

> 1 Neil can't have been / Neil couldn't have been unhappy with the meal. He really enjoyed it.
> 2 He might / may / could have felt a bit ill after eating too much.
> 3 The waiter might / may / could have made a mistake in the bill, and Neil noticed it.
> 4 Or Vic might / may / could have said something that upset Neil.
> 5 But the waiter must have been upset about something, too.
> 6 Neil may well have been embarrassed by the waiter's strange expression.

Note: Grammar practice

You could do the grammar practice on p136 at this point.

SPEAKING

5 a Learners go back to the pictures at the top of the section and speculate about situations 2 and 3 in the same way as the sentences in **4** speculate about situation 1. Learners choose expressions from **3**, based on how certain they feel about their speculations.

b Learners compare their ideas with other pairs and find out how many different ideas they had about the two situations.

 You could use photocopiable activity 8A on the Teacher's DVD-ROM at this point.

... and the other

READING

1 *Reading for main idea.* To find out what was going on in pictures 1–3 from the Listening, learners read the three postings on the website 'Cross-cultural misunderstandings'. They identify the reasons why Neil, Daniela and Haneul acted and felt as they did at the time. They can compare answers with a partner before you check the answers.

> Neil: He was embarrassed because the tip Vic left in the restaurant was too small.
> Haneul: She was very embarrassed because kissing and hugging is not usually done in public in her country.
> Daniela: She couldn't understand why there was no music and dancing at the party. In her own country, parties always have music and dancing.

2 👥 *Responding to the text*. Learners discuss the questions in groups. Find out afterwards what they would have felt and done in those situations.

VOCABULARY Describing strong feelings

3 a 👤/👥 Learners match the six highlighted expressions in the web postings with meanings a–f. They should use the context to help them.

> a4 b1 c6 d5 e3 f2

To clarify pronunciation, model and drill the six expressions.

b 👤/👥 Learners now match six more words with the meanings in **a**.

> 1e 2f 3d 4a 5c 6b

Model and drill the six words.

> **Optional extra**
>
> Learners work in A/B pairs. A says expressions 1–6 from the web postings while B closes their book and tries to remember expressions with the same meaning from **3b**. Then B says the definitions in **3a** while A tries to remember both expressions (from the postings and from **3b**) for each meaning.

SPEAKING

4 a 👤 *Preparation for discussion*. Learners think of one or two incidents in their lives when a misunderstanding occurred. They choose from the listed situations or think of their own ideas. Then they use the three bullet points as a guideline for preparation. Encourage them to use expressions from **3** and from the Grammar focus, Making deductions about the past, on p62.

b 👥 *Discussion*. Learners tell each other about their incidents. The other members of the group listen and say whether they agree with the speaker's speculations, possibly adding some speculations of their own.

Round-up. Ask someone from each group to describe one or two of the incidents they discussed and say what their speculations were.

 You could use photocopiable activity 8B on the Teacher's DVD-ROM at this point.

8.2

Goals: say how you feel about past events in your life
speculate about consequences of past actions

Core language:

VOCABULARY	Reflecting on the past
GRAMMAR	Conditionals – past and present
PRONUNCIATION	Prominent words 1

Turning points

LISTENING

1 👥 To introduce the topic, write on the board: *In everyone's life, there are a number of major turning points*. Ask learners what *turning points* means (= *a time when an important change begins to happen*).

👥 Then, as a warmer, learners discuss the questions, looking at the list of suggested turning points.

2 *Listening for main idea*. Learners look at the pictures. Play recording **2.22** while they listen and identify the important moment that each picture represents.

> *Jeanette's graduating from college with a degree in law. Fernando's going to ask his girlfriend to marry him. Tristan's getting to know an interesting young woman during a flight.*

3 *Listening for detail*. Give learners time to read the three questions. Then play recording **2.22** again, while they note down their answers.

> Jeanette
> 1 Her company decided to move. She went back to college instead of going with the company or getting a new job.
> 2 She got a job with a law firm in Boston.
> 3 She's happy about it.
> Fernando
> 1 He told his father he wanted to marry Juli. His father didn't approve. They argued. Fernando decided to ask her anyway.
> 2 He didn't ask Juli to marry him. They split up a few months later. He's still single.
> 3 He seems unsure about it: 'I really don't know. I wish I'd thought about it more carefully.'
> Tristan
> 1 He got the address of a boy in China from his school headmaster. The boys became pen pals. Later, Tristan visited him in China.
> 2 He married the woman he met on the plane. They have kids.
> 3 He's happy about it.

4 👥/👥 *Post-reading discussion*. Learners say whether they know anyone who's had turning points similar to the ones that the three people in the recording experienced. Avoid personalisation here, as learners will have a chance to talk about their own turning points in Speaking on p65.

VOCABULARY Reflecting on the past

5 a 👤/👥 Learners read the three groups of sentences. They identify the three sentences that came from recording **2.22** and recall who said them.

> 2 Jeanette   5 Tristan   7 Fernando

b 👤/👥 Learners look at the highlighted parts of the sentences and answer the questions.

> 1 a positive feelings: 2, 4, 5, 6
>   b negative feelings: 1, 3, 7, 8
> 2 a things that really happened: 1, 2, 3, 4, 5, 6
>   b imaginary situations: 7, 8

All the sentences express regret or lack of regret about the past. Draw learners' attention to the form used after the highlighted expressions, particularly the use of the past perfect after *I wish* and *If only*.

6 👤 *Preparation for discussion*. Learners think of something they did recently, looking at the listed ideas or using their own. They write a sentence about how they feel now about each thing they did, choosing suitable expressions from **5a**. Their ideas and sentences will form the basis for the Speaking task in **7**.

SPEAKING

7 👥 *Discussion*. Learners discuss what they did recently and how they feel about those things now. The listeners can ask questions to find out more, as shown in the speech bubbles.

Round-up. Find out who has the fewest regrets in each group.

Speculation

GRAMMAR Conditionals – past and present

1 👤/👥 Learners read the four sentences in the grammar box and answer questions 1–3.

> 1 They're imagining them.
> 2 Both parts of sentences a and b are about the past. In sentences c and d, the 'If' clauses are about the past, but the main clauses (the second clauses) are about the present.
> 3 'if' + 'had' + past participle
>   modal verb + 'have' + past participle
>   modal verb + infinitive
>   modal verb + 'be' + '-ing' form

> **Language note**
>
> Sentences a and b are sometimes called third conditionals. In these sentences, an imaginary action in the past is linked with an imaginary result also in the past. Sentences c and d are sometimes called 'mixed conditionals'. In these sentences, an imaginary action in the past is linked with an imaginary result in the present.

2 a 👤 *Practice*. Learners work alone and complete the sentence beginnings about the three people from recording **2.22** with their own ideas.

> **Alternative for weaker classes**
>
> Do the first sentence together, eliciting sentences from the class and writing them on the board. For example: *If she hadn't looked in that newspaper, she wouldn't have gone to college. / … she wouldn't be a lawyer. / … she'd still be working at the same company.* Then learners continue with the rest of the sentence beginnings.

b 👥/👥 Learners compare their sentences. Elicit a few of their ideas for completing the sentences.

> **Note: Grammar practice**
>
> You could do the grammar practice on p137 at this point.

PRONUNCIATION Prominent words 1

3 a Play recording **2.23**. Learners read and listen to the four sentences and notice that in each group of words (separated with //), one word has an extra-strong stress (the strongly stressed syllable of that word is in capital letters). That is, this word is stressed even more strongly than words that have ordinary sentence stress. The word with extra-strong stress is said to be 'prominent'. It's a matter of speaker choice which word to make prominent, but there's a general guideline – it's often the last important word (e.g. noun, adjective, verb …) in a group of words.

b 👥 *Practice*. Learners practise saying sentences 1–4 in a natural way, being particularly careful to speak

in groups of words and making the marked word prominent. There will be more Pronunciation sections on prominence in Units 11 and 13. This section (Part 1) is to raise learners' awareness of this pronunciation feature.

SPEAKING

4 a 👤 *Preparation for discussion*. Learners think about a turning point in their life that they'd like to tell the others about. They look at the ideas listed or think of one of their own.

b 👤 Learners use questions 1–5 as guidelines for preparation. Remind them to use expressions from VOCABULARY Reflecting on the past, as well as conditional sentences. They might want to think about which words to make prominent in their conditional sentences.

c 👥 *Discussion*. Learners discuss their turning points in groups and find out if any of them had similar experiences.

Round-up. Find out which were the most common turning points in the class and which two were the most unusual ones.

> You could use photocopiable activity 8C on the Teacher's DVD-ROM at this point.

8.3 Target activity

Goals: make deductions about the past ♻
speculate about consequences of past actions ♻
disagree with speculations about the past

Core language:

TASK VOCABULARY	Disagreeing with speculations
8.1 GRAMMAR	Making deductions about the past
8.2 GRAMMAR	Conditionals – past and present

Work out what happened

TASK LISTENING

1 a 👥 *Prediction, Listening for main idea*. Learners look at the picture, read the caption and say how they think the people are feeling. Play recording **2.24**, the first part of Jo and Angela's conversation. Learners listen and try to guess what the problem is. They compare their ideas.

> Something – a pet – has disappeared from the flat. The two women can't find it.

b *Listening for main idea*. Play recording **2.25**. Learners check their ideas from **a**.

> A pet cat is missing. It belongs to someone else, who's away. They're taking care of it.

2 a *Listening for detail*. Give learners time to read sentences 1–5. Then play recordings **2.24** and **2.25** again (the whole conversation). Learners note down their answers.

> 1 *It's too high for the cat to escape from.*
> 2 *The cat could have gone out the front door while they were bringing in their shopping.*
> 3 *They would have told Angela and Jo if they'd seen the cat.*
> 4 *They fed the cat late last night, and it ate the food. Therefore, it was in the flat during the night, or part of it.*
> 5 *Maybe she didn't notice the cat escaping when she went out to get sugar in the morning. She wasn't properly awake.*

b 👥 Learners compare their answers, then read scripts **2.24** and **2.25** on p151 to check.

TASK VOCABULARY Disagreeing with past speculations

3 👤/👥 Learners put the words in the right order.

> 1 *No, we'd have seen it outside.*
> 2 *Yeah, but somebody would've seen it on the stairs.*

You can use *would have / wouldn't have* + past participle to disagree with speculations about the past that you think are unlikely or impossible, explaining why you disagree.

4 **a** ✍ *Practice.* Learners write a sentence disagreeing with what the first speaker in each exchange says, using *would have* and their own ideas.

b 👥/👥 Learners compare their answers.

> *Possible answers*
> 1 *No, she would have called us on her mobile.*
>   *No, the traffic would have been light at that time.*
> 2 *No, you would have noticed that when you got home.*
>   *No, none of our friends would have taken it.*
> 3 *But they would have told us.*
>   *But they wouldn't have cancelled it – it was too important.*
> 4 *But he would have found them and called me.*
>   *But somebody would have seen them and told me.*

TASK

5 **a** *Preparation for role play.* Divide learners into A/B pairs. They read their individual situation cards and underline the key information. Then they plan what to say and how to say it. Encourage them to use the structures from GRAMMAR Making deductions about the past and GRAMMAR Conditionals – past and present.

b 👥 *Role play.* Remind learners to use expressions from **3** and **4** during the role play. The pairs do Situation 1.

6 👥 *Preparation, Role play.* Learners repeat steps **5a** and **5b** for Situation 2.

7 👥 Learners compare their conclusions about the two situations with another pair. Afterwards, they look at the suggested explanations on p128 and see if they had similar ideas.

Round-up. Find out who had similar ideas to the suggested explanations and whether they came up with any other interesting possibilities.

8 Explore

Across cultures: Languages

Goal: to make learners aware of the character of and attitudes to language in different cultures

Core language:

VOCABULARY   Languages: *a language; a dialect; an accent; an official language; a regional language; a common language; a mother tongue; a first language; a second language; monolingual; bilingual; multilingual*

SPEAKING

1 **a** 👥 As a warmer, learners read the instructions, the words and languages, then try matching each word with the language it came from.

b 👥 Learners check their ideas on p121, then discuss the two questions. Elicit some of their ideas after a while.

> *alphabet: Greek   boss: Dutch   cotton: Arabic*
> *hamburger: German   ketchup: Cantonese*
> *marriage: French   opera: Italian   plaza: Spanish*
> *robot: Czech   sauna: Finnish   shampoo: Hindi*
> *ski: Norwegian   tsunami: Japanese   yoghurt: Turkish*

LISTENING

2 **a** 👥 *Prediction.* Learners look at the pictures and read the captions (note that Sahana is pronounced 'Shahana'). They discuss what they know about languages in India and the Netherlands.

b *Listening for main idea.* Play recording **2.26**. Learners note down answers to the questions.

> Sahana
> 1 *Many different languages and even more dialects are spoken in India. English is the common language. Hindi is spoken by the majority.*
> 2 *A lot of people learn Hindi in school.*
> Liesbeth
> 1 *Dutch, Frisian and English are spoken in the Netherlands.*
> 2 *Lots of people learn other languages in school besides Dutch, Frisian and English.*

3 **a** *Listening for main idea.* Give learners time to read the six questions. Play recording **2.27** while learners identify the three questions that Sahana and Liesbeth answer.

> *Sahana answers questions 1 and 3; Liesbeth answers question 6.*

b 👥 *Listening for detail.* Play recording **2.27** again for learners to listen and note down two or three details about each of the three questions identified in **a**. They compare answers and check in script **2.27** on pp151–2.

> *Possible answers*
> 1 *Hindi and Bengali are a lot less rigid than before. People mix a lot of English words into their sentences.*
> 3 *Older people aren't happy about young people mixing English with Hindi and Bengali.*
> 6 *Dutch is direct because the character of the people is direct. They say what they mean. They don't mean to be rude, but people from other countries might think they are.*

VOCABULARY Languages

4 👤/👥 Learners discuss the differences in meaning within each group of three expressions. After a while, elicit their ideas. If more clarification is needed, you can use these dictionary definitions.

> 1 *a language: a system of communication consisting of sounds, words and grammar*
> *a dialect: the form of a language that people speak in a particular part of a country, containing some different words and grammar, etc.*
> *an accent: the way in which people in a particular area, country or social group pronounce words*
> 2 *an official language: the language used by the state. A country may have more than one official language.*
> *a regional language: a language spoken in a particular area of a country*
> *a common language: a language spoken by the majority of (or all) the people in a country*
> 3 *a mother tongue: the language you learn when you're a baby.*
> *a first language: the language you learn first, your mother tongue*
> *a second language: the language you acquire after your mother tongue*
> 4 *monolingual: speaking or using only one language*
> *bilingual: able to use two languages for communication*
> *multilingual: able to use more than two languages for communication*
> Note: *a mother tongue and a first language are the only two with the same meaning.*

SPEAKING

5 a 👤 *Preparation for talk*. Learners look at the questions in **2b** and **3a** again and choose a few to talk about. They plan what to say and what expressions to use from **4**.

b 👥 *Talk*. Learners give their talks in pairs, then answer the two follow-up questions.

Round-up. Find out what learners discussed, and what facts they thought a visitor might want to know.

Explore writing

Goal: write a complaint about a service

Core language:

Stating your intention: *I'd like to make a complaint about ...; I'm writing to express my dissatisfaction with ...; This is to inform you of ...; I think you should know about ...*
Stating what you want: *I would like ...; I expect ...*
Making suggestions or recommendations: *I also suggest ...; I strongly recommend ...*
Ending: *I hope that ...; I trust that ...*

1 👥/👥 To introduce the topic and the context, learners discuss the questions. Find out from a few of them what they said.

2 👤 Learners read the online complaint form filed by a hotel guest after his stay at a hotel. They answer the four questions.

> 1 He was charged £75 for use of the gym. It should have been free.
> 2 The clerk was rude and refused to believe him.
> 3 The manager cancelled the charge, but did not tell the clerk to apologise.
> 4 He wants them to send him a formal apology and an assurance that the clerk has been disciplined. He also wants them to take steps to ensure that such an incident doesn't happen again.

3 👥/👥 *Responding to the text*. Learners say what they'd have done in the guest's position.

4 👥 Explain that some people write an online complaint in one paragraph, but others divide it into paragraphs. Learners decide how many paragraphs they'd divide the guest's complaint into, where they'd divide it, and why.

👥 Then they compare their ideas with another pair.

> **Suggested answer**
> *Create a second paragraph before 'I stayed at your hotel ...', where the guest describes what happened. The first paragraph states the reason why he's writing. Create a third paragraph before 'I would like to receive ...', where the guest states what he would like the hotel to do. Create a fourth paragraph before 'I look forward to ...', where he ends his email, saying he looks forward to their reply.*

5 👥/👥 Draw learners' attention to the four highlighted expressions in the guest's complaint. They decide which expressions a–f could replace the four highlighted ones (i.e. they identify where a–f would fit grammatically and make sense). You may need to explain to weaker students that three of the expressions a–f relate to the same (the first) highlighted expression.

> *1 b, e, f   2 d   3 a   4 c*

6 👥 Tell learners to cover the complaint. They try to remember and work out what the missing word is in each expression. Then they quickly check their answers in the guest's complaint.

> *1 occurred   2 told   3 pointed   4 was   5 regret*
> *6 apology   7 assurance   8 steps   9 confidence*

Clarify any points of meaning and pronunciation. For example, *an assurance* means 'a promise'.

7 a 👤 Learners read the situation. If they wish, they may think of their own.

b 👤 *Preparation for writing*. Learners plan how many paragraphs to use, what to say and what language they'll need from **5** and **6**. They can also use expressions from VOCABULARY Describing strong feelings and VOCABULARY Reflecting on the past.

c 👤 *Writing*. Learners write their complaints. If you wish, this can be done as homework and brought in the next day.

8 👥/👥 Learners read a few of each other's complaints. They comment on how clearly the incidents are described and say what they think of the solutions the writers asked for.

8 Look again

Review

VOCABULARY Reflecting on the past

1 a 👤/👥 Learners rewrite the 'a' sentences with the new beginnings, keeping the meaning the same.

> 1 I'm glad I got married.
> 2 I'm not sorry about leaving college.
> 3 I wish I'd known my grandfather.
> 4 If only I hadn't changed jobs.

b 👤 Learners imagine they're someone well known in their country, past or present, and write five or six sentences expressing regret or lack of regret about what they did or what happened to them. For example, *I wish I hadn't made that album.* They shouldn't say who they are, though, as the sentences will be used in a guessing game in **c**.

c 👥/👥👥 Learners listen to each other's sentences and try to guess who the people are. They can add more details about the people afterwards.

GRAMMAR Conditionals – past and present

2 a 👤 Explain to learners that they will listen to six situations and that you'll pause between the situations to give them time to write a conditional sentence about each situation. Then play recording **2.28**. Alternatively, you can read the situations yourself.

b 👥/👥👥 Learners compare their sentences to see how similar they are. The sort of sentences they might make (although answers depend on their ideas) are, for example:

If my alarm clock had gone off, I would have got on that flight. If I'd got on that flight, I might have got food poisoning.

If I hadn't gone to the café, I wouldn't have seen my ex-boyfriend / I wouldn't have had such a bad evening.

If Gisela had told me it was her birthday, I wouldn't have asked her to work late.

c 👥👥 *Discussion.* Learners think of similar situations they have experienced and conditional sentences they can use. They then describe the situations and, if they wish, ask and answer questions about them. Find out afterwards which were the most interesting situations from each group.

CAN YOU REMEMBER? Unit 7 – Problem-solving experiences

3 a 👤/👥 Learners complete the paragraph with the five expressions a–e.

> 1 I found it really difficult to
> 2 My biggest problem was that
> 3 My way of solving this problem was to
> 4 What we decided to do was
> 5 What I learned was

b 👤 *Preparation for discussion.* Learners think of problems they had, like Ian's, in connection with the listed situations. They choose useful expressions from **a** to describe their situations.

c 👥👥 *Discussion.* Learners describe the problems and say how they solved them.

Extension

SPELLING AND SOUNDS /e/

4 a 👤/👥 Learners underline the letters in each word that make an /e/ sound, then complete the two spelling patterns.

> speculate, dialect, education, weapon, regret, emigrate, head, instead, investigate, gesture
> 1 Only e is used at the start of words.
> 2 e or ea is used in the middle of words.

b 👤/👥 Learners find more ways of spelling /e/ in some common words.

> Six ways: ai (again, against, said), a (any, many, says), u (bury), ie (friendly), ei (leisure), eo (leopard)

c 👥 Learners take turns to choose ten words from **a** and **b** and test each other's spelling.

> **Alternative**
>
> Learners close their books. You dictate ten of the words. They compare their spelling, then check it in their books.

NOTICE Expressions with *and* and *or*

5 a 👤/👥 This section focuses on word pairs linked with *and* and *or*. Learners complete the four sentences from the unit.

> 1 or   2 and   3 and   4 or

b 👤/👥 Learners complete the eight sentences, using context to help them choose the right expression.

> 1 sick and tired   2 sooner or later   3 rain or shine
> 4 clean and tidy   5 trial and error   6 more or less
> 7 odds and ends   8 black and blue

> **Optional extra**
>
> Learners work in pairs and take turns to test each other on all 12 expressions from **5a** and **5b**. For example, A says: *sick*; B then gives the whole expression: *sick and tired*.

Self-assessment

To help focus learners on the self-assessment, read it through and get learners to give you a few examples of the language they have learned in each section. Give an example to start them off if necessary. Then learners circle the numbers on each line.

Unit 8 Extra activities on the Teacher's DVD-ROM

Printable worksheets, activity instructions and answer keys are on your Teacher's DVD-ROM.

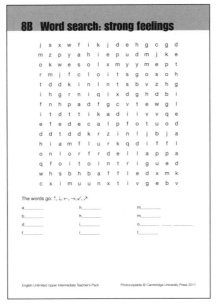

8A Mysteries of the world

Activity type: Reading and speaking – Information gap / Making deductions – Individuals / Small groups

Aim: To make deductions about mysterious events in the past

Language: Making deductions about the past – Use at any point from 8.1.

Preparation: Make one copy of the worksheet for every three learners. Cut up each worksheet to make three stories.

Time: 35 minutes

8B Word search: strong feelings

Activity type: Vocabulary – Game – Pairs

Aim: To revise adjectives describing strong feelings

Language: Describing strong feelings – Use at any point from 8.1.

Preparation: Make a copy of the worksheet for every pair of learners.

Time: 15 minutes

8C No regrets?

Activity type: Reading and speaking – Guessing / Information gap – Pairs/ Groups

Aim: To express regret or lack of regret about the past

Language: Reflecting on the past / Conditionals – past and present – Use at any point from 8.2.

Preparation: Make one copy of the worksheet for every four learners. Cut up each worksheet to make a set of four stories.

Time: 40 minutes

Unit 8 Self-study Pack

In the Workbook

Unit 8 of the *English Unlimited Upper Intermediate Workbook* offers additional ways to practise the vocabulary and grammar taught in the Coursebook. There are also activities which build reading and writing skills and a whole page of listening and speaking tasks to use with the Interview video, giving your learners the opportunity to hear and react to authentic spoken English.

- **Vocabulary:** Making deductions about the past; Describing strong feelings; Reflecting on the past; Disagreeing with speculations; Languages
- **Grammar:** Conditionals – past and present
- **Explore reading:** Article: Immobile on the phone
- **Interview:** Cultural difference – Aurora and Monica

On the DVD-ROM

Unit 8 of the *English Unlimited Upper Intermediate Self-study DVD-ROM* contains interactive games and activities for your learners to practise and improve their vocabulary, grammar and pronunciation, and also their speaking and listening, with the possibility for learners to record themselves, and a video of authentic spoken English to use with the Workbook.

- **Vocabulary and grammar:** Extra practice activities
- **Pronunciation:** Prominent words
- **Explore speaking:** *right*
- **Listening:** Talking about a turning point
- **Video:** Cultural difference

How it's done

9.1

Goals: explain how something is made
organise a description

Core language:

GRAMMAR	Verbs with adverbs and prepositions 1
PRONUNCIATION	Stress in multi-word verbs
VOCABULARY	Organising a description

Printing press

LISTENING

1   *Pre-listening discussion.* To introduce the topic of the listening, learners discuss the questions in groups.

Follow this stage by eliciting and comparing answers and ideas from different groups in open class. Then tell learners that they're going to hear a description of how books are made.

2 a   *Prediction.* Learners look at the pictures and guess the order of the stages A–E.

b   *Listening for main ideas.* Play recording **3.1**. Learners listen and check their guesses from **a**, correcting the order of the stages A–E as necessary.

> **1D   2C   3A   4E   5B**

3 a   *Listening for details.* Before listening for a second time, give learners a chance to read the questions and tell each other if they can remember any of the answers. Then play recording **3.1** once again.

b   Learners read script **3.1** on p152 to check and complete their answers as necessary.

> | | |
> |---|---|
> | Part 1 | *The press can print 16 pages at once. It can print about 10,000 sheets an hour.* |
> | Part 2 | *The paper is folded four times. The pages are printed in a particular sequence so they come out in order when folded.* |
> | Part 3 | *A book block is all the sections of the book (except the cover) gathered together, but not glued or trimmed.* |
> | Part 4 | *The notches in the spine help the glue to stick the cover on.* |
> | Part 5 | *The temperature of the glue is about 250˚C.* |

4   *Discussion.* Learners discuss the two questions.

Round-up. Ask learners which were the most interesting tours they discussed, and if there are any they would particularly recommend.

GRAMMAR Verbs with adverbs and prepositions 1

> **Note**
>
> This is the first of two grammar sections in this course on verbs. The second section is in Unit 13.

5 a   *Presentation.* Learners complete the summary of the book-making process using the prepositions and adverbs in the box.

They compare their answers before checking as a class.

> **1** *into*   **2** *onto*   **3** *from*   **4** *through*   **5** *up*   **6** *to*   **7** *along*   **8** *off*

b   Ask students to discuss the questions in pairs before checking as a class.

> *into* **is a preposition because it describes** where *the paper goes. It has an object: the printing press.*
> *over* **is an adverb because it modifies the verb. It says** how *the paper is turned. The paper is the object of* turn, *not the object of* over.
> *You can change the word order in 3, saying* The press turns over the paper *instead. You cannot change the word order in 1 or 2.*

This is likely to be a discussion point in many classes, as students may be unfamiliar with the idea that words like *over* can be adverbs as well as prepositions. The best way through these complications, and for students to recognise the underlying rules about word order, is for students to think about the logical meanings of different combinations of words from the sentences and to recognise which make sense and which don't. It is often possible to grasp the syntax simply by considering the meaning of the sentences, and encouraging students to do this is likely to help more than learning lists of verbs with different 'patterns'. Some boardwork can help:

Sentence 1

into the printing press

Sheets of paper go into the printing press

Sheets of paper ~~go the printing press into~~

In sentence 1, *the printing press* is the object of the *preposition* into, but not the object of the verb: it does not make sense to put *the printing press* next to the verb. To put it another way, *into the printing press* makes sense as a single meaning-unit and cannot be changed.

Sentence 2

The operator pours ink into the printing press.
ink is the object of *pours*; *the printing press* is the object of *into*. Again, *into the printing press* is a fixed unit. Discussing why ~~The operator pours the printing press into the ink~~ doesn't make sense could help students with this.

Sentence 3

turns the paper

Here, *the paper* is the object of the *verb*: it is the thing which the press *turns*.

turns over

Over is an adverb because it describes the verb: it says *how* the paper turns.

In these cases it makes sense to say either *turns the paper over* or *turns over the paper*, so this is why you can change the word order in sentence 3.

c   Learners look at all 15 highlighted verbs in the summary and notice the grammar patterns associated with them. They divide them by grammar pattern into three groups of five. For feedback, elicit the three groups onto the board. You could finish off this by asking which sentences can change their word order (those with pattern 3), and writing up the 'alternatives' on the board.

Note: Grammar practice

You could do the grammar practice on p137 at this point.

PRONUNCIATION Stress in verbs with adverbs and prepositions

6 a   / *Presentation.* Learners read the two descriptions and choose the correct words. Encourage them to try and work out the answers by saying the sentences in the box in **5b** and seeing which stress patterns sound most natural.

Then play recording **3.2**. Learners listen to check their answers.

1 verb   2 adverb

Optional extra

Summarise the 'hierarchy' of stress in multi-word verbs by writing on the board:
adverb (double underline)
verb (underline)
preposition (no underline)

---

   b *Practice.* Drill the four sentences from **5b**. Listen carefully to ensure that learners are saying them with the correct stress patterns.

1 *The operator **pours** ink **into** the printing press.*
2 *Sheets of paper **go into** the printing press.*
3 *The press **turns** the paper **over.***
   *The press **turns over** the paper.*

SPEAKING

7 *Practice (grammar and pronunciation).* Learners cover the summary in **5a** and summarise the book-making process from memory in their own words, using the 15 verbs on the board. They can look at the illustrations in **2a** to help them.

Alternative for weaker classes

Before starting the speaking, number the multi-word verbs on the board 1–15 to show the order they should occur in the summary.

While learners are doing this, monitor closely to check their pronunciation of the multi-word verbs.

First of all, …

VOCABULARY Organising a description

1 / *Presentation.* Learners add the expressions in the box to the correct groups 1–5 according to their function.

Alternative: Categorising dictation

Books closed. Give learners a copy of the table in **1a** on a handout. Read the expressions in the box aloud. Learners listen and write down each expression in the correct group. Learners compare their answers and look at **1a** in their books to check their spelling, then check answers as a class.

1 To start off, …; To begin with, …; The first thing is, …
2 After that, …; Following that, …; Once that's done, …
3 I'll explain that in a minute.
4 Earlier I mentioned …
5 And that's it.

SPEAKING

2 / *Prediction.* Learners look at the pictures and try to guess how each thing is made.

3 a *Preparation for describing a process.* Divide the class into two groups. Working together, learners in Group A read the notes about the making of Maldon salt on p127 and follow the instructions to prepare to describe the process. Learners in Group B do the same for glass bottles on p125.

Alternative

Learners prepare to describe a process (physical, administrative, etc.) associated with their work or studies.

---

   b *Describing a process.* Put the learners into A/B pairs. They listen to each other's descriptions. Encourage learners to ask questions about anything they don't understand or would like to know more about.

4 *Round-up.* Learners go back to their groups from **3a** and tell each other, in as much detail as they can, what they can remember about the process they've just heard about.

You could use photocopiable activity 9A on the Teacher's DVD-ROM at this point.

9.2

Goals: describe responsibilities and roles in different situations
explain how a team or organisation works

Core language:
VOCABULARY   Describing responsibilities
VOCABULARY   Describing roles

Responsibilities

READING

1 a / *Prediction.* Learners look at the picture and guess what the five people's jobs might involve.

Then, as a class, compare ideas for each job.

   b *Reading for main ideas.* Learners read the article quickly to check their ideas.

Optional extra: Monolingual classes

Ask learners if they know the names of these jobs in their first language. Note: in some countries, the various responsibilities described in the article are divided up differently.

2 a *Responding to the text.* Learners read again and answer the two questions for each job. Tell learners that although there are no strictly right or wrong answers, they should be ready to justify their views by referring to the text.

b 👥 / 👥👥 Learners compare their answers, justifying them by referring to specific parts of the article.

3 *Round-up.* Discuss the question as a class. Ask learners to tell you which information they found the most interesting or unexpected.

VOCABULARY Describing responsibilities

4 a *Presentation: duties.* Learners match 1–5 with a–e, looking back in the article to check if necessary.

1 d   2 c   3 b   4 a   5 e

b 👥 *Memorisation.* Pairs cover the sentence stems 1–5 in **a** and, looking at a–e, try to remember the complete sentences. They don't need to use exactly the same expressions, but their sentences should be factually and grammatically accurate and they should try to use a range of expressions for describing responsibilities.

Alternative: Matching slips

Books closed. Provide each pair of learners with the ten expressions in **4a** on slips of paper, cut up and shuffled. Learners match the slips to make five sentences, then find and underline the expressions for describing duties. Point out the *-ing* forms in d and e. Then learners turn the slips of paper 1–5 face down and try to remember the complete sentences.

5 *Presentation: hierarchies.* Learners choose expressions from the box to replace the highlighted expressions in the two sentences, keeping the meaning the same.

1 answers to, reports to
2 manages, oversees, supervises

SPEAKING

6 a 👤 *Preparation.* Learners think of a team or organisation from their experience and prepare to talk about the two questions. Encourage them to choose language from **4** and **5** to help them with their descriptions.

b 👥 / 👥👥 *Describing a team or organisation.* Learners listen to each other's descriptions. As they listen, their task is to decide which roles sound the most challenging. Encourage learners to ask follow-up questions about any points they don't understand or would like to know more about.

Optional extra

Learners write up their description of their team or organisation in the form of a page on a company/club/government/etc. website.

 You could use photocopiable activity 9B on the Teacher's DVD-ROM at this point.

Roles

LISTENING

1 *Listening for main ideas.* Play recording **3.3**. Learners listen and answer the two questions.

1 Josette writes screenplays.
2 She mentions her roles as: a parent, a teacher,
a member of a writer's guild, a member of a charity,
a football supporter.

2 *Listening in detail.* Learners tell each other any details they remember about each of Josette's life roles.

Play recording **3.3** again. Learners listen to check and add to the details about each of Josette's roles.

VOCABULARY Describing roles

3 a 👥 / 👥👥 *Presentation.* Learners look at expressions 1–8 from Josette's talk and provide the next word.

b Learners look at script **3.3** on p152 to check their answers.

1 as   2 of   3 of   4 in   5 as   6 to   7 for   8 of

SPEAKING

4 a 👤 *Preparation.* Learners prepare to talk about the three questions. Encourage them to make a list of their life roles and to choose expressions from **3a** to help describe them.

b 👥 / 👥👥 *Discussion.* Learners tell each other about their answers to the three questions.

Round-up. Ask a few learners to tell the class what new information they found out about their partner(s).

9.3 Target activity

Goals: organise a description ♻
explain how a team or organisation works ♻
give a detailed presentation on a familiar topic

Core language:

TASK VOCABULARY	Organising a talk
9.1 VOCABULARY	Organising a description
9.2 VOCABULARY	Describing responsibilities

Give a factual talk

TASK LISTENING

1 *Pre-listening discussion.* Learners look at the photo and information about Adam. Discuss the questions as a class. Elicit possible good and bad points about being a travel writer, and find out how many learners in the class would like to do this kind of job.

2 a 👥 / 👥 Tell learners they're going to listen to Adam giving a talk to a group of students about his work. Learners think of questions they'd like to ask Adam.

Compare ideas as a class.

b *Listening for main ideas.* Play recording **3.4**. Learners listen to the introduction to Adam's talk to find out what four topics he plans to talk about.

👥 / 👥 In the same pairs/groups as in **a**, learners check answers together and decide: will Adam be answering any of their questions from **a**?

> 1 what it's like to be a travel writer
> 2 money
> 3 how to get into the profession
> 4 how it's changing at the moment

3 a *Listening for details.* Tell learners they're now going to listen to the next part of Adam's talk. Give them time to read through the points 1–6 and ask: *Which topics (from 2b) are we going to hear about?* (*1, 2 and 3; not 4.*)

Play recording **3.5**. Learners listen and make notes on the six points.

b 👥 / 👥 Learners compare their notes, then read script **3.5** on p153 to make sure they have all the main points and clear up any areas of misunderstanding.

> 1 It's hard work, unglamorous.
> 2 Twelve hours of visiting various places, then writing up notes in the evening.
> 3 1) have regular work with a top magazine;
>   2) write guidebooks.
> 4 They agree a single sum to include both the writer's fee and their expenses.
> 5 $6 after costs, according to one estimate
> 6 By writing for travel magazines.

TASK VOCABULARY Organising a talk

4 a 👥 / 👥 *Presentation.* Learners look at the expressions in a–f from Adam's talk and match each with a function 1–3.

> a1 b2 c3 d2 e3 f2

b 👥 / 👥 Learners look at more expressions in the box and match them with 1–3.

> 1 I'll be looking at … main areas; I've divided my talk into … parts.
> 2 Next, I'd like to say something about …; Now let's take a look at …
> 3 So, we've talked about …; That's it as far as … is concerned.

Alternative: Board presentation

- Write the three headings on the board: *outline*, *open topic*, *close topic*. As a class, go through the sentences a–f in **4a** and write them under the correct headings.
- Now go through the expressions in **4b**. Ask learners to make whole sentences with the expressions and write them under the correct headings.
- *Books closed*. Rub out two or three key words in each expression. In pairs or groups, learners try to remember the complete expressions.

TASK

5 a 👤 *Preparation for presentation.* Learners choose one of the situations or think of their own topic.

b 👤 Learners prepare a talk on their chosen topic, following the four steps. Set a clear time limit for this preparation (e.g. 15 minutes) and be on hand to help learners if they have any questions about language. Learners should not write their talks out in full, but encourage them to make notes of key points and useful expressions from **4a** and **b**. Remind them that they may also find useful expressions in VOCABULARY Organising a description and VOCABULARY Describing responsibilities.

Alternative: More guided preparation

- Give each learner a blank 'flowchart' to help them plan their talk, consisting of five large labelled boxes joined by arrows: *Introduction > Topic 1 > Topic 2 > Topic 3 > Topic 4*.
- In the *Introduction* box, learners note down the topics they want to include in their talk. Then they write a brief introduction to their talk, choosing appropriate expressions from **4a** and **b**.
- In pairs or groups, learners listen to each other's introductions. They tell each other what questions they'd like answered in the main body of the talk.
- In the *Topics* boxes of the flowchart, learners make notes of key points. At the top of each box, they write an expression for opening the topic. At the bottom of each box, they write an expression for closing the topic.

---

c 👥 Learners practise their talks in groups.

6 👥 *Presentations.* Learners get into new groups and listen to each other's talks. After each talk, they ask questions about any points they didn't follow or would like to hear about in more detail.

Round-up. Ask for one or two volunteers to give their talk to the whole class.

9 Explore

Keyword: *way*

Goals: use expressions with *way* to describe methods and
styles of doing things
use literal and metaphorical expressions with *way*
meaning *route*

Core language:

way = method: *the best way to, an interesting way of, ...*
way = style: *in a different way, in the best way possible, ...*
way = route: *be in the way, go out of your way, work your
way up, ...*

way = method

1 a 👥/👥👥 *Reading.* Learners read through the
quotations together and discuss the questions.

Round off the discussion by asking a few pairs/groups
to tell the class if there were any quotations they
disagreed with.

> **Alternative: Round the room**
>
> *Books closed.* Copy each quotation onto a separate piece
> of paper and stick the pieces of paper on the door, walls,
> windows, etc. around the room. In their pairs/groups,
> learners move round the room, reading each quotation in
> turn. Finally, learners sit down and tell each other which were
> their favourite quotations.

b *Presentation.* Elicit answers to the questions and write
them on the board.

> 1 *way* to + infinitive; *way* of -ing form
> The meaning is the same.
> 2 *there's no way, a million ways, the best way, a way, lots
> of ways, only one way, the only way, the easiest way*

c 📖 *Practice.* Learners complete questions 3–6 with
their own ideas. While learners are writing, monitor
closely to make sure that they're using the correct
grammar patterns with *way*.

👥/👥👥 Learners ask and answer all the questions.

Round-up. Choose one or two of the more interesting
questions written by learners and discuss briefly as a
class.

way = style

2 a 👥/👥👥 *Presentation.* Learners use the words to
complete the expressions with *way* in sentences 1–4.
Then check as a class.

> 1 *fastest*   2 *imaginative*   3 *quiet*   4 *different*

> **Optional extra: Contextualisation**
>
> Learners try to remember the context of the four sentences
> (*Who said them? What were they talking about?*), then look
> back at the relevant units to find the sentences and check
> their answers to **2a**. Note that all these sentences are to be
> found in the recording scripts.
> 1 Adam the travel writer talking about his work (**3.5**)
> 2 Dominika talking about the artificial palm tree in the centre
>   of Warsaw (**1.24**)
> 3 Alex talking about his driving instructor (**1.19**)
> 4 David talking about Portugal (**1.15**)

b 👥/👥👥 Learners think of more words which could
go in each sentence (not necessarily keeping the same
meaning) and write them down. Note that sentence 1
requires an adjective in the superlative form. Then
compare ideas as a class.

> *Possible answers*
> 1 *quickest / most efficient / most accurate / most
>   discreet*
> 2 *innovative / original (or, with article 'a' instead of 'an':
>   traditional / practical, etc.)*
> 3 *calm / friendly / cheerful / ironic*
> 4 *unusual / strange / indirect / self-conscious*

c *Practice.* Play recording **3.6**, pausing between each
instruction if necessary. Learners listen and write
down names/activities in response to the instructions.

> **Alternative for weaker classes**
>
> Ask learners to read the instructions instead of listening to
> them by looking at script **3.6** on p153.

way = route

3 a *Presentation.* Write the examples 1 and 2 on the board
with *in the way* underlined. Ask learners:

a *In which sentence is 'in the way' physical, i.e. it
refers to a real, physical route?* (*1*)

b *In which sentence is 'in the way' abstract, i.e. it
refers to an imaginary route?* (*2: the way* refers to
the route to the presidency.)

Explain that many expressions with *way* can have
either a physical or an abstract meaning, depending on
the context.

b 👥/👥👥 Learners decide which expression in each
pair is more physical and which more abstract. Then
check as a class.

> *The more physical member of each pair is:*
> *1a   2a   3b   4a*

c 👥/👥👥 *Discussion.* Learners decide (monolingual
classes) / tell each other (multilingual classes) how
they would translate the expressions with *way* in **a**
and **b** into their first language, and whether the same
expressions can be used in both physical and abstract
ways.

Round-up. Discuss as a class, focusing on two or three
of the expressions.

 You could use photocopiable activity 9C on the
Teacher's DVD-ROM at this point.

Explore speaking

Goals: check that people understand
add more details
ask people to clarify or repeat things

Core language:

Expressions for:
• checking understanding: *Do you get what I mean?, ...*
• elaborating: *To be precise, ...*
• asking for clarification/repetition: *What do you mean by ... ?, ...*

1   👥 / 👥👥 *Pre-listening discussion.* Learners look at the picture and discuss the two questions. Then discuss each of the questions briefly as a class.

2   a   *Listening for main ideas.* Read through the points 1–6 with the class. Tell learners that these points will be mentioned in a conversation between a professional chocolate maker, Valeria, and a customer, Sergio.

Play recording **3.7**. Learners listen and identify which of the points 1–6 Sergio does *not* understand at first and asks for more information about.

> *Sergio doesn't understand points 2, 4 and 6 at first.*

Alternative for weaker classes

Tell learners that there are three points Sergio does not at first understand.

b   👤 *Reading for main ideas.* Learners read the conversation on the page. They check their answers to **a** and find explanations for all six of the points.

👥 / 👥👥 Learners compare their answers, then discuss as a class.

> 1 *Caramel is refrigerated so it hardens and can be hand-dipped in melted chocolate.*
> 2 *The special ingredient is a secret.*
> 3 *It makes the filling slightly harder, like putty.*
> 4 *Putty is the soft substance used to hold glass in windows.*
> 5 *The special ingredient liquefies when not in contact with oxygen in the air, i.e. when covered in chocolate.*
> 6 *Sugar can make it difficult or impossible to taste other flavours.*

3   a   *Presentation.* Divide the board into three columns and copy the group headings onto the board.

👥 / 👥👥 Learners read the conversation again and match the highlighted expressions 1–8 with the correct groups.

Go through the answers as a class, writing each expression in the appropriate column on the board as you proceed.

Checking your listener understands	Adding more detail	Asking for clarification or repetition
1 *Do you get what I mean?* 4 *Does that make sense?*	6 *To be precise, ...* 8 *What I mean is, ...*	2 *What do you mean by ... ?* 3 *What's ... exactly?* 5 *When you say ..., do you mean ...?* 7 *Sorry, did you say ... ?*

b   👥 / 👥👥 Learners match eight more expressions to the correct groups.

Again, go through the answers as a class, writing each expression in the appropriate column.

Checking your listener understands *Am I making any sense?* *Is that clear?* *Do you follow me?* *Do you see?*	Adding more details *To be more specific, ...* *In fact, ...*	Asking for clarification or repetition *Can you go over that again?* *Can you run that past me again?*

4   a   👤 *Preparation.* Learners choose one of the situations given (or think of their own) and plan what to say. Learners should make notes but should not try to plan out what they want to say in full. Encourage learners to choose expressions for *Checking your listener understands* and *Adding more details* to use during their explanations.

b   👥 *Practice.* Learners listen to each other's explanations. Emphasise that it's the responsibility of *both* learners to make sure the explanations are understood, the speaker by checking understanding and adding more details, the listener by asking for clarification or repetition whenever necessary.

Optional extra: Task repetition

Learners change pairs and practise giving their explanations a second time. Learners' explanations are likely to be significantly more fluent and coherent, allowing them to focus more attention on making sure their partner is following what they say.

5   👥 *Practice.* Learners get into new pairs and tell each other what they heard from their partner in **4b**.

9 Look again

Review

VOCABULARY Describing responsibilities

1   a   👥 / 👥👥 Learners complete the sentences 1–6 with expressions for describing people's responsibilities. Explain that different answers are possible.

> 1 *is responsible for / 's main task is / 's duties include*
> 2 *is accountable to / answers to / reports to*
> 3 *is in charge of / manages / oversees / supervises*
> 4 *up to*
> 5 *task / duty / responsibility*
> 6 *duties / responsibilities / tasks*

b   👥 Learners choose one of the occupations listed and decide how to describe its responsibilities, using expressions from **a**.

c   👥👥 Pairs listen to each other's descriptions and say whether they agree or whether they think any important points are missing.

GRAMMAR Verbs with adverbs and prepositions 1

2 a 👤 Learners complete the extracts by adding the words in brackets in the correct place. Remind learners that, with some verbs, the adverb can go in two places. As an example, put extract 1 on the board and ask learners what are the two possible places where *over* can be added:

Please don't turn <u>over</u> the page until I tell you. / turn the page <u>over</u>

👥 / 👥👥 Learners compare their answers, then check as a class.

> 1 Please don't turn <u>over</u> the page / turn the page <u>over</u> until I tell you to.
> 2 NOTE: attach a recent photograph <u>to</u> your completed application ...
> 3 The prime minister has put <u>together</u> a new team / put a new team <u>together</u> ...
> 4 Have you seen Neil today? He's cut <u>off</u> all his hair! / cut all his hair <u>off</u>!
> 5 Pour the water <u>into</u> a saucepan. Add the tomatoes, green peppers and garlic.
> 6 Stacey, will you put the milk <u>in</u> the fridge, please?

b 👥 / 👥👥 Learners suggest where they could see or hear each extract.

Then they compare their suggestions with those on p121.

Round-up. Ask learners if any of their suggestions were very different from those in the book.

CAN YOU REMEMBER? Unit 8 – Strong feelings

> **Optional lead-in: What's the word?**
>
> *Books closed.* Spell out the words in the box, pausing briefly between each letter: *A–P–P–... .* When learners think they know what the word is, they shout it out: *appalled!* If they're correct, write the word up on the board.

3 a 👤 Learners complete the questions as they wish by choosing words from the box.

b 👥 / 👥👥 Learners ask and answer their questions.

Extension

SPELLING AND SOUNDS /ʊ/

4 a 👥 / 👥👥 Learners read through the words together and underline the letters in each word which correspond to the sound /ʊ/.

Then check as a class, writing the words up on the board and underlining the appropriate parts.

> c<u>oo</u>kery, c<u>ou</u>ld, f<u>u</u>lly, g<u>oo</u>ds, guideb<u>oo</u>k, likelih<u>oo</u>d, p<u>u</u>ll, p<u>u</u>sh, sh<u>ou</u>ld, w<u>ou</u>ld

b 👥 / 👥👥 Learners answer the questions 1–3, using the words in a to help them.

> 1 oo   2 u   3 oul

> **Language note**
>
> An alternative but slightly more complicated analysis for question 3 is that the letters *ou* represent the /ʊ/ sound, while the letter *l* is silent.

c 👤 *Spellcheck.* Play recording 3.8. Learners listen to the 12 words and write them down.

👥 / 👥👥 They compare their spelling of the 12 words, then look at script 3.8 on p153 to check.

NOTICE *big* and *high*

5 a 👥 / 👥👥 Learners choose the correct adjective, *big* or *high*, in each sentence.

Compare answers as a class, then find the original sentences in the article *The Camera Crew* on p72 to check.

> 1 big   2 big-   3 high

b 👥 / 👥👥 Learners choose *big* or *high* to complete the topics 1–6.

> 1 big   2 high   3 high   4 high   5 big
> 6 high ('big' is possible, but 'high' is much more common)

c 👥 / 👥👥 Learners choose topics from 1–6 in b to ask each other about. Demonstrate by asking a few learners *Can you tell me about ... ?* + one of the topics and inviting them to ask you questions in return.

Self-assessment

To help focus learners on the self-assessment, you could read it through, giving a few examples of the language they have learned in each section (or asking learners to tell you). Then ask them to circle the numbers on each line.

Unit 9 Extra activities on the Teacher's DVD-ROM

Printable worksheets, activity instructions and answer keys are on your Teacher's DVD-ROM.

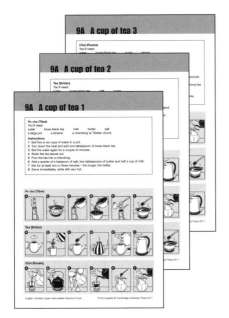

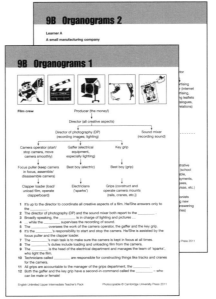

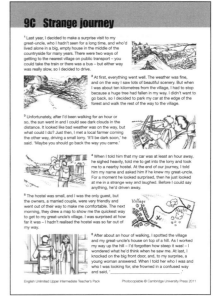

9A A cup of tea

Activity type: Reading and speaking – Completing descriptions – Groups

Aim: To practise describing a process

Language: Organising a description – Use at any point from 9.1.

Preparation: Make one copy each of Worksheets 1–3 for every three learners.

Time: 25 minutes

9B Organograms

Activity type: Writing and reading – Drawing game – Individuals/Pairs

Aim: To practise describing hierarchies and responsibilities

Language: Describing responsibilities – Use at any point from 9.2.

Preparation: Make one copy of Worksheet 1 for each learner. Make one copy of Worksheet 2 for each pair of learners. Cut up Worksheet 2 to make two organograms.

Time: 30 minutes

9C Strange journey

Activity type: Reading, speaking and listening – Story-telling – Pairs / Whole class

Aim: To practise using expressions with *way* in a narrative context

Language: Expressions with *way* – Use at any point from Keyword: *way*, p75.

Preparation: Make a copy of the worksheet for each learner.

Time: 45 minutes

Unit 9 Self-study Pack

In the Workbook

Unit 9 of the *English Unlimited Upper Intermediate Workbook* offers additional ways to practise the vocabulary and grammar taught in the Coursebook. There are also activities which build reading and writing skills and two whole pages of listening and speaking tasks to use with the Documentary video, giving your learners the opportunity to hear and react to authentic spoken English.

- **Vocabulary:** Organising a description; Describing responsibilities; Describing roles; Organising a talk
- **Grammar:** Verbs with adverbs and prepositions 1
- **Explore writing:** A handover note
- **Documentary:** The human rights lawyer

On the DVD-ROM

Unit 9 of the *English Unlimited Upper Intermediate Self-study DVD-ROM* contains interactive games and activities for your learners to practise and improve their vocabulary, grammar and pronunciation, and also their speaking and listening, with the possibility for learners to record themselves, and a video of authentic spoken English to use with the Workbook.

- **Vocabulary and grammar:** Extra practice activities
- **Pronunciation:** Stress in multi-word verbs
- **Explore speaking:** Answering *Yes/No* questions without using *Yes* or *No*
- **Listening:** A future career?
- **Video:** Documentary – The human rights lawyer

Discovery

10.1

Goals: talk about exploration and discovery
explain the benefits of something

Core language:

VOCABULARY	Exploration and discovery
VOCABULARY	Describing benefits
PRONUNCIATION	Stress in compounds

Frontiers

VOCABULARY Exploration and discovery

1 👥/👥 Learners look at the four pictures, read the captions, then discuss what they think people are trying to find, or find out, by using each of the machines. Elicit a few of their ideas afterwards.

2 a 👤/👥 Learners look at the pairs of highlighted expressions and match each one with the most likely ending.

> 3 a 4 b 5 b 6 a 7 b 8 a 9 a 10 b

  b 👥/👥 Learners discuss what they think the difference is between the expressions within each pair. After a while, ask for their ideas. If more clarification is needed, you can use these dictionary definitions.

> *explore = go around a new place to find out what's there*
> *discover = find something*
> *scan = look around an area to try to find something*
> *detect = discover or notice something, especially something that's difficult to see, hear, etc.*
> *map = make a map of a particular area of land*
> *locate = find the exact position of something or someone*
> *search for = try to find something or someone*
> *do research into = study a subject in detail in order to discover new information about it*
> *find evidence of = discover something that makes you believe something is true or exists*
> *reach = arrive somewhere*

3 👥 Learners look at the pictures at the beginning of the unit again and talk about them. They can include some of the ideas they came up with in **1**, but they use the new expressions from **2a**.

Alternative

To give learners more to talk about in **3**, bring in various pictures (e.g. from the Internet) of machines used in exploration of the Earth and space to add to the four at the beginning of the unit. For instance, pictures of a volcano robot (*Dante, Dante II*), a weather balloon, an oil or rock drill, a satellite, a radio telescope and so on. Learners discuss what they think people are trying to find, or find out, with each of the machines.

READING

4 a 👥/👥 *Prediction.* Learners read the six statements about exploration of the deep sea, and discuss together whether they think they're true or false.

  b *Reading for main idea.* Learners read the article quickly to check their ideas from **a**.

> 1 True 2 False 3 False 4 False 5 True 6 False

5 *Reading for detail.* As the article is largely an opinion piece, learners focus on identifying what the writer, Frank Pope, thinks.

> 1 It's difficult to explore because of the darkness and pressure. That makes ocean research very expensive. Governments tend to spend the money on space exploration instead of ocean exploration.
> 2 To find evidence of other life forms, to help us look at the Earth with a global perspective, to understand the history of the universe
> 3 To find new species (including mysterious huge ones), to search for clues to the origin of life, to get new sources of food, drugs and energy

6 👥/👥 *Responding to the text.* Learners discuss the questions together.

Round-up. Afterwards, ask a few what they discussed and see if there's a general consensus.

 You could use photocopiable activity 10A on the Teacher's DVD-ROM at this point.

They're absolutely vital for …

VOCABULARY Describing benefits

1 👤/👥 Learners sort the ten words and expressions into the three patterns illustrated in sentences 1–3. Pattern 1 is followed by *to* + infinitive, pattern 2 is followed by *for* + *-ing* form or noun, and pattern 3 is followed by a noun.

> 1 allow us, enable us, give us the ability
> 2 crucial, essential, vital
> 3 benefit, improve, be of (considerable) benefit to, have a positive effect on

2 👥 *Practice, Preparation for discussion.* Learners work in pairs and choose four things they think are the most important to do in the next 50 years. They can also use their own ideas. They write sentences in their pairs, using useful expressions from **1**. These sentences will form the basis for the Speaking in **4**. Monitor and correct at this stage before Pronunciation and Speaking.

PRONUNCIATION Stress in compounds

3 a Play recording **3.9** while learners listen and underline which word in each compound has the main stress.

> <u>space</u> probes, the deep <u>ocean</u>, nuclear <u>power</u>, <u>power</u> stations

  b 👤/👥 Based on what they underlined in **a**, learners answer the two questions.

> 1 the first 2 the second

  c 👤/👥 Learners decide where the main stress goes in four more compounds.

d Play recording **3.10** so learners can check their answers.

> *heart* disease, global *warming*, *climate* change, alternative *energy*

Then they practise saying all eight compounds, using the correct stress.

Learners will have the chance to practise this feature of pronunciation in the Speaking task that follows. At this stage, they may want to check the sentences they wrote in **2** for compounds and make sure they know how to stress them correctly.

SPEAKING

4 👥 Put learners into new pairs, that is, with different partners from the one they worked with in **2** above. Each learner says which four things they chose in **2** and explains their choices. Then, as a pair, they make a final list of the four most important things for the human race to do in the next 50 years.

Round-up. Each pair tells the class the four things they chose and explains why they chose them. As a class, identify which are the top two or three most popular choices.

 You could use photocopiable activity 10B on the Teacher's DVD-ROM at this point.

10.2

Goals: describe important issues and priorities
talk about dedicated people and their achievements

Core language:

GRAMMAR	Using the *-ing* form
VOCABULARY	Achievements

Priorities

READING

1 👥 Learners look at the photo of the panda (you can bring in more if you wish) and get them to discuss in groups what words and ideas they associate with that animal, e.g. *endangered, cute, eats bamboo, lives in China.* Find out their ideas after a while and get them to explain them.

2 a 👥 *Prediction.* Learners discuss which of the listed things they think are, or have been, a problem for the panda and in what way.

b *Reading for main idea.* Learners read the interview, check their ideas from **a** and note down what Lu Zhi says or implies about each of the topics.

> All of them are, or have been, a problem except for tree planting.
> Farming: *Farmers are more worried about paying their bills than conservation and pandas. Lu Zhi implies they're destroying the pandas' environment to get more farming land.*
> Government policies: *It's hard to change government attitude and behaviour. Local government worries about jobs and education. Lu Zhi implies it is more concerned about people than pandas and conservation.*
> Logging: *They cut down trees and destroy the pandas' environment.*
> Tree planting: *Logging companies have begun to plant trees, benefiting the panda.*
> Road building: *It destroys the pandas' environment.*
> Tourism: *It's increasing, so more roads and facilities are needed for tourists. This causes more habitat destruction. Lu Zhi implies that more tourists will go to see the pandas, which may disturb their lives – unless the nature of tourism changes.*

3 *Reading for detail.* Learners read the article again and answer 1–3.

> 1 She liked field work and wanted to work outside of a lab. The more she learned about pandas, the more she wanted to help them.
> 2 She thinks you have to understand people's feelings and the situations they're in. That helps you come up with solutions. Complaining and scolding doesn't work.
> 3 She saw how her professor convinced the government to create a new reserve. After that, the government stopped commercial logging in western China and gave the loggers money to plant trees. She realised things can change.

4 👥 / 👥 *Responding to the text.* Learners discuss the questions.

Round-up. Afterwards, find out if they agree with each other and if not, what their reasons are.

GRAMMAR Using the *-ing* form

5 👤 / 👥 This is revision and consolidation of the main uses of the *-ing* form. Learners read the information about the different uses of the *-ing* form and match each use to a highlighted word 1–6 in Lu Zhi's interview.

> a 3   b 2   c 1   d 6   e 5   f 4

6 👤 *Practice, Preparation for discussion.* Learners work alone and complete the sentences with their own ideas. The context is different kinds of issues and priorities. Encourage them to use *-ing* forms where possible. The sentences will be used as the basis for **7**.

Note: Grammar practice

You could do the grammar practice on p138 at this point.

SPEAKING

7 👥 *Discussion.* Learners read their sentences to each other. Encourage them to just glance at the sentences and say them to each other if possible. They compare their ideas and find out how similar, or different, they are.

Round-up. Get someone from each group to summarise the main similarities, and another person from each group to summarise the main differences about priorities in their group. The other groups can listen and ask questions to find out more.

Life's work

VOCABULARY Achievements

1 👤/👥 Learners complete the highlighted expressions in the sentences with the words in the box.

> | 1 top   2 made   3 won   4 dedicated   5 used   6 faced
> | 7 changed   8 worked   9 showed   10 greatest

Get learners to identify which expressions are used in the present perfect to summarise various achievements in her life (*2, 3, 4, 5, 6, 7*).

2 👤 *Practice, Preparation for discussion.* Each learner thinks of someone they feel is very dedicated and has achieved a lot. They can get ideas from the four prompts. Once they've chosen someone, they gather their ideas and write four or five sentences describing the person's most important achievements. They choose expressions from **1** that suit their description. These sentences form the basis for discussion in **3**. Monitor and correct their sentences before the Speaking.

SPEAKING

3 👥 Learners tell each other about the people they chose. The others listen and ask questions to find out more. Afterwards, they decide together what they think each person's greatest accomplishment was. Then they decide who has probably had the biggest impact on people's lives today, and explain why.

Round-up. Each group reports to the class the results of their discussion and explains their decisions.

Alternative

The Speaking task **3** can be done as a mingle, where learners move freely around the class and tell each other about the people they chose. When they sit down, get a few to tell you about one of the people they heard about.

Optional extra

As homework, learners can write a small paragraph about the person they chose, in order to get further written practice of the expressions in **1**. They may wish to do a little research on the Internet and include a few more details in their paragraph.

 You could use photocopiable activity 10C on the Teacher's DVD-ROM at this point.

10.3 Target activity

Goals: talk about exploration and discovery ♻
talk about dedicated people and their achievements ♻
summarise information from different sources

Core language:

TASK VOCABULARY   Giving and comparing sources
10.1 VOCABULARY   Exploration and discovery
10.2 VOCABULARY   Achievements

Choose a subject for a documentary

TASK LISTENING

1 👥/👥 Learners look at the pictures and share information and ideas. The main objective here is to give them a chance to contribute information if they know something and to raise awareness of and interest in the people.

2 *Listening for main idea.* Play recording **3.11** while learners number the four places in the order Leif Eriksson visited them.

> | Labrador 3   Baffin Island 2   Vinland 4   Norway 1

3 *Listening for detail.* Give learners a chance to read the six questions. Then play recording **3.11** again while they note down their answers.

> 1 Around 970 or 975
> 2 He was blown there by a storm OR he followed the route of an earlier explorer and arrived there.
> 3 35
> 4 Very pleasant, with a mild climate, green grass, wild grapes, rivers, salmon
> 5 About 1020
> 6 The northern tip of Newfoundland in Canada

TASK VOCABULARY Giving and comparing sources

4 👤/👥 Learners find an expression in the box that has a similar meaning to each underlined expression in sentences 1–7. They then read script **3.11** on p153 to check their answers.

> 1 who you ask   2 According to   3 claim   4 mentions
> 5 make no mention of   6 are in agreement   7 vary

Optional extra

At this point, learners can take turns testing each other on the expressions in A/B pairs. Learner A reads sentences 1–7 and B gives the replacement expressions:
A *Depending on where you look, he was born around 970 or 975.*
B *Depending on who you ask, he was born around 970 or 975.*
After A has read all seven sentences, B reads the sentences with the expressions in the box and A gives the original expressions:
B *Depending on who you ask, he was …*
A *Depending on where you look, he was …*

TASK

5 a *Reading.* Explain to learners that they are going to research the other three explorers in the pictures in order to decide which one would make the best subject for a TV documentary: Uemura, Tereshkova or Villas Boas. Divide learners into groups of three and give each learner within each group a letter: A, B or C.

👤 Each learner reads their two respective articles about their explorer and makes notes of key points and facts. They should also make notes of any differences in facts, or new details, in the articles.

b 👤 *Preparation for summaries and discussion.* Each learner plans how to summarise the main points of their article to their group. They should choose expressions from **4** and they can also use expressions from earlier in the unit: VOCABULARY Exploration and discovery and VOCABULARY Achievements.

c 👥 *Summaries and discussion.* In their groups, learners A–C take turns giving summaries of their articles to the other group members. When they've finished, they discuss which one of the three would make the best subject for a TV documentary, make a decision and justify their choice.

6   👥 Each group reports which explorer they decided on, and explains why they chose him or her.

Round-up. Find out which was the most popular choice for the documentary. Find out which facts learners felt were most interesting about each of the three explorers.

10 Explore

Across cultures: Rights and obligations

Goal: to make learners aware of various rights and obligations in different cultures

Core language:

Rights and obligations: *have the right to; are obliged to; are expected to; are free to; is our duty to; have the option of; is compulsory to; have the freedom to*

LISTENING

1   👤/👥 *Listening for main idea.* To introduce the topic, write on the board *a right* and *an obligation*. Ask learners to discuss the difference in meaning. Elicit their ideas. If more clarification is needed, you can use these dictionary definitions.

> *right: something that the law allows you to do*
> *obligation: something that you do because it is your duty or because you feel you have to*

👤 Get learners to look at the pictures and read the captions. Give them time to read the two questions. Then play recording **3.12**.

> 1 Gavin: the right to roam (in England)
>   Hikari: taking care of her apartment building (in Japan)
>   Ryan: voting (in Australia)
> 2 a Hikari, Ryan   b Gavin

2   *Listening for detail.* Give learners the chance to read the nine questions. Then play recording **3.12** again. The answers are in the same order as the recording.

> 1 Hikers and walkers can walk on public or privately owned land in the countryside.
> 2 In people's gardens or special hunting and fishing areas
> 3 Close all gates carefully, don't drop litter, don't disturb the animals, don't damage plants.
> 4 The grounds and pavements around the building and the children's play area in the back
> 5 Various common expenses, like stair lights
> 6 It's not much trouble, it gives them a chance to chat.
> 7 About 95% of registered voters
> 8 You have to explain why not. If your explanation is not good, you may have to pay a small fine.
> 9 Because election results reflect the wishes of almost everyone, not just a few.

3   👥/👥 *Responding to the text.* Learners give their opinions about what the three people said. Get class feedback afterwards to find out what they think. Are the three situations different from what happens in their own country?

VOCABULARY Rights and obligations

4   👤/👥 Learners sort the expressions from the recording into two groups.

> *rights: 1, 4, 6, 8*
> *obligations: 2, 3, 5, 7*

All the expressions are followed by an infinitive without *to* except for *have the option of*, which is followed by an *-ing* form.

5   👤 *Practice, Preparation for discussion.* Each learner, working alone, chooses four or five of the topics in the list and plans how to answer the questions about them. Encourage them to make notes, choosing useful expressions from **4** for each topic.

SPEAKING

6 a 👥 *Discussion.* In groups, learners discuss and compare their ideas from **5**.

  b 👥 Learners reflect on how seriously people take these rights and obligations. For instance, people nowadays may be more relaxed about fulfilling certain obligations compared with their parents' or grandparents' generation.

7   👥 Learners add information on rights and obligations in other countries or cultures, based on experience or general knowledge.

Explore writing

Goal: write a summary of a text

> **Note**
>
> Learners did a spoken summary in Target activity 10.3, Task 5 on page 82. This is its counterpart, a more concise written summary.

1   👥/👥 To introduce the topic, learners read the short paragraph about SETI and discuss the questions.

2 a 👥/👥 *Prediction.* Learners discuss together how a director of the SETI Institute might answer the two questions.

  b *Reading for main idea.* Learners quickly read the interview to find the answers to the questions in **a**.

> 1 First, make sure it isn't a hoax by getting an independent confirmation. Then tell the world.
> 2 Not immediately. First there has to be global consensus about what to say.

3 a *Reading for detail.* Learners read both summaries. They also read the main article again in detail to check whether the summaries have picked up the main points. They answer the questions.

> Version B. It's clear and easy to understand. It presents the main points. It has good linking expressions ('first', 'then', 'however').

  b 👤/👥 Learners go through points 1–6 and check whether the summaries in **a** match or fail to match each point.

Alternative for weaker classes

Do the first point together as a class. Ask them which summary is easy to understand and why. Then allow them to continue on their own.

4 a *Preparation for writing.* Learners work alone and reread the article *Forget space travel. The ocean is our final frontier* on pp78–9. Since they've read it before, they should be familiar with the content and vocabulary. Learners make notes of the main points in the article, then compare their ideas with a partner. At this point, they can eliminate points or words that are not necessary and add ones that are. Monitor and make sure they've identified most of the main points. Get them to think of how to express the main points in their own words.

b *Writing.* Learners write a summary of the article in about 100 words.

Alternative

Learners write their summaries at home and bring them in the next day for **5**.

5 Learners exchange summaries with a partner and read them, checking they've followed the points in **3b**. If they feel a little more work is needed, they discuss those points and improve their summaries together.

6 Finally, they compare their summaries with an example summary on p121 to see whether they included the same points. Note that this is an example summary, meaning that learners can create a summary that is worded a bit differently but picks up roughly the same points. It doesn't have to be exactly the same.

10 Look again

Review

VOCABULARY Exploration and discovery

1 a Learners complete the underlined words with vowels.

> 1 done research into   2 exploring   3 searched for
> 4 locate   5 discovered   6 reached

b Learners ask and answer the six questions. Encourage them to ask follow-up questions.

c Each group reports to the class the three most interesting answers from the group.

GRAMMAR Uses of the *-ing* form

2 a Learners read the paragraph. They find nine words that should be *-ing* forms but aren't (they're mistakes) and correct them. Then they compare their answers with a partner.

> Today, only about 1,600 giant pandas are still living in the wild in central China. Farming, logging and other changes have driven them out of the lowlands where they once lived.
> Giant pandas weigh up to 115kg and can be almost a metre high at the shoulder. Although people think these slow-moving, black and white animals are charming, they can be dangerous.
> Pandas usually eat while sitting up. Their large teeth and strong jaws are perfect for crushing the tough bamboo stems. To get enough nutrition, pandas must eat between 9 and 18kg of bamboo every day. This means that more than half their day involves searching for food and eating.

b Learners recall the different uses of the *-ing* form they learned in this unit. After a few minutes, they can check on p81. They then match the (corrected) *-ing* forms in the paragraph in **a** with the uses of the *-ing* form on p81.

> living: part of a progressive verb form ('are living')
> farming, logging: as the subject in a sentence
> slow-moving, charming: as adjectives
> sitting: after a time linker ('while')
> crushing: after prepositions ('for', 'to')
> searching, eating: after certain verbs ('involve')

CAN YOU REMEMBER? Unit 9 – Describing roles

3 a Learners read the paragraph about Martine and complete the highlighted expressions with the words in the box.

> 1 as   2 of   3 as   4 in   5 to   6 for   7 of   8 of

b *Writing.* Learners write a paragraph similar to the one in **a** about someone they know or know about (e.g. a famous person). They choose expressions from **a** which suit their topic.

Optional extra

Learners read each other's paragraphs in pairs and ask questions to find out more. Then they get into new pairs and tell their new partner what their first partner's paragraph said.

Extension

SPELLING AND SOUNDS /eɪ/

4 a Learners underline the letters that make an /eɪ/ sound.

> alien, complain, obey, failure, they, yesterday, exploration, runway

b Learners match each word in **a** with the spelling patterns 1–3.

> *1 alien   2 complain, failure, exploration*
> *3 obey, they, yesterday, runway*

c 👤/👥 Learners complete the spelling, then check in a dictionary. Alternatively, you can elicit the spelling and write the words on the board.

> *ancient, available, education, survey, break, faithful, aid,*
> *neighbour, ashtray, brain, essay, railway*

Optional extra

In pairs, learners take turns to test each other's spelling of the words in **4a** and **4c**.

NOTICE Adjectives with *something*, *anybody*, etc.

5 a 👤/👥 Learners read the sentence and complete the explanation. They then brainstorm more words like *something* and *anybody*.

> *1 before; after*
> *2 Answers can include:*
> *anything, nothing, somebody, nobody, someone,*
> *anyone, no one, somewhere, anywhere, nowhere,*
> *someplace*

Language note

The usual spelling of *no one* is two words with no hyphen.

---

b 👤 Learners change the underlined words in questions 1–3 to extend the total number of questions to six.

> *Possible answers*
> *1 somewhere cheap but good to eat, somewhere fun to*
> *visit nearby, somewhere relaxing to be in …*
> *2 somebody interesting to talk to, somebody fascinating*
> *to know, somebody knowledgeable about computers*
> *3 something useful to remember when travelling,*
> *something funny you heard recently, something*
> *important you discovered when learning another*
> *language*

c 👥/👥👥 Learners ask and answer questions 1–3, as well as the three new ones they made.

Self-assessment

To help focus learners on the self-assessment, read it through and get learners to give you a few examples of the language they have learned in each section. Give an example to start them off if necessary. Then learners circle the numbers on each line.

Unit 10 Extra activities on the Teacher's DVD-ROM

Printable worksheets, activity instructions and answer keys are on your Teacher's DVD-ROM.

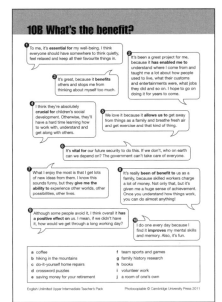

10A Important 'firsts'

Activity type: Speaking – Quiz – Pairs / Groups / Whole class

Aim: To complete and take part in a quiz on exploration, discovery and invention

Language: Exploration and discovery – Use at any point from 10.1.

Preparation: Make one copy of the worksheet for every pair.

Time: 35 minutes

10B What's the benefit?

Activity type: Reading and speaking – Discussing benefits – Individuals/Mingle

Aim: To talk about how important certain aspects of life are to you, and why

Language: Describing benefits – Use at any point from 10.1.

Preparation: Make one copy of the worksheet for each learner.

Time: 30 minutes

10C Some thoughts

Activity type: Writing and speaking – Matching and summarising – Pairs/Mingle

Aim: To write and talk about 'thoughts for the day' using the -ing form

Language: Using the -ing form – Use at any point from 10.2.

Preparation: Make one copy of the worksheet for every pair. Cut up the worksheet to make a set of 24 cards. Mix up all the cards in each set thoroughly. Make an extra copy of the worksheet to use as an answer key.

Time: 35 minutes

Unit 10 Self-study Pack

In the Workbook

Unit 10 of the *English Unlimited Upper Intermediate Workbook* offers additional ways to practise the vocabulary and grammar taught in the Coursebook. There are also activities which build reading and writing skills and a whole page of listening and speaking tasks to use with the Interview video, giving your learners the opportunity to hear and react to authentic spoken English.

- **Vocabulary:** Exploration and discovery; Describing benefits; Achievements; Giving and comparing sources; Rights and obligations
- **Grammar:** Using the -ing form
- **Explore reading:** Article: Space exploration volunteers wanted
- **Interview:** Environmental issues – Liu and Adriana

On the DVD-ROM

Unit 10 of the *English Unlimited Upper Intermediate Self-study DVD-ROM* contains interactive games and activities for your learners to practise and improve their vocabulary, grammar and pronunciation, and also their speaking and listening, with the possibility for learners to record themselves, and a video of authentic spoken English to use with the Workbook.

- **Vocabulary and grammar:** Extra practice activities
- **Pronunciation:** Stress in compounds
- **Explore speaking:** *anyway*
- **Listening:** Dedicated people and their achievements
- **Video:** Environmental issues

Questions, questions

11.1

Goals: describe people skills
carry out an interview

Core language:

VOCABULARY	Expressions with *people*
VOCABULARY	Interviewing
PRONUNCIATION	Prominent words 2

Interview with an interviewer

LISTENING

1 👥 / 👥👥 Learners discuss the four questions about interviewers in the media.

> **Alternative for monolingual classes**
>
> Discuss question 1 as a class and elicit a list of interviewers onto the board. Then put learners in pairs or groups to discuss the remaining three questions.

To round off the discussion, ask some pairs or groups to tell the class their opinions about question 4 (*What makes a good interviewer?*).

2 a 👥 / 👥👥 *Prediction.* Draw learners' attention to the photograph of Andie and Antonia and read through the caption. Then give learners time to read through the questions 1–7 and discuss what the answers could be.

   b *Listening for detail.* Play recording **3.13**. Learners listen and make notes on the answers to the questions.

> 1 His family were against the idea.
> 2 He knows how to deal with people.
> 3 A wide variety, e.g. politicians, listeners, health experts
> 4 He's interested in people and their opinions. He's also interested in current affairs and politics. He enjoys the variety of his work.
> 5 He does almost no preparation. He quickly decides on an opening question.
> 6 He simply carries on. He doesn't give up.
> 7 He doesn't have much to do with the actual interview, but may sometimes suggest questions.

3 a *Listening for detail.* Give learners time to compare their notes in pairs or groups. Then play recording **3.13** again. Learners check their notes and add as much detail as they can.

   b Learners look at script **3.13** on p154 to check their notes and read any parts of the interview which they found difficult to follow. Monitor closely during this stage and be ready to answer any queries learners may have about the content of the interview.

4 👥 / 👥👥 *Discussion.* Learners discuss the two questions.

   Round-up. Identify one or two learners who think they know someone who would make a really good radio interviewer and ask them to tell the class about it.

VOCABULARY Expressions with *people*

5 👥 / 👥👥 *Presentation.* Learners decide whether Andie said a) or b) in each pair of expressions, and discuss how each pair differs in meaning.

> 1 Andie says a. 'Handle' simply means 'deal with' or 'work with'. 'Manipulate' suggests controlling people's behaviour in a way which is dishonest or immoral.
> 2 Andie says a. If you 'get the best out of' people, you make them behave or perform in the best way possible. If you 'bring out the worst in' people, you make them behave badly. Also, 'get the best out of' suggests a skill which you can use deliberately, while 'bring out the worst in' describes an unconscious effect on other people.
> 3 Andie says b. 'Put people on edge' = 'make people nervous'; 'put people at ease' = 'make them relaxed'
> 4 Andie says a. 'Clam up' = 'stop talking because you are nervous or afraid'

> **Optional extra**
>
> Tell the class about people from your own experience (people you know, people you used to know, people you've met), each with a different attribute from **5**. For each person, write a simple sentence on the board using an expression from **5**:
> - *I used to have a boss who was very good at* <u>manipulating</u> *people.*
> - *My old chemistry teacher really knew how to* <u>get the best out of</u> *us.*
>
> Working alone, learners write similar sentences about people from their lives. Then they listen to each other's sentences in pairs or groups and ask questions to find out more about the people and their attributes.

SPEAKING

6 a 👥 *Discussion.* Learners decide on a list of three or four professions where good people skills are required. They talk about exactly what kind of people skills are required in each case. Encourage them to choose appropriate expressions from **5**.

   b 👥👥 Put pairs together to make groups of four. Learners tell each other about their ideas from **a**.

> **Alternative for smaller classes**
>
> Instead of making groups of four, ask learners to get into new pairs and tell each other about the discussion they had with their previous partner.

Is that right?

VOCABULARY Interviewing

1 a *Presentation.* Write items a–d on the board. As a class, look at the highlighted expressions in the four speech bubbles. Elicit which expressions 1–4 belong under which headings and write them on the board.

> a 1　b 3　c 2　d 4

   b 👥 / 👥👥 Learners look at expressions 5–12 and match them with the headings a–d. Then check as a class. Elicit which expressions belong under which headings and write them on the board.

> a 5, 11　b 6, 12　c 7, 9　d 8, 10

Language note

Draw learners' attention to the two useful discourse patterns which are exemplified by the speech bubbles in **1b**:
- pick up something said earlier *then* ask for more detail
- give a summary or interpretation *then* check that it's true.

2 a *Practice.* Learners choose one of the topics from the list (or a topic of their own) and prepare to talk about it briefly (for no more than a couple of minutes). They may make notes if they wish, but should not write out what they are going to say in full.

b Learners listen to each other and use expressions from **1** to develop conversations. Demonstrate this by choosing one of your more confident learners and having a conversation with them on their chosen topic in front of the class.

PRONUNCIATION Prominent words 2

3 a *Review.* Play recording **3.14**. Learners listen while reading the sentences, and repeat. Point out how:
- the speaker uses groups of words (introduced in Units 5 and 6) to make her speech easier to follow;
- she chooses one key word in each group of words to have prominence (introduced in Unit 8).

b *Practice.* Learners look at the other three speech bubbles in **1b** and decide how they would divide the speech into groups of words and where they would use prominence. Emphasise that there are no strictly right or wrong answers; the important thing is to make groups of words which belong together logically and give prominence to key words so that your message is easier for people to understand.

> *Possible answers*
> *// You SEEM to be saying // that it's best NOT to plan too much. // Have I got that RIGHT? //*
> *// BAsically, // the producer ISn't very involved in the interview. // Am I RIGHT? //*
> *// You said something about being offered a JOB // on pirate RAdio. // Tell me MORE about that. //*

c Put pairs together to make groups of four, or put learners into new pairs, to compare the ways in which they've used groups of words and prominence.

SPEAKING

4 a *Preparation for interview.* Tell learners they're going to be interviewed, but that they will be able to choose what topic they're interviewed about and what kinds of question they'll be asked. On a piece of paper, learners write down their chosen topic and three questions they'd like to be asked.

b Learners then exchange papers with a partner and add two more questions: one to open the interview and one other.

5 *Interview.* Learners number the questions in the (provisional) order they'd like to ask them. They interview each other about their chosen topics, using the questions on their papers as starting points and using expressions from **1** to develop the interview, clarify points, get more details, etc.

6 *Round-up.* Learners get into new pairs and report on the interviews they've just carried out: what did they learn, and do they think they got the best out of their interviewee?

 You could use photocopiable activity 11A on the Teacher's DVD-ROM at this point.

11.2

Goal: report what people say
Core language:

VOCABULARY	Reporting verbs
GRAMMAR	Patterns after verbs

Unusual behaviour

READING

1 a *Pre-reading discussion.* Learners imagine they're giving advice to someone attending their first-ever job interview and make a list of 'dos and don'ts'.

b Elicit each pair/group's ideas and write them on the board to make a class list of 'dos and don'ts'. As you elicit each point, invite learners to say whether or not they agree with it. If they disagree, ask them to suggest how it should be changed.

2 *Prediction.* Ask learners to cover the main part of the article. Learners read the introduction only, then guess what kinds of 'unusual behaviour' might be described in the rest of the article.

Ask a few pairs/groups to tell the class about their ideas.

3 *Reading for main ideas.* Learners read the rest of the article. They decide which one (or two or three) of the examples of unusual behaviour they find most difficult to believe.

Learners compare their ideas.

4 a *Reading for interpretation.* Learners read again and decide which of the applicants (if any) they would describe in the ways listed.

b Learners compare their ideas.

Round-up. Read out the suggested answers below, explaining that these represent just one possible way of interpreting the article. Learners listen and say whether or not they agree, and why.

> *Suggested answers*
> *desperate to get the job: 7, 8, 9, 10*
> *over-confident: 1, 2, 5, 15*
> *aggressive: 1, 4, 5, 9*

SPEAKING

5 *Discussion.* Learners discuss the four questions.

He challenged me to …

VOCABULARY Reporting verbs

1 / *Presentation.* Learners choose verbs from the box to replace the underlined parts of the sentences (= focus on meaning), making changes to the forms of the sentences as necessary (= focus on form). Then they check their answers by looking back in the article and finding the original sentences.

> 3 She <u>complained (that)</u> she hadn't had lunch.
> 4 He <u>promised to</u> have the corporate logo tattooed on his forearm.
> 5 The therapist <u>advised him to</u> ignore the question I'd just asked.
> 6 She <u>refused to</u> get out of the chair.
> 7 She <u>threatened to</u> stay in my office until I hired her.
> 8 He <u>apologised</u> for the interruption.
> 9 A candidate <u>thanked</u> me for seeing him.
> 10 He <u>admitted (that)</u> he didn't want a job.

2 *Memorisation.* Learner A (book open) says one of the original sentences in **1**. Learner B (book closed) gives the equivalent sentence using a verb from the box. Then they swap roles.

GRAMMAR Patterns after verbs

3 / *Presentation.* Learners read the information in the box. Emphasise that there are no simple rules governing verb patterns, so the patterns associated with each verb simply have to be learned. Two good ways of doing this are: 1) getting into the habit of noticing patterns in things you read (or perhaps hear); 2) checking patterns in dictionaries, particularly when writing.

Learners match the sentences they wrote in **1** with the six patterns a–f.

> a 1, 3, 7
> b –
> c 4, 5
> d –
> e 6
> f 2

4 a *Learner training.* As a class, look at the dictionary entry together and find two more patterns with *admit*.

> 1 admit + doing something
> 2 admit + to + doing something

b / Learners choose three more verbs from **1**. For each verb, they suggest possible patterns, making an example sentence to show each pattern.

c Provide learner dictionaries so learners can check their ideas, or invite learners to ask you about any patterns they're not sure of.

5 a *Practice.* Learners choose four stems to complete with their own ideas to make questions for the other people in the class. Monitor closely to ensure that learners are using correct verb patterns.

b Learners get into new pairs and ask each other their questions.

SPEAKING

6 a *Preparation for anecdotes.* Learners prepare to talk about three or four experiences, using the list of situations and the four prompts to guide them. Learners may make notes if they wish, but should not write out their anecdotes in full. Encourage learners to use reporting verbs where possible.

b *Anecdotes.* Learners listen to each other's anecdotes and decide which is the most interesting.

Round-up. The class listens to the most interesting anecdote from each group.

 You could use photocopiable activity 11B on the Teacher's DVD-ROM at this point.

11.3 Target activity

Goals: carry out an interview ♻
report what people say ♻
give statistics

Core language:

TASK VOCABULARY	Giving statistics
11.1 VOCABULARY	Interviewing
11.2 GRAMMAR	Patterns after verbs

Carry out a survey

TASK LISTENING

1 Look at the picture of Vicki and read through the caption with the class.

/ Learners look at the summary of Vicki's survey and work out what kinds of people she spoke to, and what questions she asked.

Then check as a class.

> Vicki spoke to two main groups of people: people who live locally, and office workers.
> Possible questions she asked:
> • (local people) Where do you buy bread? How often do you need cakes for special occasions?
> • (office workers) Where do you get your lunch? If you don't get your lunch from us, why not? If we had a lunch delivery service, would you be interested in using it?

2 *Listening for main points.* Play recording **3.15**. Learners listen and put the topics a–e in the order Vicki discusses them.

> c, b, e, d, a

3 *Listening for details.* Play recording **3.15** again. Learners listen and complete the missing information 1–6 in the survey summary.

> 1 *150* 2 *cheaper* 3 *two* 4 *two* 5 *ten* 6 *ten*

4 🙎/🙎🙎 *Responding to the text.* Learners discuss what Vicki and her colleagues should do next.

Round-up. Learners discuss and compare their ideas as a class.

TASK VOCABULARY Giving statistics

5 a 🙎/🙎🙎 *Presentation: modifiers, proportions.* Learners look at the ten expressions in the box. They decide which five could go in sentence 1, and which five could go in sentence 2.

> 1 *about, almost, exactly, just under, nearly*
> 2 *all, almost none, half, most, none*

Language notes

- The expressions in sentence 1 are for modifying numbers: *150 → almost 150, just over 150*, etc.
- The expressions in sentence 2 are for describing proportions: *nearly all of them, half of them*, etc.
- You can say *almost all, nearly all* and *almost none*, but *nearly none* sounds rather unnatural.
---

b 🙎/🙎🙎 *Presentation: fractions.* Learners look at the examples from Vicki's talk, then think of two ways to say each fraction.

> *one out of four, a quarter (a fourth (AmE))*
> *one out of three, a third*
> *two out of three, two-thirds*
> *two out of five, two-fifths*
> *seven out of ten, seven-tenths*

Alternative

Books closed. Write on the board:
$\frac{3}{4}$ *local people said they need cakes for special occasions.*
Ask, pointing to $\frac{3}{4}$: *How can we say this?* (*three out of four, three-quarters of / three-fourths of (AmE)*)
Then put the fractions from **5b** on the board one by one, and elicit two ways of saying each one.

TASK

6 🙎🙎 *Preparation for survey.* Put learners into small groups. Groups choose an idea for a local business from the list, or think of their own.

Ask each group to tell the class which idea they've chosen, and make sure each group has a different idea.

Learners design a survey of five or six questions, similar to Vicki's. They need to find out: 1) what people's needs and habits are now in relation to their chosen business idea; 2) whether (or under what circumstances) they'd be interested in using their business. Questions can be yes/no, open or multiple-choice.

Make sure that *all* the learners in a group write down the questions.

7 🙎🙎 *Survey.* Put learners into new groups of one person from each old group. Learners take turns to survey the other people in their group and note down their responses. Remind learners they can use expressions from VOCABULARY Interviewing.

8 a 🙎🙎 *Report.* Learners get back into their groups from **6**. They put their survey results together to make a single set of results.

Then they plan a brief presentation of their results for the rest of the class, and decide who will give the presentation. Encourage learners to use expressions as appropriate from **5** and from GRAMMAR Patterns after verbs.

Option: Guidance for presenting results

Guide learners to produce fuller and more carefully structured summaries by putting a presentation structure on the board for them to follow:
- *a brief description of your business idea*
- *how many people you spoke to*
- *question 1 > results*
- *question 2 > results*
- *question 3 > etc.*
- *conclusions from your survey*
---

b Listen to each group's summary as a class.

🙎/🙎🙎 Learners discuss which seems to be the most promising business idea.

Round-up. Ask a few learners which business idea seems most promising to them, or have a class vote (learners are not allowed to vote for their own group).

 You could use photocopiable activity 11C on the Teacher's DVD-ROM at this point.

11 Explore

Keywords: *up* and *down*

Goals: understand the range of meanings of *up* and *down*
use multi-word verbs with *up* and *down*
use *up* and *down* as verbs and adjectives

Core language:
Multi-word verbs with *up* and *down*: *break up; close down*; …
Verbal uses of *up* and *down*: *up the price; down your coffee*; …
Adjectival uses of *up* and *down*: *your time's up; profits are down*; …

Meanings

1 a 🙎/🙎🙎 Learners choose the correct word, *up* or *down*, in the sentences 1–6.

> 1 *up* 2 *up* 3 *down* 4 *down* 5 *down* 6 *up*

b *Presentation.* Read through the information in the box with the learners.

🙎/🙎🙎 Learners look again at sentences 1–6 in **a** and categorise them according to whether *up*/*down* has meaning a, b or c.

> a 4   b 3, 6   c 1, 2, 5

Verbs with *up* and *down*

2 **a** 👥 / 👥👥 *Presentation.* Learners replace the underlined parts of the sentences 1–8 with verbs from the box in the correct form.

> 1 cut down on   2 give up   3 broke up   4 set up
> 5 close down   6 ended up   7 took up   8 turned down

   b *Practice.* Give learners a few examples of sentences about your own life over the last five years, each including a multi-word verb from **a**, e.g. *I took up jogging, I turned down a job offer from another school.*

   👤 Learners write sentences about themselves or people they know. As learners are writing, monitor closely to make sure that they are using the multi-word verbs correctly and to assist as required.

   👥 / 👥👥 Learners listen to or read each other's sentences and ask questions to find out more.

Verbs and adjectives

3 **a** 👥 / 👥👥 *Presentation.* Learners guess the meanings of the verbs and adjectives *up* and *down* in each sentence.

> 1 increased, improved (must have an object, i.e. you up something)
> 2 drank completely
> 3 finished (only used to talk about time, e.g. you can't say 'my money's up')
> 4 not working (only used to talk about communications, e.g. you can't say 'my car's down')
> 5 higher/lower than before
> 6 sad/depressed; awake

   b 👤 *Practice.* Learners complete the sentences with *up* and *down.*

> 1 up   2 down   3 up   4 down
> 5 up or down (more natural than 'down or up')

   Learners ask and answer the questions.

   Round-up. Discuss the first two or three questions as a class.

Explore speaking

Goal: give emphasis to different kinds of information

Core language:

Topic headers: *Audio books, where do they go?*
Fronted objects: *Fiction you put on the right.*

1   👥 / 👥👥 Learners read the definition of *work experience* and discuss the three questions. To round off the discussion, ask learners to tell the class about any work experience they've done.

2 **a** *Listening for detail.* Use the photograph and caption to introduce Shawna. Give learners time to read through the questions 1–5.

   Play recording **3.16**. Learners listen and answer the questions.

   b 👥 / 👥👥 Learners compare their answers, then read the conversation on the page to make sure all their answers are correct.

> 1 Put them on the right-hand trolley.
> 2 Put them on the left-hand trolley.
> 3 Put them on the third, silver trolley.
> 4 Give them back to the customer.
> 5 Put them in the cash drawer.

3 **a** *Presentation.* Learners find four sentences in the conversation with the same meaning as those given in the exercise.

> 1 Fiction you put on the right.
> 2 Non-fiction you put on the left.
> 3 Audio books, where do they go?
> 4 Fines, do I have to handle them too?

   b 👥 / 👥👥 Learners match the sentences 1–4 with the explanations a and b.

> a 3 and 4   b 1 and 2

4 a *Practice*. Learners change the sentences to give emphasis to the underlined parts. They use fronting for 1–3 and headers for 4–6.

They compare their answers.

b Play recording **3.17**. Learners listen to the sentences 1–6 to check their answers from **a**. They practise saying the sentences using appropriate word groups and stress.

> 1 The TV you can use, but the DVD player's not working.
> 2 Milk you'll find in the fridge and the sugar's on the shelf.
> 3 This door you open with the big key and that door you open with the small key.
> 4 Yesterday's newspaper, what did you do with it?
> 5 This coffee machine, can you tell me how it works?
> 6 These chairs, where do you want me to put them?

5 a *Preparation for role play.* Put learners into pairs and label them A and B. Explain the context for the role play: B is going on holiday. While B is away, A is going to stay in their home. B is showing A round the kitchen.

Give learners a few minutes to prepare for the role play. Learner A thinks of five or six things they want to ask about B's kitchen: what's there, where things are, how to use them. Learner B thinks of things they need to tell A. Encourage learners to think of things to say using sentences and questions like those in **4a**.

b *Role play.* Learners have a conversation, imagining they are in B's kitchen.

c Learners reverse roles, prepare for and have another conversation. This time, B is going to stay in A's home, and the conversation takes place in A's living room.

6 *Round-up.* Learners get into new pairs and tell each other what they remember about their previous partner's kitchen / living room.

11 Look again

Review

GRAMMAR Patterns after verbs

> **Optional lead-in: Reverse alphabet dictation**
>
> *Books closed*. Spell the list of reporting verbs backwards and as a continuous string of letters:
> NETAERHTESUFERESIGOLOPAECNUONNAESIMORPNIA
> LPMOCTIMDAEGNELLAHC
> Learners listen and write down the letters. Then they read the letters backwards to find eight reporting verbs and open their books to check.

1 a Learners use the reporting verbs in the box to complete the article. Remind learners that they need to make sure the verbs are in the correct form.

> 1 announced   2 admitted   3 complained
> 4 challenged   5 threatened   6 apologised
> 7 promised   8 refusing

b Learners underline the patterns after each verb. Go through the answers as a class, writing the verbs and patterns up on the board.

> 1 announced that he has … (that clause)
> 2 admitted that he had … (that clause)
> 3 complained that he was … (that clause)
> 4 challenged 'The Correspondent' to provide … (object + infinitive)
> 5 threatened to take … (infinitive)
> 6 apologised to the Prime Minister … (preposition 'to' + object)
> 7 promised to make … (infinitive)
> 8 refusing to say … (infinitive)

c *Books closed*. Working together, learners recall what the minister said, using the verbs and patterns on the board to help them.

VOCABULARY Expressions with *people*

2 a Learners think of people they know (or know about) who match the descriptions 1–6.

b Learners go through the descriptions 1–6 in **a** one by one, telling each other about the people they thought of.

Round-up. They tell each other which of the six people they've heard about they'd most like to meet, and why.

CAN YOU REMEMBER? Unit 10 – Describing benefits

3 a As a class, look at the expressions in 1–3. Ask learners which word(s) could come next in each case.

> 1 to (infinitive)
> 2 to (preposition), for, that
> 3 on

To check learners' grasp of these structures, ask them to suggest a few possible sentences about, for example, computers:
They allow us to buy things over the Internet.
They're crucial to/for a lot of businesses.
They've had a positive effect on education.

b 👤 Learners think about the question and write their reasons, using expressions from **a**.

c 👥 / 👥👥 Learners listen to each other's reasons and say whether they agree.

Extension

SPELLING AND SOUNDS Stressed /ɪ/

4 a 👥 / 👥👥 Learners read through the words together and identify the three spellings which correspond to the sound /ɪ/.

> *i, y, ui*

b 👥 / 👥👥 Learners identify more spellings which make the sound /ɪ/ in the list of common words.

> u: b*u*sy, b*u*siness
> e: *E*ngland, pr*e*tty, wom*e*n
> o: w*o*men

c 👤 *Spellcheck.* Play recording **3.18**. Learners listen to the ten words and write them down.

👥 / 👥👥 They compare their spelling of the ten words, then look at script **3.18** on p155 to check.

NOTICE Verbs with *off*

5 a As a class, look at the extract and focus on the highlighted verbs 1 and 2. Ask learners: *In which verb does 'off' have the meaning of something starting, and in which does it mean something finishing?*

> *starting: went off*
> *finishing: turned off*

b 👥 / 👥👥 Learners complete the questions 1–6 using the verbs in the box. Remind learners that they should use the verbs in the correct form.

> *1 goes   2 switch/turn off   3 kick off   4 round off*
> *5 cut off   6 broken off   7 call off   8 set*

Optional extra

Learners decide which of the verbs in 1–6 have the meaning of something starting/finishing.

> *Starting: 2   Finishing: 1, 3, 4, 5, 6*

---

c 👥 / 👥👥 Learners discuss the questions in **b**.

Self-assessment

To help focus learners on the self-assessment, you could read it through, giving a few examples of the language they have learned in each section (or asking learners to tell you). Then ask them to circle the numbers on each line.

Unit 11 Extra activities on the Teacher's DVD-ROM

Printable worksheets, activity instructions and answer keys are on your Teacher's DVD-ROM.

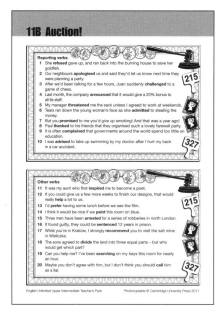

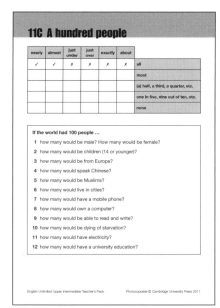

11A Lie detectors

Activity type: Listening and speaking – Interview and guessing game – Whole class

Aim: To practise language for developing a topic and getting more details in an interview

Language: Interviewing – Use at any point from 11.1.

Preparation: Make one copy of the worksheet for the class. Cut up the worksheet to make a set of 36 cards.

Time: 45 minutes

11B Auction!

Activity type: Reading and error correction – Grammar auction – Groups / Whole class

Aim: To raise awareness of grammar patterns after verbs

Language: Reporting verbs / Patterns after verbs – Use at any point from 11.2.

Preparation: Make one copy of the worksheet for each learner.

Time: 35 minutes

11C A hundred people

Activity type: Speaking – Quiz – Groups

Aim: To practise expressions, including vague expressions, for describing numbers and proportions

Language: Giving statistics – Use at any point from 11.3.

Preparation: Make a copy of the worksheet for each learner.

Time: 25 minutes

Unit 11 Self-study Pack

In the Workbook

Unit 11 of the *English Unlimited Upper Intermediate Workbook* offers additional ways to practise the vocabulary and grammar taught in the Coursebook. There are also activities which build reading and writing skills and a whole page of listening and speaking tasks to use with the Interview video, giving your learners the opportunity to hear and react to authentic spoken English.

- **Vocabulary:** Expressions with *people*; Interviewing; Reporting verbs; Giving statistics
- **Grammar:** Patterns after verbs
- **Explore writing:** A report using statistics
- **Interview:** How not to get the job – Raquel and Anna Laura

On the DVD-ROM

Unit 11 of the *English Unlimited Upper Intermediate Self-study DVD-ROM* contains interactive games and activities for your learners to practise and improve their vocabulary, grammar and pronunciation, and also their speaking and listening, with the possibility for learners to record themselves, and a video of authentic spoken English to use with the Workbook.

- **Vocabulary and grammar:** Extra practice activities
- **Pronunciation:** Prominent words
- **Explore speaking:** *absolutely*
- **Listening:** After a job interview
- **Video:** How not to get the job

12 Alternatives

12.1

Goals: talk about health treatments
express belief and scepticism

Core language:

VOCABULARY	Health and treatments
VOCABULARY	Belief and scepticism
PRONUNCIATION	Fluent speech 3 – *It's* and *'s*

Placebo?

VOCABULARY Health and treatments

1   👥 / 👥👥 *Prediction*. To introduce the topic, learners look at the picture and discuss the questions. Then they read the short description to check their ideas.

2   👥 / 👥👥 Learners discuss the differences between the expressions from the short text in **1**. After a while, ask for their ideas. If more clarification is needed, you can use these dictionary definitions, along with some examples.

> 1 *an illness* = a disease of the body or mind (influenza, measles)
> *symptoms* = a physical feeling or problem which shows you have a particular illness (a fever, a cough, red spots)
> 2 *a treatment* = something you do to try and cure an illness or injury (taking antibiotics, doing physiotherapy)
> *a remedy* = something that makes you better when you are ill (an aspirin, cough medicine)
> 3 *effect* = a change, reaction or result that is caused by something (blood pressure is lower, pain disappears)
> *side effects* = other effects a drug has on your body in addition to the main effect of the medicine (usually something negative or unwanted, such as an allergic reaction, weight gain, headaches)
> 4 *a medicine* = a substance used to cure an illness or injury (cough medicine, penicillin)
> *a placebo* = a harmless substance (a sugar pill) given to someone who's told it's a real medicine

3   👥 / 👥👥 Learners look at the list of treatments and answer the questions. Their answers will vary depending on opinion, experience and culture, so flexibility is recommended.

> *Possible answers*
> 1 acupuncture: back pain, headaches, joint pain
> antibiotics: infections
> hypnosis: to stop smoking, to reduce stress
> massage: to reduce stress, to reduce pain
> painkillers: headaches and other minor pain
> physiotherapy: after surgery or injury
> surgery: heart problems, broken bones
> vaccinations: to prevent diseases like influenza, mumps, rubella, measles, etc.
> 2 conventional medicine: antibiotics, painkillers, physiotherapy, surgery, vaccinations
> alternative medicine: acupuncture, hypnosis, massage

READING

4   👥👥 *Reading for main idea*. Learners work in two groups, A and B, reading separate articles. Each person in the group reads individually and identifies the main arguments in their article. Then they check with someone else in their group. Check the answers by going to Group A, then Group B, rather than having an all-class check.

> Group A: Ben Goldacre
> 1 *Homeopathic pills are no better than placebos. (para. 1)*
> 2 *The placebo effect works. (para. 2)*
> 3 *Homeopaths basically rely on the placebo effect, not on any special power in homeopathic medicine. (paras 2 and 3 – implied and stated)*
> 4 *Homeopaths are unethical, they deceive by giving sugar pills to unknowing patients. (para. 4)*
> 5 *Some homeopaths endanger their patients by giving them 'sugar pills' to prevent them getting serious diseases such as malaria. (para. 5)*
>
> Group B: Jeanette Winterson
> 1 *Just because we don't understand it is no reason to dismiss it. (para. 3)*
> 2 *People often visit homeopaths as a last resort when nothing's working, and they improve. (para. 4)*
> 3 *Recent discoveries indicate new rules for the behaviour of substances in small quantities. (para. 5)*
> 4 *We shouldn't dismiss millions of people's testimony that the remedies worked for them. (para. 7)*

5   *Reading for detail*. Learners individually read the article again and answer questions 1–3. Then they check with someone in their group. Note: the instruction and questions for Group B are on p129 underneath their article.

> Group A: Ben
> 1 *four placebo sugar pills a day will clear up an illness quicker than two sugar pills*
> *an injection is a more effective treatment for pain than a pill*
> *green pills are more effective for stress than red pills*
> *brand packaging on painkillers increases pain relief (para. 2)*
> 2 *back pain, stress at work, medically unexplained fatigue, most common colds (para. 3)*
> 3 *Some homeopaths have given patients sugar pills to protect them against fatal diseases like malaria but have not given basic advice on prevention.*
> *Some have given dangerous advice on vaccines. (para. 5)*
>
> Group B: Jeanette
> 1 *She once had a temperature of 39°C, spots on her throat and delirium. She tried a remedy called Lachesis, made from snake venom. Four hours later, she had no symptoms at all. (para. 1)*
> 2 *They say it's nonsense, without clinical proof or scientific basis, worthless, potentially lethal. (para. 2) They criticise it because it's so diluted that it must be useless. (para. 5, stated and implied)*
> 3 *She'd like to see homeopathy better regulated. She'd like to see homeopaths debating publicly with their critics, as well as initiating more research. (para. 6)*

6   👥 *Speaking*. In A/B pairs, learners tell each other about their articles.

Responding to the text. Then they give their opinions about each writer's viewpoint.

Round-up. Afterwards, find out what the class thinks as a whole, and why.

It works for me

VOCABULARY Belief and scepticism

1 👤 / 👥 Learners sort the sentences as a whole (not just the highlighted expressions) into two groups.

> Belief: 1, 3, 6, 7, 11
> Scepticism: 2, 4, 5, 8, 9, 10, 12

2 👤 *Preparation for discussion*. Learners read the six quotations and write their own reactions to them, using expressions from **1**. They can write one or two sentences in response to each. This will form the basis of their discussion in **4**, so keep this as a writing stage, while you monitor and correct.

PRONUNCIATION Fluent speech 3 – *It's* and *'s*

3 a Play recording **3.19** while learners listen to how *It's* is pronounced at the beginning of sentences in fast natural speech.

b 👥 Learners take the A/B roles and practise saying the four short conversations with *It's* pronounced as *'s*. They'll have a chance to use this pronunciation focus in **4** (*'s worthless because …*).

SPEAKING

4 👥 *Discussion*. Learners move freely around the class in a mingle, telling three or four people how they feel about the quotations in **2**. They try to find someone who shares most of their ideas.

> **Alternative**
>
> This can also be done in groups, where learners exchange ideas and find out who shares most of their ideas.

Round-up. Find out from a number of learners who shared most of their ideas. If you have time, find out the majority reaction to each of the quotations in **2**.

12.2

Goals: persuade someone of your point of view
tell people what to expect
support an argument

Core language:

GRAMMAR	*will be -ing*
VOCABULARY	Supporting an argument

A school with a difference

LISTENING

1 👥 To introduce the topic of unconventional schools, get learners to read the descriptions a–g and discuss questions 1 and 2. Find out afterwards how they feel about each description, and why.

2 *Listening for main idea*. Draw learners' attention to the picture of Fay and tell them to read the caption. Explain they're going to listen to the introduction to a talk Fay gives, then answer the two questions. Play recording **3.20**.

> *She's talking to parents who might enrol their children in her school. Some children are also present.*
> *It's an open day, where people can go on tours, see the school and ask questions.*

3 *Listening for main idea*. Explain to learners that they'll now listen to the main part of Fay's talk. They should look at the descriptions a–g in **1** again and find out which are true and which are false for Southglen. Play recording **3.21**.

> True: a, f, g
> False: b, c, d, e

4 a *Listening for detail*. Give learners time to read questions 1–5, then play recording **3.21** again. Learners note down the answers.

b Learners read script **3.21** on p155 to check.

> 1 *Weekly; anyone connected with the school can attend and make a proposal, but only teachers and students can vote.*
> 2 *How to spend the school budget, whether to hire a new teacher, how to deal with cases of bullying*
> 3 *Because the students take their responsibilities seriously and are capable of making decisions for the good of the school.*
> 4 *Try a wide range of subjects, so they can work out what they're good at or interested in.*
> 5 *Work on further projects connected with their studies, make a practical contribution like taking care of the school gardens – and do their homework.*

5 👥 *Responding to the text*. Learners discuss the questions.

Round-up. Afterwards, find out from each group what they thought. Ask them if they have learned in, or know of, a school like Southglen.

GRAMMAR *will be -ing*

6 👤 / 👥 Learners read the information in the grammar box. Then they match examples 1–4 with speakers a–d.

> 1 b   2 d   3 c   4 a

> **Language note**
>
> This use of *will be -ing* is not the 'prediction' use (see Unit 14), nor the use for stating will or intention, but rather the 'matter of course' use, i.e. stating something that's viewed as a natural fact or sequence of facts. It's often used at the beginning of talks, meetings, courses, flights, etc.

7 a *Practice*. Learners write one other possible sentence that each speaker a–d in **6** might say, using *will be -ing*.

b 👥 / 👥 They compare their ideas.

Possible answers
a We'll be starting Unit 12 today.
  We'll be revising the past perfect.
  You'll be working in groups for the first 20 minutes.
b I'll be showing you a short film about our company
  and its products.
  To start, I'll be presenting the results of our survey.
c First, we'll be hearing from Jane.
  I'll be telling you about our scholarship programme.
  I'll be summarising the results of our recent
  questionnaire.
d We'll be flying over Siberia around 3pm.
  We'll be taking off shortly.
  The flight attendants will be serving lunch in an hour.

Note: Grammar practice

You could do the grammar practice on p139 at this point.

SPEAKING

8 a *Preparation for talk.* Learners choose one of the situations 1–3 to prepare a short, informal talk about.

  b Working alone, learners prepare what to say and how to say it. Encourage them to use *will be -ing*, especially at the beginning of the talk when they outline to their listeners what they're going to talk about, and in what order.

  c *Talk.* Learners talk in pairs or small groups. They can take questions afterwards. Then the listeners say which was the most interesting part of each talk.

Alternative

If you have a small class of strong learners, they may wish to make their presentations to the whole class. Because this can be time-consuming, it's only recommended for small classes.

 You could use photocopiable activities 12A and 12B on the Teacher's DVD-ROM at this point.

My experience is that ...

VOCABULARY Supporting an argument

1 / Learners read the instruction, the information and examples 1–3. They decide which of the six extra expressions could replace the highlighted expressions in 1–3.

  1 *in my experience, I've always found that*
  2 *experts have shown that, research suggests that*
  3 *for instance, to give you an example*

SPEAKING

2 a *Preparation for talk.* Learners, in pairs, read through the statements and find one they hold opposite opinions on. If they can't find one, they can switch pairs or write their own statement which they hold opposite views on.

  b They now work alone and prepare a short talk in which they present and explain their point of view. They should consider how to outline their talk using *will be -ing* (*I'll be talking about …*), how to organise the talk (which order to present various points in) and what expressions they want to use from **1**.

c *Practice.* Learners rehearse their talks in the same pairs as in **a**.

3 *Talk.* Each pair listens to talks from at least two other pairs – more if time allows. The listeners decide whose arguments are most persuasive to them.

12.3 Target activity

Goals: persuade someone of your point of view ♻
make and justify recommendations

Core language:

TASK VOCABULARY   Recommending and justifying
12.2 VOCABULARY   Supporting an argument

Present a proposal

TASK LISTENING

1 To introduce the topic, write *team-building* on the board and ask learners if they know what it means, particularly among colleagues in a business context (= *various activities that improve team performance by encouraging communication, cooperation and trust within the team*).

   / Learners read the caption, then brainstorm a number of activities they think would be suitable for team-building. After a while, elicit a number of their ideas.

2 *Listening for main idea.* Give learners time to read the options. Explain that they can tick the options Ji-Sun discusses and circle the one she recommends. Play recording **3.22**.

> *She discusses an acting workshop, a camping weekend, learning ballroom dancing, and a treasure hunt. She recommends the treasure hunt.*

3 *Listening for detail.* Play recording **3.22** again. Learners listen and note down the pros and cons of each of the four options Ji-Sun discusses.

> Acting workshop
> *pros: everyone works together, entertaining, creative*
> *cons: not everyone feels comfortable on stage, a few strong personalities could dominate it, everyone may not be equally involved*
> Camping weekend
> *pros: requires group planning, cooperation, sharing practical skills, supplying entertainment*
> *cons: might be chilly, people might not like sleeping in a cold tent*
> Ballroom dancing
> *pros: very popular, several people are keen to do it, fun, good for fitness*
> *cons: it's a pair activity, not a team activity*
> Treasure hunt
> *pros: tried-and-tested team-building activity, involves teamwork and cooperation, offers value for money, is ideal for their purpose*
> *cons: none*

4 *Listening for main idea.* Play recording **3.23**. Learners listen to Bryn's decision and, afterwards, say whether they agree with him.

TASK VOCABULARY Recommending and justifying

5 a 👤/👥 Learners read the five sentences, look at the
highlighted expressions for recommending, and decide
which are used to say you're in favour of an option and
which are used to say you're against an option.

> in favour: 3, 5
> against: 1, 2, 4

b 👤/👥 Learners now underline the word or words
in sentences 1–5 that introduce the *reasons* for the
recommendations. These expressions are used when
justifying recommendations and arguments. With
weaker classes, you might want to tell them that there
is no introductory expression in one of the sentences
(sentence 3).

> 1 since   2 because   3 –   4 on the grounds that   5 as

TASK

6 👤 *Preparation for proposal.* Stages **6** to **8a** are all
preparation stages. Learners read the situation and
underline the key points. Then they look at the
pictures and read about each venue. They may find it
useful to underline or make a list of key points.

7 👥 Divide learners into groups of three or four.
The groups discuss the pros and cons of each of the
four venues, considering the six aspects listed (size,
price, etc.). Then they decide which venue they'd
recommend and why.

8 a 👥 Still in their groups, learners prepare to present
their proposal to the other groups. They decide what
language to use. Remind them to choose useful
expressions from **5** and also from VOCABULARY
Supporting an argument. Then learners decide how to
divide up their proposal among the group members so
each has a chance to talk.

b 👥 *Proposal.* Learners listen to the proposals from
the other groups. They identify which is the most
popular venue in general.

Round-up. Ask if anyone would like to change their
decision now that they've heard the other groups'
arguments.

 You could use photocopiable activity 12C on the
Teacher's DVD-ROM at this point.

12 Explore

Across cultures: Health and healthcare

Goal: to make learners aware of health and healthcare in
different cultures

Core language:

VOCABULARY	Healthcare: *have health insurance; cover (medical) treatment; be free of charge; have check-ups; make an appointment at/with; have a high status; be entitled to; have a (formal) manner towards; have access to; discuss (treatment) openly with; have a choice between; treat people; stay in; help out with; provide information about*

LISTENING

1 a 👥 Learners work in pairs to prepare their lists. Give
them a few minutes to do this.

b 👥 Allow learners to compare their lists with as many
other pairs as possible. Have a quick feedback session
and write their ideas on the board.

2 *Listening for main idea.* Learners look at the four
pictures and read the names and countries. They're
going to match the speakers to the statements they
make. Tell them the statements are not in the same
order as the recording and the wording may be slightly
different. Give learners a chance to read items 1–8
before you play recording **3.24**. Remind learners that
they can simply write the first letter of the speaker's
name (i.e. *L, R, H* or *S*) beside each statement.

> 1 Liesbeth   2 Reginald   3 Hugo   4 Sahana
> 5 Reginald   6 Hugo   7 Liesbeth   8 Sahana

3 👥 Learners discuss the statements in **2**, comparing
them with the situation where they live.

VOCABULARY Healthcare

4 👤/👥 Learners complete the highlighted expressions
in each section A–C with the words for that section.

> 1 have   2 cover   3 Are   4 have   5 make   6 have
> 7 Are   8 have   9 given   10 discuss   11 have   12 treat
> 13 stay   14 help out   15 provide

SPEAKING

5 👥 Divide learners into three groups, A–C. These
correspond with the three sections A–C in **4**. Each group
discusses the particular set of questions for their group.

6 👥 Learners tell the other groups what they
discussed. The others listen and add more
information, thoughts or examples if they can.

7 👥 They discuss their experience or knowledge of
healthcare in other countries and compare it with
healthcare in their own country or culture.

Explore writing

Goal: write a proposal

Core language:

Stating the aim: *The purpose of this proposal is to summarise; [The purpose of this proposal is] to present some suggestions*
Introducing background information: *As you know, ...; As we understand it, ...*
Giving opinions and reactions: *This would certainly ...; We do not feel that ...; We believe that ...*
Introducing proposals: *We also propose that ...; Our proposals are ...; Would it be possible to ...*
Concluding: *We hope that our proposals will be given serious consideration; We look forward to discussing them with you at a convenient time.*

> **Note**
>
> Learners did a spoken proposal in Target activity 12.3. This is its counterpart, a more formal written proposal.

1   👥 / 👥👥 To introduce the topic, draw learners' attention to the picture and get them to discuss the questions. Find out afterwards what they think is important and what they added to the list.

2   *Reading for main idea.* Learners read the proposal and answer the three questions. They can compare their answers with a partner before you check them.

> 1 It's for Li Ming Chen, the company's Managing Director. It's written by Constanza Brookes, Staff Representative. It's to summarise staff reaction to the Board's proposals and to present some suggestions of their own.
> 2 The board has proposed to repaint the walls and hang curtains, to buy longer tables and more chairs, and to brighten up the café with plants. The staff like the idea of repainting and curtains, but don't think new furniture or plants are necessary.
> 3 The staff propose that the company buy several poster-size prints, invest in a new dishwashing machine, purchase a new coffee machine, buy more salt and pepper sets and buy new uniforms for the café staff. The most important staff proposals are about the dishwashing machine and the coffee machine.

3   *Reading for detail.* Learners read the proposal again to find reasons for what the staff want and don't want.

> Repainting and curtains: will make the café more attractive.
> New furniture: not necessary as the present furniture's in good condition and the present small tables encourage a friendlier feeling than long tables would.
> Plants: not a good use of money.
> Posters: will brighten up the walls.
> New dishwashing machine: the present one is of poor quality and doesn't always clean things thoroughly.
> New coffee machine: the present one breaks down constantly and takes a long time to get repaired.
> More salt and pepper shakers: so there's one set for every table.
> New uniforms: café staff find their present uniforms uncomfortable and unattractive.

4   👥 Learners decide on a title for the proposal (a) and headings for the three main paragraphs (b–d). Then they compare their ideas with another pair.

> *Possible answers*
> a *Proposal for improvements to the café / Improvements to the café*
> b *Introduction*
> c *Your suggestions / Your proposals / Board proposals*
> d *Our suggestions / Our proposals / Staff proposals*

5   👤 / 👥 Learners sort the 12 numbered expressions in the proposal into five functions.

> 1   2, 3
> 2   1, 4
> 3   5, 7, 8
> 4   6, 9, 10
> 5   11, 12

6 a   👥👥👥 Learners choose one of the places listed, or think of another one that's common to the class as a whole. They brainstorm a list of ways in which they think the place could be improved.

  b   👥 Learners write a proposal in pairs.

> **Alternative**
>
> Instead of doing **6**, each learner chooses a place they know well that could be improved, e.g. a lunchroom at work, a library at college, a changing room at their gym, a station waiting room, etc. Working alone, they make a list of ways in which it could be improved, then write their proposal at home and bring it in the next day. Learners read a few of each other's proposals (pairs / small groups) and ask more questions about the places. If you wish, ask some of them to tell the class about a partner's proposal.

7   👥 Learners swap with two or three other pairs. Encourage them to give constructive feedback on the other proposals, even if they disagree with the ideas.

12 Look again

Review

VOCABULARY Health and treatments

1 a   👤 / 👥 Learners complete the conversation between a doctor and patient, using the initial letter in each gap to help them remember the expressions. Then they check on p94.

> 1 symptoms   2 remedy   3 effect   4 illness
> 5 medicines   6 antibiotic   7 painkiller   8 side effects

  b   👥 Learners write down a word (or two) to help them remember each line of the conversation, e.g. line 1: *symptoms*, line 2: *painful*, line 3: *remedy* and so on. Then in pairs, they cover the conversation and try to recall it, checking when necessary. They take turns being the doctor and patient.

> **Alternative**
>
> Instead of **1b**, photocopy and cut up the lines of the completed conversation. In pairs, learners re-assemble the conversation, read it aloud, then gradually take out one line at a time and try to recall it. Eventually, all the lines will be gone and they'll reproduce the whole conversation from memory.

GRAMMAR *will be -ing*

2 a 👤/👥 Learners complete the short conversations with their own ideas, using *will be -ing*, e.g.
   A: *Are you working late tonight?*
   B: *No, not tonight, but I'll definitely be working late on Friday.*

   b Learners compare their ideas and see how many different ones they've come up with.

Extension
In pairs, learners write two or three more short conversations of their own. Then they read them in groups or to the class.

CAN YOU REMEMBER? Unit 11 – Giving statistics

3 a 👤/👥 Learners match the expressions (words) and percentages (numerals).

about two-thirds of them: 65% *almost none of them: 2%* *exactly half of them: 50%* *just over half of them: 51%* *just under a quarter of them: 23%* *most of them: 80%* *nearly all of them: 97%* *six out of ten: 60%*

   b 👥 Learners look around at the other people in the class and discuss questions 1–5 in pairs, choosing suitable expressions from **a**, e.g.
   Well, nearly half of the people / the students / us are male.

   c 👥👥 Learners compare their answers with another pair and find out if they agree.

Extension

SPELLING AND SOUNDS /eə/

4 a 👤/👥 Learners complete the spelling of the words with the four options.

aerobics, repair, software, airline, vegetarian, parent, prepare, chair, airport, aeroplane

   b 👤/👥 Learners match each word in **a** with one of the spelling patterns a–c.

a ae, air   b a   c air, are

Language note
In many accents, *air* and *are* would also be pronounced with an /r/. Also, in American English, /eə/ is usually just said as /e/.

   c 👤/👥 Learners identify more ways of spelling the sound /eə/ in a few exceptions.

Five ways: aire, ayer, ear, eir, ere

   d 👥 Learners take turns to test each other's spelling, choosing nine words each from **a** and **c**.

NOTICE *-ly* adverbs

5 a 👤/👥 Learners complete the sentences from various reading and listening texts from this unit.

1 *thoroughly*   2 *publicly*   3 *potentially*   4 *seriously* 5 *independently*   6 *reasonably*   7 *strongly*   8 *constantly*

   b 👥 Learners test each other on the sentences in **a**. Encourage the learner remembering the adverbs to do so without looking at the book.

Optional extra
Write this on the board: *Tell me about:* *1   a restaurant in your town which …* *2   something in your home which …* *3   something you think politicians should …* *4   someone you think is good at …* Learners complete each sentence with their own ideas, including a suitable adverb from **5a**. For example: *Tell me about a restaurant in your town which is constantly busy and hard to get into.* Then they listen to each other's sentences and ask questions to find out more.

Self-assessment

To help focus learners on the self-assessment, read it through and get learners to give you a few examples of the language they have learned in each section. Give an example to start them off if necessary. Then learners circle the numbers on each line.

Unit 12 Extra activities on the Teacher's DVD-ROM

Printable worksheets, activity instructions and answer keys are on your Teacher's DVD-ROM.

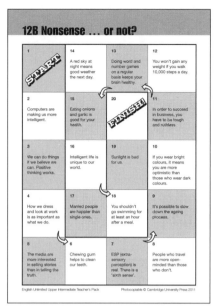

12A What we'll be doing is …

Activity type: Reading and speaking – Mingle – Pairs / Whole class

Aim: To plan the content of a short course

Language: *will be -ing* – Use at any point from 12.2.

Preparation: Make one copy of the worksheet for every pair.

Time: 40 minutes

12B Nonsense … or not?

Activity type: Speaking – Board game – Groups / Whole class

Aim: To express belief and scepticism about a variety of topics, and say why

Language: Belief and scepticism / Supporting an argument – Use at any point from 12.2.

Preparation: Make one copy of the worksheet for every three learners. Prepare dice: one for each group. Make three small, different-coloured markers out of paper for each group (or learners can use a small personal item such as a ring, a coin, an eraser, etc.).

Time: 35 minutes

12C Advice columnist

Activity type: Reading and speaking – Advising on problems – Groups

Aim: To give advice by making recommendations and justifying them

Language: Recommending and justifying – Use at any point from 12.3.

Preparation: Make one copy of the worksheet for each learner.

Time: 45 minutes

Unit 12 Self-study Pack

In the Workbook

Unit 12 of the *English Unlimited Upper Intermediate Workbook* offers additional ways to practise the vocabulary and grammar taught in the Coursebook. There are also activities which build reading and writing skills and a whole page of listening and speaking tasks to use with the Interview video, giving your learners the opportunity to hear and react to authentic spoken English.

- **Vocabulary:** Health and treatments; Belief and scepticism; Supporting an argument; Recommending and justifying; Healthcare
- **Grammar:** *will be -ing*
- **Explore reading:** Article: Laughter
- **Interview:** Alternative treatments – Leo and Anna Laura

On the DVD-ROM

Unit 12 of the *English Unlimited Upper Intermediate Self-study DVD-ROM* contains interactive games and activities for your learners to practise and improve their vocabulary, grammar and pronunciation, and also their speaking and listening, with the possibility for learners to record themselves, and a video of authentic spoken English to use with the Workbook.

- **Vocabulary and grammar:** Extra practice activities
- **Pronunciation:** Fluent speech – *It's* and *'s*
- **Explore speaking:** *now*
- **Listening:** A doctor's recommendations
- **Video:** Alternative treatments

13 Compromise

13.1

Goals: describe disagreements and compromises
make your case in a disagreement

Core language:

VOCABULARY	Disagreement and compromise
VOCABULARY	Making your case
PRONUNCIATION	Prominent words 3

Living space

LISTENING

1 a 👥 / 👥👥 *Prediction.* Learners look at the pictures
and guess what the disagreement in Liesbeth's
neighbourhood was about.

Ask a few pairs/groups to tell the class about their ideas.

b *Listening for main idea.* Play recording **3.25**. Learners
listen to find out what the disagreement was about.

> *Some people living at the end of the cul-de-sac wanted
> the green to be turned into a car park. Other people (for
> example those with children) disagreed.*

2 *Listening for detail.* Learners read through the
statements 1–6 and see if they can remember which
are true and which are false.

Then play recording **3.25** once again. Learners listen
and mark the statements true or false.

> 1 False   2 False   3 True   4 True   5 False   6 True

3 👥 / 👥👥 *Personal reaction.* Learners discuss the three
questions.

Round-up. Ask pairs/groups to explain to the class
their views on the second question (*Do you agree that
the compromise was 'a good deal all round'?*).

VOCABULARY Disagreement and compromise

4 a 👥 / 👥👥 *Presentation.* Learners explain how the
expressions in each pair are different (or similar) in
meaning.

1 a *get everyone's opinion* = find out what people think
  b *organise a petition* = collect the signatures of
    people who agree with a particular opinion
2 a *call a meeting* = invite people to come together and
    talk
  b *organise a demonstration* = organise for a group
    of people with the same opinion to come together
    in a public place to express how they feel about a
    particular issue
3 a *have a word with someone* = talk to someone
    quietly and unofficially
  b *make an official complaint* = complain to an
    organisation in writing
4 a *thrash something out* = reach an agreement by
    having a long, maybe difficult conversation
  b *talk something over* = discuss a difficult or
    complicated question slowly and carefully
5 a *propose an alternative* = suggest a new or different
    idea
  b *propose a compromise* = suggest an agreement in
    which both sides get something (but not everything)
    of what they want
6 a *take legal advice* = ask a lawyer for advice
  b *take legal action* = for example, ask a court to stop
    something, or take someone to court

b Learners say which of the actions in **a** were taken by
Liesbeth or her neighbours.

> 1 a   2 a   3 –   4 a   5 b   6 –

SPEAKING

5 👥 / 👥👥 *Practice.* Learners say what they would do
in the four situations listed. Encourage learners to use
the expressions in **4a** as well as their own ideas.

Compare ideas as a class.

6 👥 / 👥👥 *Anecdote.* Give learners a minute or so to
think about the questions, then ask them to discuss.

Workspace

LISTENING

1 *Pre-listening discussion.* With the class, look at the
photograph of Yousef at work and discuss the two
questions.

2 *Listening for main ideas.* Tell learners that they're
going to listen to a conversation between Yousef and
his manager, Leo, about the lack of workspace in the
office. Play recording **3.26**. Learners listen and answer
the questions.

> *Yousef wants his own private office. He doesn't get what
> he wants, but Leo suggests an alternative.*

3 a 👥 / 👥👥 *Listening for details.* Learners tell each other
what they can remember about topics 1–3 and start
making notes.

Play recording **3.26** once again. Learners listen to
check their notes and add more details.

b 👥/👥👥 Learners compare their expanded notes, then read script **3.26** on pp156–7 to make sure they've grasped all the important points accurately.

> **Suggested answers**
> Yousef's ideas:
> • *to rent rooms from the company upstairs*
> • *to move into the photocopying room and move the photocopier into the corridor, next to the drinks machine*
> Leo's objections:
> • *Renting rooms will cost money, but the financial situation of the company is not very strong at the moment and his boss (Karin) will not agree.*
> • *He's not sure there's room in the corridor for the photocopier.*
> • *Yousef's colleagues (Agustin and Rachel) will not be happy if only Yousef gets his own office.*
> What they agree:
> *Leo will give his office to Yousef, Agustin and Rachel; he will move into the photocopying room; the photocopier will move to the corridor or, if there isn't enough room in the corridor, into the space in the main office which has been vacated by Yousef and his two colleagues.*

VOCABULARY Making your case

4 👥/👥👥 *Presentation.* Learners read the three extracts from the conversation and complete them with the expressions in the boxes.

> 1 *I've been thinking* 2 *And besides* 3 *I've thought about that* 4 *you know* 5 *I'm afraid* 6 *in that case* 7 *But what about* 8 *That's no problem* 9 *In any case*

5 *Practice.* As a class, brainstorm a list of things which managers and employees, or tutors and students, might argue about. Write learners' ideas up on the board.

👥 Then in pairs, learners write a conversation about one of the things from the list on the board, similar to Yousef and Leo's. They should include some of the expressions from **4**. Set a clear time limit for this task, monitoring closely and assisting as necessary. If a pair finishes early, ask them to add a few more lines to their conversation.

PRONUNCIATION Prominent words 3

6 a *Review.* Draw learners' attention to the extract from Yousef and Leo's conversation, marked with // to show the groups of words. Remind them that:
- proficient users of English divide their speech into groups of words (introduced in Units 5 and 6);
- in each group of words, there's usually one word which is prominent, i.e. it has extra-strong stress (introduced in Units 8 and 11).

Play recording **3.27**. Learners listen to the extract and underline the prominent word in each word group. They compare their answers in pairs or groups, then check as a class.

> // I've been THINking // would it be POssible // for me to have my own Office //
> // We just don't have the ROOM // And beSIDES // it's not just YOU //

b 👥 *Practice.* Learners divide the conversation they wrote in **5** into groups of words, and choose the prominent syllable in each word group. Emphasise

that there is not just one possible way of doing this: word groups and prominence are a matter of speaker choice, but word groups should hang together logically, and prominence should be placed on words carrying key or new information. The important thing is to make speech easier for people to understand.

Then learners practise reading their conversations aloud.

c 👥👥 Put pairs together to make groups of four. Pairs listen to each other's conversations and answer the questions.

> **Alternative for small classes**
> Learners perform their conversations in open class.

SPEAKING

7 a 👤 *Preparation for debates.* Label learners A and B. Working alone, learners read the two situations and prepare to have a conversation for each, thinking of reasons to support their point of view.

> **Alternative for weaker classes**
> Instead of learners preparing for the conversations on their own, divide the class into two groups, A and B. The learners in each group work together to prepare. Then, for **7b**, put the learners into A/B pairs.

b 👥 *Debates.* Learners have the two conversations in their pairs. Their aim is not to 'win' the argument but to try to come up with a compromise which both sides are happy with. Encourage them to use expressions from **4**.

8 *Round-up.* For each situation, pairs tell the class what compromises they came up with. Find out which were the most popular and the most creative compromises.

 You could use photocopiable activity 13A on the Teacher's DVD-ROM at this point.

13.2

Goal: talk about dealing with conflict
Core language:
GRAMMAR   Verbs with adverbs and prepositions 2

In the middle

READING

> **Optional lead-in**
> *Books closed.* Dictate the definition of *mediate* or write it on the board. Ask learners to guess which word the definition describes. Provide a few letters if necessary to help learners guess. After they've made a few suggestions, they open their books and look at the dictionary entry to check.

1 👥/👥👥 To introduce the topic of the interview, learners read the dictionary entry for *mediate* and discuss the two questions.

To round off the discussion, ask pairs/groups to tell the class about their ideas for question 2 (skills and qualities of a good mediator).

2 a 👥 / 👥👥 *Prediction.* Learners read the statements about professional mediation and predict which are true and which are false.

b *Reading for detail.* Learners read the interview quickly to check their ideas from **a**.

> 1 True
> 2 True
> 3 False (mediators do not suggest solutions or compromises)
> 4 False (about two hours is the maximum)
> 5 True

3 *Reading for detail.* Learners read again and find reasons for 1–6. They compare answers in pairs/groups before checking as a class.

> 1 One set of neighbours didn't like the mess and noise created by the other's hobbies, but didn't express this.
> 2 Both parties were reasonable people. They just needed to communicate more openly.
> 3 Because of the fact that the parties in a mediation are different.
> 4 Mediators become tired. No progress is likely to be made if there's been no breakthrough.
> 5 To show what the real problems are and how people are feeling.
> 6 To help participants see the situation in a more objective way.

SPEAKING

4 👥 / 👥👥 *Discussion.* Learners discuss the three questions.

Round-up. Ask pairs/groups to choose one person in the class who they think would make a good mediator, and explain why.

Let's talk it over

GRAMMAR Verbs with adverbs and prepositions 2

> **Note**
>
> This is the second of two grammar sections in this course on multi-word verbs. The first section is in Unit 9.

1 *Presentation.* Read through the information in the box with the class.

> **Alternative**
>
> Write on the board:
> 1 They hoped the problem would go away.
> 2 We invite each participant to bring along a supporter.
> 3 They simply put up with the problem.
> Ask learners:
> • what are the multi-word verbs? (1 *go away*, 2 *bring along*, 3 *put up with*) Underline them.
> • what are the objects of the multi-word verbs? (1 –, 2 *a supporter*, 3 *the problem*) Put a box around them.
> • how else could we say sentence 2? (*We invite each participant to bring a supporter along*.) Write it down.
> Add the labels *verb* (or *V*), *preposition* (P), *adverb* (A), *object* (O) to show the grammar patterns of the three kinds of multi-word verb.

👥 / 👥👥 Learners find the nine verbs in the interview and notice the grammar patterns associated with them. They divide them by grammar pattern into three groups. For feedback, elicit the three groups onto the board.

> Pattern 1: *go on, break down, sit down*
> Pattern 2: *talk over, set up, sort out, keep up*
> Pattern 3: *come up with, face up to*

2 👥 / 👥👥 Learners decide which one of the four sentences is wrong, and try to explain why. Then discuss as a class.

> Sentence 3 is wrong. When a multi-word verb with an adverb (pattern 2) has a pronoun object ('it'), the pronoun must go before the adverb. (When the object is a full noun, it can go before or after the adverb.)

3 👥 / 👥👥 Learners find verbs in **1** with similar meanings to the normal verbs a–f.

> a face up to   b go on   c go away   d break down
> e set up   f put up with

4 a 👤 *Practice.* Learners read the sentences 1–8 in the quiz and add the missing word to each one. In some sentences, the missing word can go in two different places.

Learners compare their answers in pairs or groups, then compare as a class.

> 2 keep <u>up</u> the pressure / keep the pressure <u>up</u>
> 3 go <u>away</u>   4 put up <u>with</u>   5 talk <u>over</u> problems / talk problems <u>over</u>   6 goes <u>on</u>   7 face up <u>to</u>
> 8 sort <u>out</u> a problem / sort a problem <u>out</u>

b 👤 Learners answer the quiz, giving each statement a score from 1–4 according to the key above the statements.

> **Note: Grammar practice**
>
> You could do the grammar practice on p139 at this point.

SPEAKING

5 👥 / 👥👥 *Discussion.* Learners talk about each of the statements in the quiz in turn, explaining their answers and giving reasons and examples from their own experience.

6 Learners look at the Analysis on p130 and work out which is their main style of conflict management.

In the same pairs/groups as **5**, they tell each other their result from the Analysis and whether they agree with it.

Round-up. Ask learners to tell the class which is their main style of conflict management. Find out which are the most and least common styles in the class.

 You could use photocopiable activity 13B on the Teacher's DVD-ROM at this point.

13.3 Target activity

Goals: describe disagreements and compromises ♻
make your case in a disagreement ♻
negotiate a formal agreement

Core language:

TASK VOCABULARY	Negotiating an agreement
13.1 VOCABULARY	Making your case
13.2 GRAMMAR	Verbs with adverbs and prepositions 2

Negotiate an agreement

TASK LISTENING

1   To establish the context for the listening, look at the photograph and read through the caption with the class. Ask a few questions to check they've understood the key points: *What does Caitlin do? What was the purpose of the event at the hotel? Why is Caitlin meeting Ethan?*

👥 / 👥👥 *Prediction.* Learners guess what kind of mistake the hotel might have made.

Compare ideas as a class.

2   *Listening for main ideas.* Give learners time to read the three questions, then play recording **3.28**. Learners listen and answer the questions.

> 1 The hotel wasn't prepared for enough people. They prepared for 75 guests, when the actual number was 175.
> 2 They opened a buffet in a side room.
> 3 Yes

3 a 👥 / 👥👥 *Listening for details.* Learners look at the figures a–f and see if they can remember what each figure refers to.

Play recording **3.28** again. Learners listen and identify the significance of the figures.

   b Learners compare their answers, then scan script **3.28** on p157 to check.

> a the expected number of guests
> b the real number of guests
> c the cost of the emergency buffet meal
> d the cost of the dinner for 75 people
> e the total compensation offered by the hotel
> f the proposed discount on the next booking with the hotel

TASK VOCABULARY Negotiating an agreement

4 a 👥 / 👥👥 *Presentation.* Learners complete the expressions in 1–10 using the words from the box.

> 1 compensated   2 entitled   3 gather   4 have
> 5 prepared   6 offer   7 agree   8 accept   9 depends
> 10 be

   b 👥 / 👥👥 *Memorisation.* Learners write two or three key words to help them remember each sentence in **a**. Then they cover the sentences and, working together, try to remember them.

> **Optional extra**
>
> When learners are confident that they can remember the sentences reasonably well, they test each other: Learner A (book open) gives two or three key words; Learner B (book closed) listens to the key words and says the complete sentence. Then they swap.

TASK

5   👥👥👥 *Preparation for negotiation.* Divide the class into two groups, A and B. Learners in Group A look at the situation for the Hailey Arts Club on p129. Learners in Group B look at the situation for the Torrington Hotel on p130. The learners in each group read the situation and prepare for the negotiation by thinking about the three questions.

6 a 👥👥 *Negotiation.* Learners get into pairs of one learner from Group A and one learner from Group B. They negotiate together. Set a time limit (e.g. 15 minutes). The learners' aim is to reach an agreement within this time, getting the best possible deal for their side. Remind learners that they can use expressions from **4a** and VOCABULARY Making your case.

   b 👥👥 Learners return to their groups from **5** and tell each other what they agreed. Remind learners that they can use appropriate multi-word verbs from GRAMMAR Verbs with adverbs and prepositions 2. They decide who managed to negotiate the best deal.

   Round-up. Ask each group to tell the class who managed to negotiate the best deal for their side. What were the details of the deal?

13 Explore

Keyword: *put*

Goals: use *put* to talk about moving or placing things
use multi-word verbs with *put*

Core language:

put + object + prepositional phrase: *put things on the tables*; *put the blame on someone*; …
Multi-word verbs with *put*: *put something on*; *put somebody off*; …

put = place or move something

1 a *Listening for main ideas.* Direct learners' attention to the photograph of Caitlin on p106. Ask learners to remind you: *What are Caitlin and Ethan talking about?* (*Caitlin is negotiating with Ethan for compensation from his hotel.*) *Why?* (*Caitlin works for a charity which recently organised a fundraising event at Ethan's hotel, but the event was not a success because the hotel had not prepared for enough guests.*)

   Play recording **3.29**. Learners listen to four people and answer the two questions.

   b 👥 / 👥👥 Learners compare their answers. (Note that question 2 is a matter of personal interpretation, so there are no strictly right or wrong answers.)

   Then learners read script **3.29** on p157 and decide if they'd like to change any of their answers.

2 a 👥 / 👥👥 *Presentation.* Draw the table on the board with the example sentence. Learners copy and complete the table with seven more expressions from script **3.29** on p157.

Go through the answers with the class and complete the table on the board.

put	something	preposition	something
put	half the guests	in	a little side room
putting	things	on	the tables
put	the blame	on	us
putting	pressure	on	the management (for ...)
put	her	in	a terrible mood
put	her	in	a really difficult situation
put	a lot of time, money and effort	into	our catering services
put	our reputation	in	danger

b Go through the expressions one by one and ask learners which expressions describe physical movement, and which have a more abstract meaning. Use underlining as shown in the key above to help learners see which parts of the expressions are 'fixed' and which are flexible.

3 a 👤 *Practice.* Demonstrate by giving learners a few examples of sentences describing your own life or opinions, each using an expression with *put*, e.g. *My daughter's always putting pressure on me to buy her a mobile phone. I need to put more effort into keeping fit.* Encourage them to ask questions to find out more about the things described in your sentences.

Then learners write four or five sentences of their own. As they are writing, monitor closely to make sure that they are using the expressions correctly and to assist as required.

b 👥 / 👥👥 Learners listen to one another's sentences and ask follow-up questions to develop conversations.

Multi-word verbs with *put*

4 a *Presentation.* As a class, look at the sentences 1–4. Ask learners to suggest what the multi-word verbs mean by, for example, providing synonyms or miming.

b 👥 / 👥👥 Explain that many of the most common multi-word verbs have two or more distinct meanings. Learners look at the same four multi-word verbs in four new sentences and guess what they mean.

5 a 👤 *Practice.* Learners cover **4a** and **4b** and complete 1–8.

They compare answers, then uncover **4a** and **4b** to check.

b *Find someone who.* Learners walk around the room talking to different people. Their task is to find at least one person who does each thing 1–8 in **a**, then to find out more by asking follow-up questions.

Demonstrate the activity by asking learners what question they would ask for 1 (*When you're working, do you like to put music on?*). Ask a few learners this question. When a learner says yes, ask the rest of the class to suggest possible follow-up questions.

👥 / 👥👥 *Round-up.* Learners tell each other what they found out about other people in the class.

Explore speaking

Goal: use different ways of adding emphasis

Core language:

Expressions for adding emphasis: *absolutely* awful; *far* too big; what *on earth*; ...
Emphatic use of auxiliary verbs: We *have* tried our best; I *do* see your point; She *did* work really hard; ...

1 *Listening for main ideas.* Play recording **3.30**. Learners listen to the three conversations and answer the questions.

👥 / 👥👥 They compare answers, then check as a class.

2 a 👥 / 👥👥 *Presentation: emphatic expressions.* Learners read and complete the recording scripts on the page with the expressions in the box.

b Play recording **3.30** again. Learners listen to check their answers.

> **Note**
> The answer to 5 is *complete*, but *total* would also be possible.
> The answer to 6 is *total*, but *complete* would also be possible.

c 👥 *Practice.* Put learners into pairs and label them A and B. Learner A (book open) reads sentences from the recording scripts *without* the emphatic expressions. Learner B (book closed) repeats the sentence, adding an appropriate emphatic expression.
A: *That's the best price we can manage.*
B: *That's definitely the best price we can manage.*

After a few minutes, learners swap roles so Bs 'test' As.

3 a *Presentation: emphatic auxiliaries.* As a class, look at the two groups of sentences, a and b. Ask learners: *Which group is used in the conversations? Why?* (*Group b, because the speakers want to give extra emphasis to the points they're making.*)

b 👥 / 👥👥 Learners answer the questions, using the sentences in **a** to help them.

> 1 will, can, could, may, might, shall, should, must
> 2 do (does, did)

c 👥 *Practice.* Put learners into pairs and label them A and B. Learner A (book open) reads sentences from group a in **a**. Learner B (book closed) repeats the sentence, adding and/or stressing an auxiliary verb to make it more emphatic.
A: *I like it usually.*
B: *I do like it usually.*

After a few minutes, learners swap roles so Bs 'test' As.

4 👤 *Practice.* Learners use language from **2** (expressions) and **3** (auxiliaries) to make the sentences more emphatic. Explain that there are different ways of doing this, and hence no strictly right or wrong answers.

👥 / 👥👥 Learners compare their ideas, then discuss as a class.

> **Possible answers**
> 2 I *absolutely* hated my first job. However, I *did* learn a lot.
> 3 I'm not very good at cooking *at all*, but I *do* make *terribly* good lasagne.
> 4 I don't normally watch horror films, but I *would* go and see 'The Descent'.
> 5 I think it's *far, far* better to be happy than famous.
> 6 For me, voting in elections is a *complete* waste of time.
> 7 When I was at school, I found chemistry *absolutely* impossible.
> 8 I think I'm *far, far* more sensible now than I was ten years ago.

5 a 👤 *Personalisation.* Learners alter the emphatic sentences they wrote in **4** so that they are true for them. Learners may alter the sentences as little or as much as they wish.

Demonstrate this stage by asking learners to suggest different ways of changing the first two or three sentences and writing their ideas on the board, for example:

Although I don't usually like biographies at all, I did enjoy 'Bruce Lee: Fighting Spirit'.

Although I generally love sports on TV, I don't like watching golf at all.

Although I'm a very, very big Woody Allen fan, I thought 'Scoop' was terribly disappointing.

Monitor closely while learners are writing to make sure they are using emphatic expressions and auxiliaries correctly and to provide assistance as required.

b 👥 / 👥👥 Learners listen to each other's sentences and ask follow-up questions to develop conversations.

Round-up. Ask pairs/groups to tell the class about any sentences they strongly disagreed about. Find out what the rest of the class thinks about the sentence.

 You could use photocopiable activity 13C on the Teacher's DVD-ROM at this point.

13 Look again

Review

VOCABULARY Disagreement and compromise

1 a 👥 / 👥👥 Learners complete the expressions 1–8 with verbs, using the first letters to help them.

> 1 get   2 call   3 have   4 thrash out   5 organise
> 6 make   7 propose   8 take

b 👥 / 👥👥 As a class, look at the picture and read through the situation. Ask learners: *What's the first thing (1–8) you'd do in this situation?* Elicit a few possible answers.

Then learners continue the discussion in their pairs/groups, putting the actions 1–8 in **a** in the order they'd do them.

Round-up. Ask one or two pairs/groups to tell the class what they decided.

GRAMMAR Verbs with adverbs and prepositions 2

2 a Play recording **3.31**. Learners listen to the seven extracts and answer the questions for each one.

👥 / 👥👥 Learners compare their ideas in pairs or groups, then check as a class.

> **Possible answers**
> 1 A father talking to his children at home
> 2 A student inviting a classmate to a party
> 3 A father at home, talking to his wife about their daughter's boyfriend
> 4 A businessman talking to an unhappy client at work
> 5 A woman gossiping with friends in a café
> 6 A manager talking to her assistant in a business meeting
> 7 A father talking to his son at home

b Play recording **3.31** again. Learners listen and note down the multi-word verb in each extract.

> 1 go away   2 bring … along   3 puts up with
> 4 sit down   5 going on   6 set … up   7 face up to

c 👥 Learners try to remember and write down the seven extracts, including the verbs.

CAN YOU REMEMBER? Unit 12 – Belief and scepticism

3　**a** 👥 / 👥👥 Learners put the jumbled words in order to make six expressions. They must use all the words.

> **Alternative: Jumbled dictation**
>
> *Books closed.* Dictate the jumbled words, pausing briefly between each expression. Learners listen and write down the words in the correct order. Then they compare their answers and check as a class.

> 1　*It works for me.*
> 2　*It's tried and tested.*
> 3　*There's no proof that it works.*
> 4　*You can see its effects.*
> 5　*It's nothing more than a placebo.*
> 6　*It has no scientific basis.*

　　b 👥 / 👥👥 Learners compare and discuss their opinions of the advice for a happier life, using expressions from **a**.

　　Round-up. Discuss as a class. Find out which points most people agree with and are sceptical about.

Extension

SPELLING AND SOUNDS /əʊ/

4　**a** 👥 / 👥👥 Learners read through the words together and underline the letters in each word which correspond to the sound /əʊ/.

　　Then check as a class, writing the words up on the board and underlining the appropriate parts.

> plac**o**, neg**o**tiate, appr**oa**ch, **o**cean, downl**oa**d, arr**ow**, her**o**, h**o**mework, bungal**ow**, **o**verseas

　　b 👥 / 👥👥 Learners read the patterns 1–3. For each one, they find example words from **a**.

　　Then check as a class, crossing out the words on the board as you match them to the descriptions.

> 1　*placebo, negotiate, ocean, hero, homework, overseas*
> 2　*approach, download*
> 3　*arrow, bungalow*

　　c 👥 / 👥👥 Learners identify the letters which make the /əʊ/ in the list of words.

> ou: sh**ou**lder, s**ou**l
> oe: t**oe**
> ough: th**ough**
> au: m**au**ve

　　d 🎧 *Spellcheck.* Play recording **3.32**. Learners listen to the 11 words and write them down.

　　👥 / 👥👥 They compare their spelling of the words, then look at script **3.32** on p157 to check.

NOTICE Expressions with *keep*

5　**a** As a class, look at the extract and focus on the two highlighted expressions. Ask learners to suggest what the missing words could be, then look in script **3.25** on p156 to check.

> *a keep the peace　b keep everybody happy*

　　Write these expressions on the board under two headings:
　　a: keep + something
　　b: keep + something/someone + description

　　b 👥 / 👥👥 Learners decide which of the highlighted expressions in 1–7 belong under heading a, and which under heading b.

> a 1 *keep a diary;* 2 *keep my appointments;* 4 *keep a secret;* 7 *keep an open mind*
> b 3 *keep someone waiting;* 5 *keeps me up;* 6 *keep my fingers crossed*

> **Language note**
>
> *up* (= *awake*) in 5 is regarded as an adjective. See Unit 11 Keywords *up* and *down*.

　　c 👥 / 👥👥 Learners discuss each of the sentences 1–7 in turn, saying which are true for them.

Self-assessment

To help focus learners on the self-assessment, you could read it through, giving a few examples of the language they have learned in each section (or asking learners to tell you). Then ask them to circle the numbers on each line.

Unit 13 Extra activities on the Teacher's DVD-ROM

Printable worksheets, activity instructions and answer keys are on your Teacher's DVD-ROM.

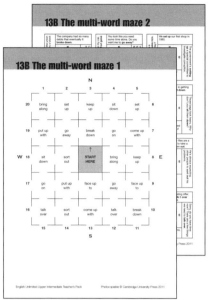

13A Ladies and gentlemen

Activity type: Speaking and pronunciation – Practising short announcements – Pairs

Aim: To practise using word groups and prominence to make announcements more intelligible

Language: Groups of words (Units 5 and 6) / Prominence (Units 8, 11 and 13) – Use at any point from 13.1.

Preparation: Make one copy of the worksheet and one copy of the suggested answers for each learner.

Time: 25 minutes

13B The multi-word maze

Activity type: Reading – Identifying mistakes / Maze game – Pairs/Groups

Aim: To raise learners' awareness of the range of meaning of some common multi-word verbs

Language: Verbs with adverbs and prepositions 2 – Use at any point from 13.2.

Preparation: Make one copy each of Worksheets 1 and 2 for every pair or group of learners. Ensure that each learner has a counter (e.g. a button or a coin).

Time: 25 minutes

13C Snap!

Activity type: Reading and reformulating – 'Snap' game – Pairs

Aim: To practise expressions for adding emphasis to sentences

Language: Emphatic expressions – Use at any point from Explore speaking, p108.

Preparation: Make one copy of the worksheet for every pair. Cut up the worksheet to make a set of 16 Learner A cards and 16 Learner B cards.

Time: 20 minutes

Unit 13 Self-study Pack

In the Workbook

Unit 13 of the *English Unlimited Upper Intermediate Workbook* offers additional ways to practise the vocabulary and grammar taught in the Coursebook. There are also activities which build reading and writing skills and a whole page of listening and speaking tasks to use with the Interview video, giving your learners the opportunity to hear and react to authentic spoken English.

- **Vocabulary:** Disagreement and compromise; Making your case; Negotiating an agreement
- **Grammar:** Verbs with adverbs and prepositions 2
- **Explore writing:** Describing a dispute
- **Interview:** Negotiation styles – Andrés and Di Fan

On the DVD-ROM

Unit 13 of the *English Unlimited Upper Intermediate Self-study DVD-ROM* contains interactive games and activities for your learners to practise and improve their vocabulary, grammar and pronunciation, and also their speaking and listening, with the possibility for learners to record themselves, and a video of authentic spoken English to use with the Workbook.

- **Vocabulary and grammar:** Extra practice activities
- **Pronunciation:** Prominent words
- **Explore speaking:** Apologising to a customer
- **Listening:** Problems at work
- **Video:** Negotiation styles

14 Changes

14.1

Goals: talk about the future
make predictions about the world

Core language:
VOCABULARY   Predicting the future
VOCABULARY   Future time expressions

Reading the future

READING

1   *Reading for detail*. To introduce the topic, ask learners if they think it's possible to 'read' the future and if so, how. Listen to some of their ideas. Then draw their attention to the picture of Ian Pearson and say they're going to find out about his unusual job.

Learners read the short paragraph and answer the questions.

> He's a futurologist. He tracks developments in technology and society and makes predictions about what will happen and how it will affect our lives.
> His skills and attributes: has a strong background in science and engineering, is good at trends analysis, has common sense, has reasonable business insight, knows when to listen to other people, does lots of thinking.

2 a   *Prediction*. Get learners to cover the text. They look at the six inventions in the list and discuss together how each might work.

   b *Reading for main idea*. Learners read through the article to check if their ideas in **a** were similar to what Ian describes.

> 1 It's like a contact lens, but tiny lasers project a picture onto your retina. The picture will be included in your normal vision.
> 2 Electronic circuits will be printed on your skin. When combined with active contact lenses, you can touch your skin to access the Internet or call a friend and see them in the lens.
> 3 It looks like jewellery but will connect and dial someone when you say a word because of voice recognition.
> 4 Solar panels covering 10% of the Sahara desert could supply energy to the rest of Africa and the world using superconducting cables.
> 5 Self-driving cars would run on electrified rails all over the country. You'll tell the car where to go and relax while it gets on the rails, then off the rails and drives you to your destination.
> 6 Probes would collect signals from your brain, put them in a brain model, speed up the thought processes, then put them back into your brain – making you super-intelligent.

3   *Reading for detail*. Learners read the article again and mark the statements true or false according to what Ian Pearson says.

> 1 True   2 False   3 True   4 False   5 False   6 True

SPEAKING

4   *Responding to the text*. Learners discuss the three questions in groups.

Round-up. After a while, find out what their thoughts were and whether they generally agreed with each other.

I'd be surprised if ...

VOCABULARY Predicting the future

1   Learners read the three groups of sentences and answer the questions.

> a The expressions in Group A express the most certainty (Ian uses 'will' and 'won't' to show he's quite certain).
> b The expressions in Group C express the least certainty (Ian's just expressing possibility).
> Group B falls somewhere in the middle.

> **Language note**
>
> The use of *can* in sentence 5 does not mean 'possibility' but rather 'ability' (*I can see*). In sentence 6, *could* for possibility is strengthened by *very well* so it becomes a stronger possibility than the sentences in Group C.

> **Note**
>
> The practice for this vocabulary is in **3** and is combined with practice for VOCABULARY Future time expressions.

VOCABULARY Future time expressions

2 a   Learners complete the time expressions 1–4 by finding the missing words in the sentences in **1**. The number of words required to complete 1–4 is indicated by the number of gaps.

> 1 in the future   2 by 2020   3 in about five years
> 4 Further into the future

   b   Learners put 1–12 from **a** into groups a–c, which establishes approximate time frames for the 12 expressions. Learners can then compare their answers in pairs. To some extent, answers will depend on learner opinion, since they may have different perceptions of relatively near or distant time, and this could start a useful class discussion.

> *Suggested answers*
> a 2, 3, 5, 7, 9, 11   b 6, 8, 10   c 1, 4, 12

> **Alternative**
>
> Instead of **2a** and **2b**, prepare 12 cards with one expression on each (complete 1–4 yourself). On different coloured cards, write the three headings in **2b**. Learners, as a class, sort the 12 cards into three groups under the headings. You can keep the groups of cards on the floor or on the board so they can refer to them in **4** and **5**.

   c   To clarify the differences between a few of the time expressions, learners look at three pairs of sentences. They decide whether the 'a' and 'b' sentences within each pair mean the same or not. Elicit their ideas, then confirm the answers.

> 1 They're different: in 2020 means exactly in that year; by 2020 means not later than 2020.
> 2 They mean the same. Draw learners' attention to the apostrophe after 'years' in the expression in five years' time.
> 3 They're different: in a few years means after a few years; within a few years means sometime during the next few years.

3 👤 *Preparation for discussion.* Working alone, learners look at the topics and choose six of them to write predictions about. They write sentences, choosing suitable expressions from **1** and **2a**. Monitor and correct before they do the Speaking in **4**.

 You could use photocopiable activity 14A on the Teacher's DVD-ROM at this point.

SPEAKING

4 👥 *Discussion.* Learners use the sentences they prepared in **3** as the basis for discussion. They tell each other their predictions and say why they think they're likely to happen. Then they choose, from among their group's predictions, which two they think are the most likely and which two are the least likely to come true.

5 👥 Learners tell the other groups which predictions they chose as most and least likely to come true, and why. The class then decides which are the two most and the two least likely predictions from the whole class.

14.2

Goals: talk about the future
describe personal hopes and expectations

Core language:

GRAMMAR	Future progressive and future perfect
PRONUNCIATION	Fluent speech 4 – double contractions

Yes Man

READING

1 a 👤/👥 *Prediction.* Learners look at the cover of Danny's book and try to guess from the picture, title and any other clues what it might be about. You might want to mention that the book was made into a popular film starring Jim Carrey, and ask if anyone has seen it.

b *Reading for main idea.* Learners read the short publisher's 'blurb' (= a short description to advertise a product, especially a book) from the back of the book to check their ideas from **a**, then say how they think this decision could affect Danny's life.

2 *Reading for main idea.* Learners read the extract and answer the three questions.

> 1 He feels angry at first for wasting time. Then he feels excited about the idea of saying 'Yes' to everything.
> 2 For one day
> 3 He already has some.

3 👥/👥 *Reading for detail.* Learners find the six expressions in the extract and discuss what they think the words might mean from the context in which they appear. After they've finished discussing the expressions, listen to their ideas. If more clarification is needed, you can use these definitions.

> 1 dump = to suddenly end a romantic relationship you have been having with someone. be dumped means the other person made the decision.
> 2 get back into the world outside his house, start meeting people and doing things
> 3 A rut is a boring routine, where you do the same things all the time and never seem to make progress. Danny wants to escape from that.
> 4 to make someone have a feeling that they had in the past
> 5 something that makes things start to happen. Danny wants a 'kickstart' to get his life going again. The expression comes from a way of starting a motorbike using a foot lever.
> 6 never stopping, never getting less extreme

SPEAKING

4 👥/👥 *Responding to the text.* Learners discuss the two questions.

Round-up. Find out from a few of them what they said. The others can ask them more questions if they wish.

I'll have published ...

LISTENING

1 *Listening for main idea.* Explain to learners that they are going to listen to two people talking about their lives and making predictions about what they think will happen in the future. Learners look at the pictures of Eamonn (/ˈeɪmən/) and Liliya, then read the two questions to find out what to listen for. Play recording **3.33**.

> 1 Liliya likes planning things. Eamonn is more spontaneous.
> 2 Eamonn: writing, work (his work is writing), home, money
> Liliya: holidays, flying, work, children

2 *Listening for detail.* Play recording **3.33** again for learners to identify the three predictions or hopes which each speaker mentions. They note down one or two details about each one.

> Eamonn
> 1 hope: He'll have published another novel.
>   prediction: He and his wife will probably be living in Portugal.
>   prediction: He'll have saved enough money to buy a house with a sea view.
> 2 novel: He'll have published it by the end of next year, ideally a best-seller.
>   Portugal: Maybe they'll be living in the Algarve (region of Portugal).
>   house with a sea view: He'll have enough money to buy it in ten years, he's always wanted that kind of house.
> Liliya
> 1 prediction: She should have earned her helicopter pilot's licence.
>   prediction: She'll be running her whole department at work.
>   hope: She'll have brought her children up as happy people.
> 2 helicopter pilot's licence: She'll have it by the end of the year, she's really excited about it.
>   job: She'll be running her department in a year or so, it's the accounting department.
>   her children: She wants them to be emotionally stable and successful, most parents would say the same.

GRAMMAR Future progressive and future perfect

3 **a** 👤/👥 Learners read the descriptions a and b and match them with sentences 1 and 2 from Eamonn's talk.

> a2 b1

b 👤/👥 Learners complete the form of the two structures.

> 1 will + be + -ing form
> 2 will + have + past participle

4 👥/👥👥 Explain to learners that they are going to look at other ways of expressing predictions or hopes about the future. Give them time to discuss the difference between each expression and *will* (which is used to make a confident prediction).

Language note

In Unit 12, learners used *will be -ing* to let someone know what to expect and to give the impression that the future event is a simple, natural fact.
In Unit 14, however, *will be -ing* is used to express a confident prediction.

> 1 *May* expresses possibility and is less certain than *will*.
> 2 *Hope to* expresses a hope for the future, not a prediction.
> 3 *Might* is similar to *may*.
> 4 *Should* expresses an expectation about the future.
> 5 *Expect* also expresses an expectation about the future.

5 👤/👥 Learners read script **3.33** on pp157–8 to find more examples of the progressive and perfect forms to talk about the future. There are four.

> Eamonn
> *By that time, I'll have saved up enough money to buy a place with a sea view.*
> Liliya
> *By the end of the year, I should have earned my helicopter pilot's licence.*
> *In a year or so, I'll be running my whole department at work.*
> *I hope to have brought my children up as happy people.*

 You could use photocopiable activity 14B on the Teacher's DVD-ROM at this point.

Note: Grammar practice

You could do the grammar practice on p140 at this point.

PRONUNCIATION Fluent speech 4 – double contractions

6 **a** Play recording **3.34**. Learners listen to and read the two sentences and notice how the speaker uses double contractions for *I will have* (*I'll've*). They try saying the sentences with double contractions. Then they answer the question about the pronunciation of *will not have*.

> won't've /ˈwəʊntəv/

b 👥 Learners practise reading the sentences aloud, using double contractions. Model them if necessary beforehand.

> 1 She'll've   2 They'll've   3 won't've   4 It'll've
> 5 won't've

Language note

In fast natural speech, double contractions are often used. They seldom appear in writing, however. Exceptions might be in plays (where the writer wants the actors to use that pronunciation) or novels (where the writer wants the reader to 'hear' how the characters talk). People might also use them in text messages to reduce the number of characters used.

SPEAKING

7 👥 *Discussion*. Give learners a few minutes to gather their thoughts for this Speaking task. They choose from the topics listed and use the sentence beginnings suggested. Learners tell a partner about their predictions, hopes and expectations for the future, and give reasons.

8 👥 *Discussion*. Learners get into new pairs and tell each other what they learned about their first partner. Then they decide, based on their first partner's predictions, whether their lives seem more planned or more spontaneous.

Round-up. Find out from each pair what they thought of their first partner's life, then decide whether the class in general tends to have more planned or more spontaneous lives.

14.3 Target activity

Goals: talk about the future ♻
describe personal hopes and expectations ♻
take part in a job interview

Core language:

TASK VOCABULARY	Interview questions
14.1 VOCABULARY	Future time expressions
14.2 GRAMMAR	Future progressive and future perfect

Choose the right candidate

TASK READING

1 a 👥/👥👥 *Prediction*. Learners look at the picture and discuss the questions. If you wish, you can bring in more pictures of Antarctic stations (e.g. from the Internet), showing various aspects of life inside the stations.

b *Reading for main idea*. Learners read the advert quickly to check their ideas from **a**.

> 1 Up to 70 employees
> 2 Human resources staff, scientists, mechanics, engineers, chef, doctor
> 3 Skiing, snowboarding, dog sledding, bird and animal watching, photography, films

2 *Reading for detail*. Learners read the advert again to find key information about the job that's advertised. These are the points they'd look for in real life if they were reading a job advert.

> 1 Human Resources Assistant
> 2 Two years
> 3 March 1
> 4 Provides support to the HR manager, handles all issues with total confidentiality, helps to create and maintain employee files, assists the HR manager in matters related to salaries, employee evaluation and training
> 5 Have a degree and/or professional experience, be good with computers especially Excel and Word, be attentive to detail, be able to work independently, have strong organisational and people skills, be in good health
> 6 Can contribute significantly to the social life of the station

TASK VOCABULARY Interview questions

3 👤/👥 Learners read questions 1–8. Then they replace each underlined part with a suitable expression a–h that fits grammatically and makes sense after each highlighted sentence beginning.

> 1d 2h 3b 4f 5c 6a 7e 8g

TASK

4 👥 *Preparation for interview*. Learners work in pairs to prepare a set of questions to ask another person who will be applying for the job of HR Assistant advertised in **1b**. They prepare their questions, choosing from **3** and using their own ideas if they wish. Then, since they themselves will eventually be interviewed, they discuss how they'd answer their own questions.

5 👥 *Interview*. Learners now get into new pairs and take turns interviewing each other.

6 a 👥 Learners return to their original partners from **4** and discuss the people they interviewed (one person each). Then they decide which of the two people they'd offer the job to, and why.

b 👥👥 As a follow-up to the task, the class discusses the three questions.

14 Explore

Across cultures: Recruitment

Goal: to make learners aware of job recruitment in different cultures

Core language:

VOCABULARY	Recruitment: *CV; objective; experience; references; covering letter; clients; salaries; graduates; psychology; internship experience; interview stage; candidates*

READING

1 *Reading for detail*. Learners read the advice from a website on how to prepare for a job interview abroad.

👥👥 They then discuss what information they'd give, for each point, to people coming for an interview in their country. Ask someone from each group to summarise a few of the points they discussed.

LISTENING

2 *Listening for main idea*. Draw learners' attention to the pictures of the speakers and the countries they're from. They will speak in pairs, with Iain and Barbara first, then Lixing (pronounced 'Lee-shing') and Cian (pronounced 'Kee-an'). Play recording **3.35**. Learners identify which pairs talk about the seven topics.

> covering letters: both
> CVs: both
> internships: Lixing and Cian
> interviews: both
> job advertisements: Iain and Barbara
> personalities: both
> salaries: Iain and Barbara

3 a *Listening for detail*. Explain that learners should listen and note down which country or countries each sentence refers to, according to the speakers. The wording of sentences 1–8 may differ a little from what the speakers say, but the meaning is the same. Give learners a chance to read 1–8, then play recording **3.35** again.

b Learners read script **3.35** on p158 to check their ideas.

> 1 Venezuela   2 Venezuela, Ireland   3 England
> 4 Venezuela   5 China   6 China   7 Ireland   8 Ireland

VOCABULARY Recruitment

4 a 👥 Learners look at the sentences in **3a** again. In pairs, they note down one or two useful expressions from each sentence that they think would be useful for talking about recruitment.

b 👥 Learners compare the useful expressions they chose with another pair, or as a class. They can adjust their list at this point.

> *Possible answers*
> *Nouns: CV, a main objective, experience, references, covering letter, clients, salaries, graduates, psychology, internship experience, interview stage, candidates*
> *Verbs: include, submit, show, deal with, offer, focus on, sell yourself, observe, interact*

You can clarify any aspects of meaning or usage at this point.

SPEAKING

5 *Reading for main idea.* The focus now moves from differences in recruitment between countries to differences in recruitment between professions and organisations (micro-culture). Learners read some advice from the website to find out why it's a good idea to research a company or organisation before going for an interview there.

> • *to find out about the 'culture' within a particular profession or organisation*
> • *to find out if there are any guidelines you should follow before your interview at an organisation*

6 a 👤 *Preparation for discussion.* Learners prepare to talk about how recruitment is done in a field of work they know about (e.g. one they're in or would like to be in). They choose topics from **2** (or any others that are particular to that field of work) and note down expressions from **4a** that will be useful for their discussion.

b 👥 *Discussion.* Learners discuss recruitment in their chosen fields and find out what the main differences are.

Round-up. Ask if anyone in the class (or anyone they know) has ever applied for a job in another country and find out what happened. Find out how many learners would like to work in another country one day, and why.

Explore writing

Goal: write a formal letter or email of refusal

Core language:

Thanking people or expressing appreciation: *We'd like to thank you for …; We were pleased to have the opportunity to …; Many thanks for …; We very much appreciated …; We'd like to take this opportunity to thank you …; We'd like to express our gratitude for …*
Saying 'no': *We regret to inform you that …; We are unable to …; I am sorry to say that …; We will not be needing …; Unfortunately, it is not possible to …; We're sorry to have to tell you that …*
Referring to possible future contact: *Would you mind if we keep your records on file?; We will certainly contact you if …; We have your contact details; We will be sure to get in touch if …; We will let you know if …; I have made a note of your telephone number …*

1 👥 / 👥👥 To introduce the topic, get learners to think of various situations in which they might have to write a formal letter or email saying no to something.

> *Possible answers*
> • *turning down an invitation to give a speech, a seminar or a presentation*
> • *refusing to attend a formal event (e.g. a fundraising event, a political meeting, a formal party, a graduation ceremony …)*
> • *refusing a job offer, refusing a university place or scholarship, refusing an award*

2 *Reading for main idea.* Learners read the letter and email to find out what the writers are refusing and why.

> *Christopher Pattinson says no to Mr Brackley's job application because there were many applicants who had much more experience in banking than Mr Brackley. Gudrun Olsen says no to Estelle's offer to help with preparations for the Community Autumn Festival because she has enough volunteers for that event.*

3 a 👤 / 👥 Learners sort the 12 highlighted expressions in the letter and email into three groups, a–c.

> **a** 1, 2, 7, 8   **b** 3, 4, 9, 10   **c** 5, 6, 11, 12

b 👤 / 👥 Learners add more expressions to the three groups in **a**.

> **a** We'd like to take this opportunity to thank you …; We'd like to express our gratitude for …
> **b** Unfortunately, it is not possible to …; We're sorry to have to tell you that …
> **c** We will let you know if …; I have made a note of your telephone number …

4 a 👥 *Preparation for writing.* Working in pairs, learners choose one of the situations to reply to.

b 👥 Together, they plan a formal letter or email saying no. They use the three points given as a guideline for their planning.

5 👤 *Writing.* Learners work alone and write their email or letter. If you wish, they can begin in class (doing the first paragraph, for instance) and complete the rest of the letter at home, then bring it in for correction the next day.

6 👥 Learners exchange letters with their partner from **4** (or a different one, if you prefer) and say whether they think it's clear and polite.

14 Look again

Review

VOCABULARY Predicting the future

1 a 👤 / 👥 Learners complete the paragraph with the six expressions.

> **1** I predict that   **2** I'd be surprised if
> **3** there's the possibility that   **4** could very well
> **5** the next step could be   **6** I can see

b 👤 *Writing.* Learners write a short paragraph like Kimi's, making predictions about someone they know well. They can choose useful expressions from **a**.

> **Alternative**
> The writing stage can be done as homework and brought in the next day for **c**.

c 👥 Learners read someone else's paragraph and ask questions about the person. If you prefer, they can read a few paragraphs in small groups and ask each other questions.

Round-up. Ask each pair (or group) to choose one person to tell the class about.

GRAMMAR Future progressive and future perfect

2 a 👤 Learners complete the questions with the future progressive or the future perfect. The time expressions will help them decide which form to choose. They then write two more similar questions of their own.

> 1 What will you have achieved in a year's time?
> 2 What will you be doing at 1.30 pm tomorrow?
> 3 How many people will you have spoken to by the end of today?
> 4 What will you be doing at midnight on New Year's Eve?

b 👥 / 👥👥 Learners ask and answer the questions.

Round-up. Find out how each pair or group answered one or two of the questions.

CAN YOU REMEMBER? Unit 13 – Making your case

3 a 👤 / 👥 Learners put the lines of the conversation in order.

> 1 How about going to the cinema tonight?
> 2 Good idea, but what about the shopping?
> 3 That's no problem. We can do it tomorrow.
> 4 You know I'm working all day tomorrow!
> 5 So I can do the shopping. In any case, you need an evening off.

b 👤 / 👥 Learners replace the four expressions in **a** with four new ones that fit grammatically and make sense.

> That's no problem can be replaced by I've thought about that.
> You know can be replaced by I'm afraid.
> So can be replaced by In that case.
> In any case can be replaced by And besides.

c 👥 In pairs, learners think of one or two short conversations like the one in **a**. The context is that they're friends who have different ideas about what to do this weekend. They include useful expressions from **a** and **b**, and practise saying their conversations, taking turns to start. For example:
I've been thinking, how about having a barbecue this weekend?
Nice idea, but we haven't got a barbecue.
I've already thought about that. We can borrow the one my parents have.
Well, OK, but I'm afraid I'm not very good at cooking.
Well, I am, so I'll do the cooking. And besides, you'll be busy inside making salad, cutting bread, pouring drinks ...

Extension

SPELLING AND SOUNDS /ɪə/

4 a 👤 / 👥 Learners complete the spelling of the words with the four options.

> *earphones, earrings, career, clear, disappear, engineer, period, serious, sincere, sphere*

b 👤 / 👥 Learners look at the words in **a** and answer the questions about spelling patterns.

> a ear
> b e
> at the end: eer, ear, ere

c Play recording **3.36**. Learners write down the words, then check their spelling in script **3.36** on p158. If you wish, you can elicit the spelling and write it on the board.

> atmosphere, earpiece, gear, hero, interfere, interior, overhear, steer, volunteer, experience

NOTICE Planning and spontaneity

5 a 👤 / 👥 Learners locate and complete the seven expressions in script **3.33** on pp157–8.

> 1 circumstances 2 going 3 spur 4 ahead 5 place
> 6 spontaneously 7 day-to-day

b 👥 / 👥👥 Learners discuss how people they know, or know of, behave, using the expressions in **a**. They can add examples of the people's behaviour, like this:
I have a friend who always plans ahead. For instance, she'll phone me in August and ask me what I'm doing on March 14 next year because she wants to buy tickets for a concert on that date.

 You could use photocopiable activity 14C on the Teacher's DVD-ROM at this point.

Self-assessment

To help focus learners on the self-assessment, read it through and get learners to give you a few examples of the language they have learned in each section. Give an example to start them off if necessary. Then learners circle the numbers on each line.

Unit 14 Extra activities on the Teacher's DVD-ROM

Printable worksheets, activity instructions and answer keys are on your Teacher's DVD-ROM.

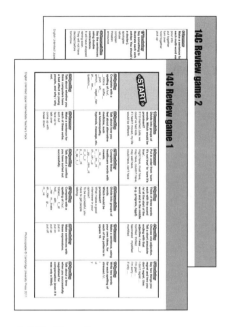

14A Science fiction?

Activity type: Reading and speaking – Sentence re-ordering / Discussion – Individuals / Pairs / Whole class

Aim: To discuss the timing and likelihood of predictions for the future

Language: Future time expressions – Use at any point from 14.1.

Preparation: Make one copy of the worksheet for every learner and fold along the line.

Time: 35 minutes

14B Families of the future

Activity type: Speaking – Presentation – Groups / Whole class

Aim: To make predictions about the future of families and family life

Language: Future progressive and future perfect – Use at any point from 14.2.

Preparation: Make one copy of the worksheet for the class. Cut up the worksheet to make a set of 12 cards.

Time: 40 minutes

14C Review game

Activity type: Vocabulary, speaking, grammar, spelling and pronunciation – Dice game – Groups

Aim: To review language from Units 8–14

Language: Various language taken from across Units 8–14 – Use at the end of Unit 14.

Preparation: Make one copy of both pages of the worksheet for every three or four learners and stick them together (short end to short end) to form a board game. You will need a die for each group and a counter for each learner.

Time: 40 minutes

Unit 14 Self-study Pack

In the Workbook

Unit 14 of the *English Unlimited Upper Intermediate Workbook* offers additional ways to practise the vocabulary and grammar taught in the Coursebook. There are also activities which build reading and writing skills and two whole pages of listening and speaking tasks to use with the Documentary video, giving your learners the opportunity to hear and react to authentic spoken English.

- **Vocabulary:** Predicting the future; Future time expressions; Interview questions; Recruitment
- **Grammar:** Future progressive and future perfect
- **Explore reading:** Article: Threats to life on our planet
- **Documentary:** The Antarctic researcher

On the DVD-ROM

Unit 14 of the *English Unlimited Upper Intermediate Self-study DVD-ROM* contains interactive games and activities for your learners to practise and improve their vocabulary, grammar and pronunciation, and also their speaking and listening, with the possibility for learners to record themselves, and a video of authentic spoken English to use with the Workbook.

- **Vocabulary and grammar:** Extra practice activities
- **Pronunciation:** Fluent speech – double contractions
- **Explore speaking:** Interrupting people
- **Listening:** Talking about hopes and expectations
- **Video:** Documentary – The Antarctic researcher

Grammar reference – Coursebook pp131–140: Answer key

Unit 1
Present perfect simple and progressive
1 Adam has been cycling competitively since he was a teenager.
2 Guess what! I've finally joined the sports club.
3 I have an awful feeling that I've broken my toe!
4 Mia's been preparing for her final exams for months.
5 I'm not really crying. I've been cutting onions!
6 Sonia's been married since she was 18.
7 Have you ever thought about becoming a vegetarian?
8 You look exhausted! What have you been doing?
9 Not again! You've already watched this film twice.
10 Sorry I didn't hear the phone. I've been working in the garden.
11 Have you finished your coffee? Would you like another?
12 I've only seen Ben a couple of times since we left school.

Unit 2
Past simple and past perfect simple
1 realised; had lost   2 had decided; was   3 texted; had got
4 loved; had never seen   5 had promised; was
6 told; had found

Past progressive and past perfect progressive
1 was just closing up   2 'd been negotiating
3 was still working   4 was living   5 'd been living
6 'd been waiting

Unit 3
Habits and tendencies – past and present
Suggested answers
1 used to be   2 would also do   3 would do
4 would eat out   5 was always worrying   6 would tell
7 would make   8 was always asking

Unit 4
Using the passive
1 are (often) criticised   2 was invited   3 can't be repaired
4 have been imported   5 has (just) been nominated
6 should be sent   7 Have … been announced
8 was / were informed (American English prefers the singular *was* for *staff*, British English prefers *were*.)

Unit 5
Describing objects – past participle clauses
1 made   2 directed   3 grown   4 located   5 imported
6 built   7 taken   8 called

Unit 6
Conditional clauses – present and future
1 is; we'll think   2 ordered; we'd consider
3 I'd (probably) think; passed   4 win; will be
5 gave; I'd be   6 I'll turn off; don't stop

In sentences 1, 4 and 6, the people use real conditionals because they are, respectively, confident, optimistic and impatient, and they consider the situations likely to happen.

In sentences 2, 3 and 5, the people use unreal conditionals because they are cautious, pessimistic and poorly qualified respectively, so they consider the situations less likely to happen.

Unit 7
Describing scenes – present and past participle clauses
1 having   2 dedicated   3 used   4 practising   5 attached
6 discussing   7 connected   8 pouring

Unit 8
Making deductions about the past
1 must have   2 may well have   3 might have
4 couldn't have   5 could have   6 must have   7 can't have
8 may have

Conditionals – past and present
1 If she'd arrived a little earlier, she <u>could have got</u> the express train.
2 I might still <u>be</u> working in an office if I hadn't won the lottery.
3 He might <u>have</u> become a landscape gardener if he hadn't been allergic to flowers.
4 If he'd locked the window, the cat couldn't have <u>got</u> out.
5 The party would <u>have</u> been successful if there hadn't been a power failure.
6 If that taxi hadn't stopped for us, we'd still <u>be standing</u> at the bus stop in the rain.
7 This soup would have been perfect <u>if</u> you hadn't added that last teaspoon of salt!
8 If she'd come back for a second interview, we <u>would</u> have offered her the job.
9 She<u>'d</u> have seen everything much better if she'd had her glasses with her.
10 If everyone <u>had come</u> by public transport, we wouldn't have this parking problem now.

Unit 9
Verbs with adverbs and prepositions 1
1 pour the milk into the bowl
2 print an address onto this envelope
3 turn over the worksheet / turn the worksheet over
4 pick up the kids from school / pick the kids up from school
5 attach the agenda to this morning's email
6 put a lot of money into this project
7 put these two single beds together
8 cut off your finger / cut your finger off

Unit 10
Using the -ing form
1 It's been <u>raining</u> heavily like this all week, so everything's wet.
2 I don't usually find horror films <u>disturbing</u>. They're just funny.
3 I sometimes feel ill when <u>riding</u> in the back of a car.
4 Excuse me. Would you be interested in <u>completing</u> a questionnaire on your local government?
5 After work, I enjoy <u>relaxing</u> in front of the TV with a cold drink.
6 Because my mother's French, <u>learning</u> the language has been fairly easy for me.
7 You can do it by <u>pressing</u> the 'Control' and the 'S' key at the same time.
8 This is an absolutely <u>fascinating</u> book. You must read it!
9 <u>Playing</u> computer games won't help you pass your exams!
10 His job involves <u>giving</u> presentations around the world.

1 5, 6, 9
2 4, 7
3 10
4 1
5 2, 8
6 3

Unit 11
Patterns after verbs
1 to go
2 (that) she hadn't checked
3 to Frank for being
4 (that) TV isn't / about TV not being
5 Brandon College to a football match
6 everybody for coming / everybody who came
7 to wait
8 you to get rid of / that you get rid of
9 (that) they're getting married / (that) they're going to get married
10 to write / (that) you'd write

Unit 12
Will be -ing
1 will be meeting   2 will be starting   3 will (also) be presenting   4 will be getting   5 will be bringing
6 will be having   7 will be watching   8 will be joining
9 will be trying out

Unit 13
Verbs with adverbs and prepositions 2
1 i (faced up to)   2 d (set it up)   3 l (put up with)
4 b (go away)   5 g (talk them over)   6 h (go on)
7 j (bring her along)   8 a (sit down)   9 e (broken down)
10 f (came up with)   11 c (sorted it out)   12 k (keep up)

Unit 14
Future progressive and future perfect
1 may have run out   2 might be working
3 will definitely have told   4 will probably be lying
5 should have had   6 will be waiting
7 expect to be living   8 hope to have spoken